Borders and Beyond
Orient-Occident Crossings in Literature

Edited by

Adam Bednarczyk

Magdalena Kubarek

Maciej Szatkowski

Nicolaus Copernicus University in Torun
Poland

Series in Literary Studies

VERNON PRESS

www.vernonpress.com

In the Americas:
Vernon Press
1000 N West Street,
Suite 1200, Wilmington,
Delaware 19801
United States

In the rest of the world:
Vernon Press
C/Sancti Espiritu 17,
Malaga, 29006
Spain

Series in Literary Studies

Library of Congress Control Number: 2018940271

ISBN: 978-1-62273-500-6

Table of Contents

Foreword

Arkadiusz Jabłoński

First of all, it is a pleasure and an honor to be invited by my colleagues from the Nicolaus Copernicus University Faculty of Languages to write a short introduction to this volume. I have always been of the opinion that interdisciplinary projects are a new and challenging direction, in the area of linguistic and literary studies – and not only. On the other hand, on the level of bare facts, I have to mention that I was not personally involved in the actual process of compilation of the volume. My area of research is definitely not literature, but general and Japanese linguistics, the pragmatics of Japanese language, including translation/interpretation studies and applied research on the effective means to describe the grammar of the language. For these reasons, doubts may arise whether it is me who should write the introduction.

Linguistic and literary studies have traditionally been separated while belonging to the same area of philological studies. Moreover, even within the same area, the determination of linguists to hold the position of science, focused on tangible objects and mathematically oriented results, may be perceived as strikingly different from the attitude of literary scholars, who seem to have nothing against being identified with the area of humanities, despite the allegedly intangible character of their statements. According to the practice of the present-day interdisciplinary research, it may not be surprising to unite the two approaches. Again, the famous interdisciplinary research may also be viewed as a mere temporary fashion, not leading to any promising synthesis in a longer perspective. Similarly, as in the contemporary circulation of information, the rise in quantity may not necessarily foster substantial gain in quality as well as the quality and regularity of its complete decoding by the target parties of the communication processes.

Why may my introduction be necessary for this volume? I think the answer is because it seems right to assume that it is in the first place the language, in its multiple, multi-dimensioned emanations, that is challenged and researched in the philological studies. At the same time, it is the language that both creates and makes it possible to discuss the innumerous incompatibilities (and: the compatibilities) between the so-called science and the humanities. It is thanks to the language that we can, as I often do mention during my linguistic classes with the university students, both complain that the mathematicians are unable to compute the number pi and to claim that its irrational properties or even devise a system in which all factors are going to be computed with the number pi as the base parameter. It is finally the language and linguistics-related statements that I shall use below, in the possibly most simple and comprehensible manner, in order to allude to several concepts from the history of linguistics and inter-cultural studies which explain the background of this volume.

The facts mentioned below are of classical, traditional nature, some of them being widely known, some other being unpopular and already forgotten or neglected. I believe that this short synthesis may contribute to bringing the reception of this volume a bit closer to reaching the ultimate goal of the philological, that is, the language studies – namely, to achieve "a scientific understanding of how people communicate," as Victor Yngve once put it. My further objective, as compared to the Yngve's objective, is to broaden the notion of communication with the phenomena of inter-cultural communication, a kind of "non-face-to-face" communication, which is in most of its aspects not different from its "face-to-face" counterpart mentioned originally. A short list of references may provide further hints to what has already happened throughout the history of the language, culture and communication studies in this aspect.

It is rather widely known what Eduard Sapir (born, which is not a commonly recognised fact, in a then German town Lauenburg, contemporarily, due to a number of complicated historical reasons, Lębork in the Republic of Poland) once mentioned on "the exotic languages of Eskimos and Hottentots." According to his point of view, there would be absolutely no obstacle in translating the *Critique of Pure Reason* by Immanuel Kant into any of those languages laying in their formal nature. It is hence not the languages, but the cultures of "those primitive peoples," not (yet?) developed enough in order get their users interested in the abstract philosophical concepts, that make a difference. The statement may reveal some minor issues while compared to the beginning of the 21st century. It is for sure not common nowadays to classify peoples as "primitive" – and probably even Sapir himself did not mean to be xenophobic, but rather chose a common expression of the time in order to allude to the rather vague concept of distant cultures, by their very definition not considered civilised. Still, the relation of a message content to the phenomena of a culture remains one of the unsolved or, at best, scarcely known issues, both for linguists in general and for the researchers in the area of intercultural communication.

Benjamin Lee Whorf wrote in one of his papers that one is immersed in language and culture in a self-evident and an almost invisible manner, similar to the influence of the dust in the air and the phenomenon of air perspective resulting from it on human vision. Also in this statement, after the decades of discussion on whether and to what extent can this claim be related to culture and to the extralinguistic reality, it is not clear, exactly how much and what kind of dust causes what results in the process of communication. Accordingly, live language data and communication-related facts seem to prove that without the link any exchange of messages turns up to be futile or at best superficial. In other words, it may not be an extremely elaborate activity to test whether almost any source message is going to have the same target effect across different cultures. It is probably not. At the same time, to define the variables of the process is neither obvious nor intuitive. It is not clear what exactly happens and what exactly changes when the messages are transferred in the process of the inter-cultural communication.

Sapir and Whorf at the time their crucial hypotheses on the dependencies between the language and the reality were formed represented the new kind of an approach to the phenomena of communication. While the strict manner of the structural approach to "the language by itself and for itself", formed according to the manifesto expressed in the famous last sentence of the most representative work by Ferdinand de Saussure did not take into account the multi-layered character of communication activity, it was for sure not due to the actual non-existence of relations between language and culture. Language functions also on the basic level of mutual, arbitrary linking between the signs and the designates. Studies undertaken on this level are crucial for discovering the nature of basic relations, such as between the few, simple and meaningless cenemes and the numerous, compound and meaning-bearing pleremes, as pointed out at a time by Louis Trolle Hjelmslev. Even though such relations reveal, at least to some point, the properties of purely mathematical or even mechanical character, it does not seem apt to transfer them in an automatic manner to the more complex levels on which communication processes are usually performed – to the links between words and phrases, phrases and sentences, sentences and paragraphs, paragraphs and chapters, chapters and texts, texts and cultural images of the world, images and behavioral schemes and so on.

What is even more important, the simplicity of the original opposition between the cenemes and the pleremes can be achieved only on the assumption that the former are abstract concepts, not immediately linked to the actual, tangible sounds. This further obscures the fact of fundamental character of approximation implemented in the process of mapping the actual results of the actual articulation activities (technically speaking, huge groups of tangible sounds, in their internal structure similar rather to what is known in the extension of the classical set theory as fuzzy set) onto the abstract, ideal phonemic patterns. The actual sounds are not equal to the phonemes (the classical sets of abstract features attributed in a conventional manner to the articulation of the latter). The way how the former is manifested in a purely physical environment, by means of the articulatory organ activities and the sound waves resulting from them, is only indirectly connected to the details of the complex processes of interpreting them in terms of cenemes. The process, usually conceptualised as a series of two-way decisions between the identification and differentiation of the actual sound with/from the ideal phoneme, should, in fact, be effectively viewed as an elaborate act of approximation. Throughout the process, the source innumerable articulation results are juxtaposed to a limited target set of perfect articulations (cenemes). The result of the process is neither obvious nor is it based on purely mathematical rules. This is exactly how the opposition between the finite and limited competence and the infinite and unlimited performance postulated by Noam Chomsky, though dated from the initial differentiation between *langue* and *parole* by de Saussure, makes it possible to manage the load of multiple language facts with the use of a relatively simple set of dimensions. Dimensions are of the mathematical or even arithmetic, predictable character. Language facts are not.

Another kind of competence necessary in the communication with the use of natural languages was rightly defined in a seemingly very simple statement made by a Polish linguist, Tadeusz Milewski: "A sign differs primarily from what is not a sound and does not refer our attention to any other object." This remark, absolutely basic for the linguistic studies, demonstrates at the same time, in an indirect but convincing manner, that it is entirely human (the language user) decision, whether, when and under what circumstances should a phenomenon be valid for the process of communication. While the detailed discussion goes beyond the set of subjects to be raised in this text, it is probably the core of this statement that causes disagreement between the researchers opting for the innate character of linguistic competence and their opponents, who support the hypothesis of primarily social properties of human communication skills. Accordingly, also the modern techniques of natural language processing and translation do not seem to be in the position to offer the tools in order to provide the artificial intelligence operating circuits with the means enabling them to dispel in an automatic and trustworthy manner inevitable doubts whether and with what actual consequences a piece of information should be decoded as valid in a given context of an exchange. Furthermore, nowadays, with the apparatus of computational linguistics and comparative literary studies, it is possible to work on the huge corpora of data and obtain very quickly the extremely simple answers to the extremely simple questions. They, however, are also based on approximations and do not emerge from the self-conscience of the related systems. Moreover, numerous further issues emerge and remain unsolved, such as the unbalanced character of the corpora or complex dilemmas related to their annotation. As can be seen, whether the ability of communication is innate or not to the humans, it is for sure not easily transferred to the human-designed, -made and -programmed systems.

To deal with a language requires a considerable degree of competence, measured in mathematical terms as well as some substantial linguistic and social experience, based on the trial and error processes already attempted individually and their actual results, along with the eligibility to attend a communication act, measured purely in social terms. As such, the speech or script acts are not automatic activities, nor are they effortless, with immediate consequences of this fact. Even in a seemingly homogeneous communication environment, not anyone can communicate with anyone, due both to the incompatible competence, the insufficient experience or the lack of eligibility. Such description of the communication competence sheds new light on the processes of intra- and inter-cultural communication activities, both requiring the motivation of the involved parties to commit themselves to the process of the homeostasis of a text, as defined by this author elsewhere. This includes advanced efforts towards achieving compatibility between the source text, with the source set of its projected users and the target environment in which the text is to be received and interpreted. No need to mention, the two may quite often differ in a significant manner.

Communication is much more than expressing one's thoughts or exchanging conclusions on the external states of affairs. It constitutes one of the activities most deeply embedded in the social and cultural actions of individuals and groups, with subsequent consequences related to the relations between the communication competence and performance.

The above statements apply in an obvious, though at the same time specific manner to the genre of literature. For ages written and printed texts were assumed by their very tangible existence to be the only trustworthy expressions of language. It is on the basis of such texts that the philological research was initiated and, subsequently, the theories of translation used to be created and verified. This mere fact has finally become the source of innumerable convictions (including the false ones) on the feasibility and the quality of the translation, such as the famously alleged opposition between the faithful translations and the beautiful ones or the unsolvable dilemma of a struggle against the absolute untranslatability in search of the perfect translatability. While they may have been long denied by the expert approach to language and the actual translation phenomena, they inevitably continue to exist in the lay minds of the translation and interpretation product end users.

The translators had to be painfully aware of the trivial but true rule, that although probably every kind of thought and state of affairs can be conveyed by the words and expressions of virtually any language, it is usually achieved in multiple as well as heterogeneous means. Written texts did not help much in investigating the non-written parameters of the source reality of their authors or the target reality of their readers. The obvious conclusion was that there must have existed something different than script – not instantly visible, but perhaps even more important than what has been explicitly conveyed in writing.

One of such factors is related to the fact that literature is similar to all other genres of art, as a kind of a surplus communication activity. Its reception is usually backed up by the high aesthetic standards and the elaborated schemes of interpretation based on them, which may not be automatically translatable into other language codes. Furthermore, at least some of the actual literary works may be denied or rejected by the very members of speech communities or sub-communities they have been designed for. Other sub-genres or themes, peripherally used or even most representative for the literature of one culture, may slip out of classification or even be absent from the standards and classifications considered typical for other cultures. This assumption may not necessarily allude only to the sophisticated qualities of the advanced kinds of literary works. Quite independently of the specific genre, many of such rules may be hidden, simply for the reason that they constitute, as mentioned by Harold Garfinkel, the "routine grounds of everyday activities" – acquired by their users not only *expressis verbis*, but mainly throughout the regular presence and experience of the extralinguistic context. Some genres may further reveal differences on a higher level of complexity and other may not exist at all. It is hence also in this particular sense that, as pointed out by Elżbieta Tabakowska, the "communication barriers are made of grammar" – grammar including both explicit and hidden rules of social interactions.

Even despite their invisibility in most contexts of actual social interactions, it is relatively easy to allude to the omnipresent rules of communication *in abstracto.* On the other hand, it may be close to impossible to study them while not being immersed in a certain reality. This, having been mentioned to avoid contact with actual facts and to value only written and indirect statements may lead to numerous common misunderstandings and overestimations. As Edward W. Said used to describe it, the manner of the orientalism, understood as trusting the text more than the actual phenomena, is a common weakness. This is how the concept of Oriental peoples is created, at the same time, as Said further aptly mentioned, denying their humanity. One surely cannot avoid in a perfect manner all dangers related to the inter-cultural generalisations. Still, the mere conscience of them may be crucial for understanding that the multi-cultural activities and studies may be an extremely demanding matter.

The notions of the Orient and the people of the Orient having been mentioned in the previous paragraph, the opposition between the Orient and the Occident, emphasised also in the title of this volume and frequently utilised in numerous works and conceptualisations belonging both to the Oriental and to the Occidental perspectives, is of course nothing new. It may serve well to illustrate the complicated status of the students and the researchers of the heterogeneous cultures, who experience a sudden enlightenment as well as the chronic encoding and decoding dilemmas in their inter-cultural contacts. It may also be useful in embodying the inevitably mixed impressions of tourists and casual or remote interpreters of the non-native culture facts, who may be free from obligation to strive at the universal solutions, though at the same time they are usually vividly determined to find the effective ad hoc solutions of the inter-cultural issues.

It is with no doubt the mission of the inter-cultural researchers to provide the methods and opportunities in order to confront the different points of view, be they linguistic or literary. In their research activities, they are inescapably forced to use the language, with all benefits and flaws resulting from this fact. There is, for example, much to question, whether the very distinction of the Orient and the Occident relies on some universal premises, alluding in an immediate manner to the archetypal notions of *us* and *them* or, perhaps, is but a product of tradition, embedded in languages and cultures the researchers have natively been immersed in. As such, this volume does not attempt at solving all possible problems and explaining any conceivable issues related to the actual acts of communication as a whole. It serves as yet another valuable source of facts and approximation to them, with both the tangible and the intangible results included.

The component texts, alluding in different ways to the notions of the Orient and the Occident, do by no means constitute a strictly defined, complete and featured in its classical character, set of language facts on a carefully selected area of communication. They should rather be viewed as a mere selection of approximations to the Oriental and the Occidental phenomena belonging to the widely recognized genre of literature. As can easily be seen, the possibly weakest factors of this classification are marked by the elements *Oriental* and *Occidental*. There is no Orient as such. Similarly, as there is no Occident. They are but the fuzzy sets of ideas, devised for the purpose to juxtapose the allegedly united and normalized concepts of the European (the inter-cultural *us*) cultures to the unknown and unexpected mass of events and phenomena that have happened to origin geographically from the so-called Asia (the inter-cultural *them*), located someplace to the East of Europe. "Asia" – as one of the prominent researchers of Polish literature and culture in Japan, Tokimasa Sekiguchi stated it in a convincing and reasonable manner – "does not exist."

Needless to say, the above assumption is not of a critical character towards the contents of this volume. The complex processes of cognition inevitably include the sequences of the construction and of the deconstruction of schemes and ideas. The more that is known about the objects of research, the easier and the more thorough may be the verification of the hypotheses applied to them. May the possible deconstruction of the concept of Asia (and, subsequently, the concept of Europe), resulting at least partly also from the reception of the content of this volume, contribute to a better understanding of what has for a long time been classified as the Orient and the Occident and lead to its effective re-definition. In other words, may the concept of Asia and the Orient vs. Occident opposition prove more useful in achieving the effective perspectives of approximation to the heterogeneous language and culture facts than in obscuring the unbiased view of them. This wish is of a consciously sincere and naive nature. Thank you, the editors, for making it possible for me to express it as the conclusion of this introduction.

Bibliography

Chomsky Noam (1965). *Aspects of the Theory of Syntax*. Cambridge: MIT Press.

Garfinkel Harold (1972). "Studies in the Routine Grounds of Everyday Activities." [In:] David Sudnow [ed.] *Studies in Social Interaction*. New York: The Free Press, 1–30.

Hjelmslev, Louis (1953). *Prolegomena to a theory of Language*. Transl. F. J. Whitfield. Madison: University of Wisconsin Press.

Jabłoński, Arkadiusz (2013). *Homeostaza tekstu. Tłumaczenie i komunikacja międzykulturowa w perspektywie polsko-japońskiej* [homeostasis of a text. Translation/interpretation and the inter-cultural communication from the Polish-Japanese perspective]. Poznań: Wydawnictwo Naukowe UAM.

Milewski, Tadeusz (2004). [7th edition]. *Językoznawstwo* [linguistics]. Warszawa: Wydawnictwo Naukowe PWN.

Said, Edward. W. (1978). *Orientalism*. Pantheon Books: New York.

Sapir, Eduard (1924). "The Grammarian and his Language." *American Mercury vol. 1*, 149-155.

Saussure, Ferdinand de (1977). *Course in General Linguistics*. Transl. W. Baskin. Glasgow: Fontana/Collins.

Sekiguchi Tokimasa (2008). „Azja nie istnieje [Asia does not exist]." *Teksty Drugie* 4 (112), 48–75.

Tabakowska, Elżbieta (2002). „Bariery komunikacyjne są zbudowane z gramatyki [communication barriers are built of grammar]." [In:] Roman Lewicki [ed.] 2002. *Przekład, język, kultura* [translation, language, culture]. Lublin: Wydawnictwo UMCS, 25–34.

Whorf, Benjamin Lee (1940). "Linguistics as An Exact Science." *MIT Technology Review 43*. 61-63, 80-83.

Yngve, Victor H. (1975). „Human Linguistics and Face-to-Face Interaction." [In:] Adam Kendon, Richard M. Harris i Mary Ritchie Key. [ed.] *Organization of Behavior in Face-to-Face Interaction*. The Hague–Paris: Mouton Publishers.

Introduction

In the era of domination of visual culture, literature seems to be losing its paramount role, and its researchers are increasingly moving towards social sciences, especially sociology and anthropology – disciplines that are strongly charged with Europocentrism in the research methods they adopt. The dangers of Europocentric approach in describing and familiarising the reader with foreign cultures were pointed out by, among others, J. Hillis Miller ("Cultural Studies and Reading". In *Literary Theory. A Reader Guide*, ed. Julian Wolfrey, New York 1999). According to this scholar, in the present times, as a result of the invasion of information, we are witnesses of a constant breaching of borders, and thus, without moving outside the borders of our own, familiar world, we are subject to a constant confrontation with other cultures. "Otherness", in turn, perceived as strangeness, results in the sense of danger and a fear of losing one's own identity. A reaction to this state of affairs consists in returning to nationalism or a fanatical attitude towards religion. Cultural studies – as Agnieszka Kondor-Wiercioch writes – constitute a reaction of a kind to "this invasion", but the attempt at domesticating "otherness" is frequently based on faulty assumptions, as it endeavours to translate and assess a foreign culture with the use of one's own methodological apparatus (*Dwa światy dwie pamięci. Dylemat wielokulturowości w wybranych utworach Louise Erdrich i José Marii Arguedasa*, Kraków 2009: 46–47).

Despite the scepticism characterising the approach of Miller and scholars similar to him, as well as despite various doubts concerning whether we are capable of understanding "otherness", it is certainly worth it to undertake studies and research into literature from various cultural areas, taking, however, into account difficulties which one would need to face and traps into which one might easily fall when looking for shortcuts. The assumption driving the editors of the volume *Borders and Beyond: Orient-Occident Crossings in Literature* was to inscribe the book into a current whose aim is to break away from Europocentric traditions in studies on literature, conceived of as a product of broadly understood culture, and to undertake a reflection over the experience of border beyond the common lines of linguistic, ethnic and national divisions, which continue to determine academic discourse. The articles collected in this volume are concerned with multi-faceted issues connected with the notion of borders and that which is beyond them in the context of literary studies. Their authors, both Orientalists, and researchers of native literature, propose a reflection over a work of literature, trying to re-create the course of various borders or to revise them and design them anew.

The common plane that connects texts representing diverse and distant cultures is created by an assumption regarding migration and mutual permeation of elements – repetitive and universal on the one hand, specific and particular on the other – within the field of literary tradition perceived as Western and Oriental. We will find here texts pertaining to regions such as Europe, the Arab world, Indian subcontinent or countries such as Japan, China, Iran, Turkmenistan or Turkey. However, the geographic and cultural criterion is only one of many possibilities of ordering the rich material contained in this volume. Another criterion is the historical one. The analysed subjects are presented in a broad time perspective, covering the period from the fifth/sixth century until the present day, resulting in a cross-sectional outline of the literary output of diverse national and ethnic groups. The historical perspective showcases the fluidity of the course of contemporary borders and it points out that literary work should not be considered in their context, as political or cultural borders undergo constant changes and, at the time when the work is analysed, they are not the same as the borders determining the life of the creators when the work was produced.

In the pages of the present publication, we will find familiar names, counted among the canon of world literature and shown in a new context, but also figures that are lesser known even in their own cultural circle. The authors of the articles discuss phenomena of cross-regional scope, but phenomena of local scope, such as the literature of small, isolated ethnic groups, are also analysed. Subjects from the field of theory of literature (questions concerning delineating the borders of genres) are entangled with text analysis in the aspects of identity, trans-boundary issues, liminality, and transgression.

Among the collected articles, we will find analyses and interpretations. Many of them are characterised by an interdisciplinary approach, of both diachronic and synchronic character. Obviously, it is difficult for any contemporary publication dedicated to the East-West (or West-East) relations to lack references to colonialism and postcolonialism, but they do not constitute a dominating discourse.

Adam Bednarczyk, Magdalena Kubarek, Maciek Szatkowski

I

Limitations and Borderlands in Oriental Poetry

Chapter 1

Adaptations and Evocations of Orientalism in Nāzik al-Malā'ika's Poetry

Muneerah Bader Almahasheer
Imam Abdulrahman Bin Faisal University/ Saudi Arabia

Introduction

Nāzik al-Malā'ika's poetry can be considered through the lens of Orientalism and Deorientalism respectively. A central question in the present article involves investigation as to whether the "Orient" is engaging in the process of deorientalization through the act of – physical or cultural – border crossing. An analysis of the poetry of Nāzik al-Malā'ika will seek to understand to what degree this body of work can be considered to be Oriental.

Orientalism and Deorientalism can be conceptualised in terms of literal or metaphorical crossings of borders and frontiers. In order to effectively compare the influence of the concepts of borders, frontiers, borderlands, and transgression on both Orientalism and Deorientalism, certain preliminary examinations of relevant works must be pursued. It is first necessary to examine the question of potential intertextuality between the works of authors with roots in the Middle East that have gained a Western audience. Additionally, it is essential to seek out any other Western texts that reflect a similar set of themes as those addressed by Middle-East rooted authors. When examining the literature of this area, a number of highly important questions arise. Among these foremost of these is the issue of the Orient crossing the borders and the borderlands to deorientalize itself.

Unfortunately, Middle-East literature is not translated or examined enough compared to African or East and Southeast Asian Studies, which makes it an alluring less Oriental field. In other words, it is not an easy endeavor to survey Iraqi Arabic literature or Al-Malā'ika's poems translated into English given the lack of a comprehensive bibliography of translated Middle-East literature. Nāzik al-Malā'ika, in her poetry, often appears to be associating herself with the traditions or cultural norms of the West as opposed to those of the East. It is necessary to contemplate the degree to which the works of the writer are in fact products of an oriental cultural frame. It is not entirely clear that a sharp delineation between the East and the West, the Orient and the non-Orient can be made when asking this question. It would appear, for example, that the context in which the relevant issues are taking place involves considerations that are themselves a manifestation of a certain interaction between Orientalism and Deorientalism (Biddick 2000: 1234–1249). It is, therefore, necessary to crystalise a new formulation of an original critical representation of Orientalism (Balagangadhara 1998: 101–102).

Core Questions

This study will attempt to answer these highly relevant questions by the means of comparing the life path of Nāzik al-Malā'ika in the context of an Oriental origin. Al-Malā'ika (1921–2007), who was born in Iraq, studied in Princeton, Madison/Wisconsin, and afterwards returned to the oriental world, migrating to different Middle-East Countries, had her own history of displacement. The present study will ask the central question of whether or not the Orient is crossing the borders and the borderlands to deorientalize itself? In order to effectively elaborate on this central hypothesis, it will be necessary to attempt to find the answers to two main questions: What are Orientalism and Deorientalism? How did Nāzik al-Malā'ika experience border transgressions, associating herself predominantly with the West or the East?

A Critical Representation of Orientalism and Deorientalism

Orientalism has been defined as a way in which Western artists and cultural commentators depict cultures from the global East – the Middle East, South/Southeast Asia and North Africa. The term "Orientalism" is also somewhat historically loaded as involving a rather condescending or patronizing attitude by those in the West towards the cultures that are considered non-Western. To Edward Said, the author of 1978's *Orientalism*, a discourse that labels any non-Western reality as a non-favorable, underdeveloped, immoral and violent world merely seeks to establish Western cultural hegemony. Orientalism depicts the societies which Nāzik al-Malā'ika originated from as archaic, retrograde, and primitive, and yet regards these societies as somehow exotic and mysterious.

Orientalism and Deorientalism constitute a binary-based arbitrary system; the reality of Nāzik al-Malā'ika's poetic output shows that one person and one cultural voice can include multiple or fragmented aspects of identity, heritage, cultural context and act(s) of border-crossing or transgression. The theoretical framework of Orientalism is helpful in that it gives way for researchers to discuss and understand the power dynamics and cultural exchanges that happened, and happen, between colonising and colonised peoples and regions. Said states: "because of Orientalism the Orient was not (and is not) a free subject of thought or action. This is not to say that Orientalism unilaterally determines what can be said about the Orient, but that is the whole network of interests inevitably brought to bear on (and therefore always involved in) any occasion when that peculiar entity 'the Orient' is in question" (Said 1978:3). Said apparently questions the pluralistic hegemony and demonology of the Orient. Subsequently, Deorientalism has been defined as the critique of Orientalism; it attempts to depict a more truthful picture of such regions as the Middle East, including the regions of Iraq and Syria from which Al-Malā'ika originated. Deorientalism, the study assumes, is a De-hegemonising of context, a De-centering of the marginal, a monolithic heterogeneity of a discourse, globalization from below, and a stretching of boundaries. This decolonial dichotomy is a vigorous alternative production of disciplinary knowledge that augments mainstream knowledge, claims Kumarvadivelu (2012–2015), it is an ever growing, multidirectional and non-linear dichotomy that is fluid and amorphous. Her practice of writing poems about Iraq or Middle-East in diaspora conjures a fragmented reality and makes her an eavesdropper rather than an insider. She thinks about commonality but is not really engaged in one, the process of writing or Deorientalisation helps Nāzik to identify herself and place herself within the cultural Globe.

Efforts to provide a critical representation of Orientalism and Deorientalism have become more prevalent in recent decades. Lisa Lowe argues that "Orientalism is not a unified and dominant discourse; rather, Orientalist logics often exist in a climate of challenge, ambivalence, and contestation" since Orientalism is "irregularly composed of statements and restatements, contestations, and accommodations generated from an incongruous series of writing positions" (Lowe 1992: 28, 114). Certainly, this deeply distorted image of the Arab peoples fuels the perception of an inherent dichotomy between Orientalism and Occidentalism and the parallel erroneous perception of Orientalism as somehow synonymous with Islamism. Al-Azm describes how these perceptive processes as the "phenomena of Orientalism, Occidentalism, and Islamism are at play in a variety of contexts today [...] Occidentalism, it is argued here, has taken various forms over the past few decades: the 'Orientalism in Revers'e of Hasan Hanafi and his call for the establishment of a science of *istighrab* (Occidentalism) in the Arab world; the retaliatory occidentalism of Adonis's 'Manifesto of Modernity (or Modernism)' of 1980; the Talibanish occidentalism found in a work like *The Spirit of Terrorism* by Jean Baudrillard;

and the benign and popular variety of occidentalism, which helps in some cases to reinforce shaken identities" (Al-Azm 2010: 6–13).

Orientalism and the Social Construction of Perception

Edward Said argues that "Orientalism" assigned a certain exotic or even mystical quality to persons of the regions in question, and that this perception has impacted power relations between the Western and Eastern worlds. For example, it is widely assumed that the propensity to engage in acts of terrorism is something that is somehow endemic to the character of Middle Eastern peoples as "Islamic Terrirorism" (Little 2002:155). Since the publication of Said's *Orientalism,* the world has become increasingly globalised, and it could well be argued that what was understood as comprising "the Orient" in 1978 when Said published his work can no longer be considered as Oriental in any case.

The model of Orientalism developed by Said overlaps with the theories of Berger and Luckman regarding the social construction of perception, and how these serve to form such "othering" concepts as the Oriental/Occidental dichotomy. Berger and Luckman are primarily concerned with the way in which what is perceived to be "real" is actually socially constructed. Historically, many societies have accepted a wide range of beliefs and practices that were merely thought to be "normal" at the time but which, in retrospect, only reflected the understandings of a particular time period and the limited frame of reference that was available at the time. In reality, things that are often accepted to be self-evidently normal and unquestionable can often come to be regarded as aberrational in the space of a relatively short amount of time. Examples of this include the ways that race, gender, and sexuality have been viewed in the relatively recent past as opposed to the way that these issues have come to be regarded by social scientists in more recent times (Apelrouth and Edles 2007: 279). Changes in the way the Orient has been viewed have occurred in recent years; these changes have often been focused on the ideas of good and evil. The rise of Islamism has created a situation in which there is a perception of a clash of Eastern and Western ideologies, in which Islam and Christianity are supposedly predominant religions in the East and West respectively. However, the reality is far more nuanced and multifaceted – there exist Western Islam and Eastern Christianity, in addition to other religious and cultural traditions in all geographical regions. Otherising, (subaltering), the Orient and viewing through the lens of good and evil distorts the discourse regarding Orientalism, Deorientalism, and other fields.

Jean Baudrillard developed the concept of "hyper reality" as a means of describing the ways in which the perception of reality itself is shaped by various forces that have the effect of blurring the distinction between what is "real" and what is merely a matter of perception (ibid. 415). An important illustration of this point involves the role of the mass media in shaping popular consciousness and popular perceptions regarding a wide range of phenomena. The cultural hegemony of "hyper reality" that originates from such sources as the mass media serves to perpetuate the assumption concerning "Orientalism" that have been described by Said, and the forms of "hegemonic masculinity" that have been critiqued by Connell (ibid. 360). These, in turn, serve to form the basis of the social construction of reality that has been described by Berger and Luckman. The theoretical models developed by Berger and Luckman, Connell, Said, and Baudrillard intersect with one another. The theories that are associated with each of these thinkers reflect different paradigms through which contemporary people understand the world around them, and this, in turn, generates a wide range of social, cultural, political, and economic consequences. Each of the aforementioned thinkers has sought to critique the ways in which contemporary people, particularly those of the Western world, have come to develop an understanding of social and global realities that are often depicted or at least implicitly understood as a universal mode of perception. However, critical analysis that is associated with these thinkers demonstrates that such a shared perception represents a fairly narrow set of particular values and assumptions rather than a reality. A synthesis of these theories makes it possible to develop an understanding of the operational function of Orientalism in the Western model of perception.

In their discussion of Edward Said's concept of "Orientalism," Appelrouth and Edles make this observation:

> "The source of the West's superiority lies not in its own "advanced" civilisation but, rather, in constructing non-Western cultures through negative terms that project onto the colonized all those traits that the West cannot possess if it is to legitimate its position as the center of progress and the beacon of humanity....Thus, when a politician remarks that Muslims "hate us for our freedom," this claim is dependent on a purified notion of what Western freedom has promoted around the world, in turn justifying an ennobled aggression against those who are «against freedom»" (Appelrouth and Edles 2007: 623).

Like Edward Said, they argue that it is this kind of dualism and cultural chauvinism that becomes the hallmark of the ideological oriental context which enables the Western conquest of the Islamic world. According to this false dichotomy, "the Islamic nations are plagued by political repression, anti-intellectualism, retrograde cultural values, and severe social underdevelopment. By contrast, the Western nations are believed to be manifestations of higher levels of enlightenment, progress, prosperity, 'freedom', 'democracy', and 'cultural evolution' " (ibid.). Criticism of the Western cultural superiority is revealed in biases and misconceptions that can be found in Western academic scholarship, caricatures and media. Specifically, the common perception of Western societies as centers of enlightenment and growth or "civilisations", and Islamic societies as centers of reaction and obscurantism or "traditionalism" is rooted in demonstrably false assumptions, or hyper reality (Edwards 2000).

How Did Nāzik al-Malā'ika Experience Border Transgressions in her Life?

The question of whether or not the Orient is now crossing the border to de-orientalise itself is the central area of concern that is related to this study. A wide range of thinkers and scholars are attempting to fight the presumptions that are often associated with Orientalism. According to Edward Said, Orientalism suggests that it is appropriate to group all oriental cultures together and label them as underdeveloped. Consequently, a narrative is formed that makes the culture of the West appear to be of higher value than that of the East. Thus, there are people from the Orient that migrate into the Western world and write about their experiences. These poets would have their own cultural tradition now mixed in with western culture. As a result, a person from the West cannot simply say that the oriental cultures are backwards, or that they have simply mixed with the superior cultures from the west. Césaire notes that the vast majority of "history" is told by white people; this has a self-perpetuating effect that preserves and continues the white perspective on the Orient. In the post-colonial context, views of Orientalism and Deorientalism involve the peripheries of metropolitan European geography; however, it is also necessary to remember that coloniser and colonised people and cultures are not separate and delineated throughout history, or in the post-colonial era. The relationships between the East and the West and the lines that are drawn between these cultures and cultural practices are inherently ambivalent and porous based on restructuring and destructuring of thought and historiography.

Nāzik al-Malā'ika, the Iraqi poet who is best known as the first to use the medium of free verse to express her thoughts, finds herself caught between two worlds: a yearning for a world that is different from her life as an Arab in the Orient while simultaneously being about the Orient itself. Al-Malā'ika was born in Baghdad on August 23, 1923. Her real name is Nāzik Ṣādiq al-Laḫmiyya, and she became known as "Nāzik al-Malā'ika" due to the tranquility and divine milieu of Al-Laḫmiyya's family. Her father, Ṣādiq al-Malā'ika, named her Nāzik after the Syrian rebel Nāzik al-'Ābid, who led Syrian revolutionaries against the colonising French in the year in which the poet was born. She earned her Bachelor in Arabic language and literature in 1944 and a music degree from the Institute of Fine Arts in 1949. She also obtained a scholarship to study criticism at Princeton University, New Jersey and gained her M.A. in comparative literature study at the University of Wisconsin-Madison in 1959. For a while, Nazik served as a professor at Baghdad University but fled Iraq in 1970 in order to escape the regime of Saddam Hussein. After Hussein's invasion in 1990, Al-Malā'ika left Kuwait to Cairo and lived in a self-imposed exile; she suffered from the Parkinson's disease, which heartened a group of Iraqi intellectuals to plead to the Iraqi government, protesting what they called slackness of "Iraq's greatest surviving symbol of literature". She won Al-Babtain Prize in 1996 and was honored by the Cairo Opera House on the occasion of the passage of half a century of the beginning of free verse in the Arab world in 1999.

Nāzik al-Malā'ika, who was proficient in English, French, German, and Latin, is a renowned figure in modern Arabic literature because of her experimental free verse poetry, and critical provocative issues regarding modern Middle-East and Arab literature. For almost a decade, Al-Malā'ika competed with Badr Šākir as-Sayyāb (an Iraqi poet) concerning her primacy of free verse writing rather than classical rhyme; nevertheless, she has been acknowledged to be the first Arab female poet to use free verse. She wrote her first poem at the age of ten and published her first collection of poems in 1947, titled *The Night's Lovers*, which reveals an inordinate influence of both classical Arab poets (Maḥmūd Ḥasan Ismā'īl 1910-1977, Badawī al-Ǧabal 1900-1981, Amǧad aṭ-Ṭarābulsī 1916-2001, 'Umar Abū Rīša 1910-1990 and Bišāra al-Ḫūrī 1885-1968) and English poets (Shakespeare, Keats and Shelley). However, it is the publication of *Cholera* (1947) and *Sparks and Ashes* (1949) that granted her Arab fame. Throughout her verse, she challenges the logocentricity and phallocentricity of the Arab world, Orientalising, and Deorientalising the lifestyle of the Arabs. She also published several poetry collections, such as *Sparks and Ashes* (1949), *Bottom of the Wave* (1957), *Tree of the Moon* (1968), and *The Sea changes its Color* (1970) and *Prayers and Revolution* (1978).

A number of important questions arise from an examination of the career of the writer, and her various life experiences. One issue that is immediately apparent involves the matter of how Al-Malā'ika, as a student and, later on, as a refugee, reacted to the frequent change of country (U.S, Kuwait, and Egypt). It is interesting to consider the question of to what degree the frequent change of nations of residence influenced any political or social changes that she might have experienced. In other words, it is better to develop an understanding of people from the Orient when they have lived among Western people and adopted certain Western cultural traditions to resist the Western hegemonic systems (MacKenzie 1995: 9). There is also the matter of whether or not the "transgression" in question, such as the experience of traveling to a new country or fleeing a repressive regime, had the effect of sharpening her poetry and writings. It is necessary to establish whether or not these experiences had the effect of changing her outlook on life or any other significant areas of consideration (Rotter 2000: 1205–1217).

In a study titled *Literature and Cultural Invasion*, Al-Malā'ika (1965) expressed a binary intellectual Oriental stand when she criticised the submissive reaction of the Arab World towards the Western chauvinism: "what is essential and superior to the West in our culture in order to embrace in its stead cheap and harmful commodity" (Al-Malā'ika 1965: 3–34). The matter of whether or not Nāzik al-Malā'ika is associating herself with the West or the East is also an important aspect of any analysis of her work. Within the context of this personal history, including her longtime residential status in the West, it is necessary to consider how Oriental her poems actually are. Naturally, the Western influence is apparent in her poetry, because she is also known as a translator and a critic of literature and poetry, and her interaction with traditional Western poets and poetry is momentous. Abdul-Hai (1982) notes the influence of English Romantic poets on Al-Malā'ika's work, specifically pointing to her use of pigeon imagery as resonant with Keats's *Nightingale*. It should be remembered that Al-Malā'ika returned to Egypt and chose to stay in the Arab world and to make trips to the West.

Poetic Examples and Development

The poetry of Nāzik al-Malā'ika includes various themes that relate to the idea of living in the Orient, but it also comprises elements that can be considered Deoriental, as they advance a physical and cultural departure from the Oriental life. From reading *Who Am I, Revolt Against the Sun, New Year* and *Love Song for Words* the themes that the poet explores in relation with the Orient are approached with desolation, sadness or inner frustrations, which seem to condemn Orientalism, but other themes, such as faith, spirituality, and desire of excitement are also explored. Al-Malā'ika's selected poems contain elements that can be associated with the Arabic, but also with the Occidental terminology, which is why these poems are both Oriental and Deoriental.

In *Who Am I*, the poet associates herself with the night ("I am its secrets-anxious, black, profound/ I am its rebellious silence"; al-Malā'ika 1974: 79). *Night, black, secretiveness* are aspects specific to Arab terminology because they are metaphors of the dark, long clothes that Arabic women wear, which cover their full bodies, their identities, and at a deeper level, their thoughts. The *rebellious silence* is another metaphor that relates to the Oriental spirit, overwhelmed by intrinsic frustrations, ready to explode. As she explores her nature, the poet identifies herself with the Arabic traditions and history "I, like it, am a giant, embracing centuries/ [...] I create the distant past/From the charm of the pleasant hope/ And return to bury it/ to fashion for myself a new yesterday/ whose tomorrow is ice" (ibid. 81). These verses indicate that in the poet's perception, Oriental tradition is entrenched in the past and it cannot advance in the future because the strong recurrence of its past removes even the hope for tomorrow. The association with a continuous past is in contrast with the speed of change and transformation that occurs in the Occident, which is why this stillness, with which the author associates herself, reflects Oriental terminology.

Al-Malā'ika also discusses Arabic gender relations and lifestyle by indicating "I have veiled my nature, with silence, / Wrapped my heart in doubt" (ibid. 79). She refers to the veil that women use to cover their figures, hiding themselves and erasing their individualities, living without knowing who they really are beyond the veil. From these lines, it can be deduced that the poet acknowledges that the veil is a patriarchal social instrument that keeps women silenced, therefore submissive, hence it is another aspect that speaks of Oriental values.

Edward Said believes that the Orient should be able to represent itself (Hafez 2004: 82) and in this sense, Al-Malā'ika, as a representative of the Orient, produces a desolated image of the Orient, presenting it as oppressive, restrictive, secretive and rebellious. This perception of Orientalism is similar to the way that the Western world sees it, condemning the Oriental (especially Arab) social structures that practice the oppression of women and promote violent values of rebellion (Grosfoguel 2006: 16). Throughout *Who Am I*, Al-Malā'ika takes the side of Deorientalism, as she tries to understand who she is and where she fits in the Arab world. She is unable to find any positive representations of this world, and implicitly of herself, as the representative of the

Orientalism. Furthermore, words such as *disowned, travel, resurrection* (a value pertaining to Christian tradition, hence to Deorientalism) or *tomorrow* are associated with the postcolonial terminology. The term *disowned* refers to the action of disinheriting the natives, which is a historical fact associated with the Western colonialism. The action of *travel* completes the image of the Western conquest and the colonisers' intended imposition of the Christian belief in the resurrection, or the coming back to life after death. Although Al-Malā'ika's poem describes the aspects that define the Oriental identity through negative associations and a sad tonality, *Who Am I* is, in essence, an Oriental poem. On the other hand, the terminology associated with the Occidentalism suggests accents of Deorientalism.

Furthermore, *Who Am I* can be understood in the context of border-crossing, transgression and the ambivalence of those who cross borders. Al-Malā'ika discusses and questions her identity, which is confused or confusing, ambivalent and ambiguous:

> "The night asks who am I?
> I am its secrets-anxious, black, profound
> I am its rebellious silence
> I have veiled my nature, with silence,
> Wrapped my heart in doubt
> And solemn, remained here
> gazing, while the ages ask me,
> Who am I?" (Al-Malā'ika 1974: 79)

The poem goes on to place the question of "who am I?" in the mouth of "the wind," which is an interesting use of imagery and personification as the wind naturally is a force that can cross borders and move from one physical place to another without impediment. The wind contains air from multiple locations and is therefore inherently ambiguous with regard to what it constitutes. A clear parallel can be drawn between the wind and Al-Malā'ika's poetic identity. The poem states: "I am its confused spirit, whom time has disowned / I, like it, never resting/continue to travel without end / continue to pass without pause" (ibid. 81). In terms of Orientalism, Occidentalism, and Deorientalism, as discussed earlier, it can be seen that viewpoint and perspective are important in determining how work is understood and defined. Al-Malā'ika's viewpoint is transient, shifting and ambiguous; therefore, the definition of her poetic identity as Eastern or Western, Oriental or Deoriental, is correspondingly impossible to pin down and quantify.

The temporal context of identity development and ambiguity is also considered in this poem: "I, like it, am a giant, embracing centuries / I return and grant them resurrection / I create the distant past / From the charm of the pleasant hope / And I return to bury it / to fashion for myself a new yesterday / whose tomorrow is ice". The imagery of "ice" is a Western rather than an Eastern image. This image is contrasted to the imagery of the "sun" in *Revolt Against the Sun*, which is an Oriental image, but since the speaker is female seeking power, doubt concerning identity violates the Oriental patriarchal social norms and manners.

> "She stood before the sun, screaming:
> "Sun"! You are like my rebellious heart
> Whose youth swept life away
> And whose ever-renewed light
> Gave the stars to drink.
> Careful! Do not let a bewildered sadness
> Or a sighing tear in my eyes deceives you.
> For sadness is the form of my revolt and my resistance"
> (Al-Mala'ika 2013).

The sun can be equated with al-Malā'ika's geographical identity as an Arab writer, as repeated references to the sun evoke the climate of the Arab world more so than the global West and the northern hemisphere. Similarly, the sun is an emblem of border crossing or transcending, as each day the same sun has its effects on all regions of the globe. Al-Malā'ika continues to use dialogue with the sun and references to sadness, which can be interpreted in the context of border crossings and transgressions:

> "If my bewilderment and the lines of my torrential poet's sadness
> Should appear shimmering on my brow,
> It is only the feelings that inspire pain in my soul
> And a tear at the frightening power of life" (ibid.).

Al-Malā'ika is, similarly to historical English writers from Shakespeare to Thomas Hardy, equating the sun and light with human emotion and an absence of pain or sadness. These negative emotions are connected instead to the night, which again signifies an escape from imprisonment, "Forgetting the sadness of an unjust existence":

> "Night is all life's melodies and poetry
> Where the inspirational god of beauty wanders.
> The soul, no longer imprisoned, flutters about in it

And spirits soar above the stars.
How often I have walked beneath its shadows and lights
Forgetting the sadness of an unjust existence" (ibid.).

Even if her poetry usually depicted a desire to embrace a culture that was not Oriental, the poem *Revolt Against the Sun* finds her in a dual state of mind where she rejects the Sun, representing the British that the Iraqis revolted against, for darkness, and which is probably all that she finds familiar as she was brought up in Oriental culture. There are some symbols that one can glean from this piece of poetry such as the Sun, nature, prophecy, idol, caravan, singing harp and temple that are reflective of Oriental culture over centuries.

In her disillusionment with the Sun, she now settles for the goddess of beauty since she cannot take the "deceptive glow" that the sun offers her. In fact, she feels as if these "dancing lights" are the very reason for her state of disillusionment, as her people felt under British rule. In a way, it is probably her Oriental upbringing that causes her to find it difficult to understand the ways of the Western world even if she wishes for more, given that Arab society seems plunged in "darkness" in the way it treats its women. Yet, quite uncharacteristically, she rejects the Sun because of her rebellious heart and also due to the fact that the Sun not only mocked her sadness and tears but also laughed at her bitterness and pain. This is the reason why she feels this conflicting sense of bewilderment and feels as if she can do without the gleaming rays that do nothing to evoke the emotions that are vital to a poet's ability to express herself (ibid.). Given the British oppression of Iraq after World War I, with the defeat of the Ottoman Empire, it is clear that these words probably resonate with the feelings of Iraqi society at the time she wrote this piece of poetry.

Apart from this, the poet feels a deep sadness, since it was in her youth that she embraced the Sun whose light helped her rise above pain as she considered it to be the object of her heart's dreams, "For sadness is the form of my revolt and my resistance/Beneath the night – divinity be my witness!" In all probability, and since Al-Mala'ika was known to be liberal and defiant of the way women were treated in Iraqi society even if they were educated, it would not be surprising that she found the ideology that was a part of British imperialism to be forward-thinking and in the best interests of Iraqi society, and that she accepts the imperialistic sun as a means of resistance or escape "You are the one I held holy and worshipped/As an idol when I sought refuge from pain". Unfortunately, and as she feels disparaged now, she feels no desire to buy into this deception anymore and prefers to embrace her sadness, as Iraqi women have felt, even if she wanted to be released from this burden realising that "The sum of your dancing lights, oh sun,/ Are weaker than the flame of my resistance", an Iraqi aspiration to seek freedom from British imperialism right after World War II, tiring of its oppressive and deceptive light, "And the madness of your fire will never rend my melody".

Given that she is caught between accepting and rejecting the coloniser along with his disparaging behavior, it seems as if only Mother Nature remains her solace even if there were times when the Sun was the only object of worship and holiness. In stark contrast to her youth, she now prefers the darkness and wants to stay out of the light, since this is where the inspirational god of beauty wanders "Do not be surprised if I am in love with darkness. /You goddess of the flame that melts and thaws" (ibid.). If anything, one can interpret these statements as a rejection of her source of inspiration to write poetry while embracing her Arabic 'roots' where the sights and sounds of the night are exalted through literature and song. Even if she shared a kinship with the coloniser prior to this, her disillusionment now causes her to reject what she considered to be divine and immortal in the Western tradition of religion and politics. In other words, being grounded in the Iraqi culture is what she considers as the right thing to do given that the British have not been honest with her people. In the end, she assures the reader that the past that continues to be glorified by Western culture, probably through Christianity, is something that she will not hesitate to reject now given that she feels a closer kinship to her own country's values, no matter how primitive or un-Christian they might seem.

The *New Year* poem also expresses an elegiac tone, as the poet reveals her perception about the stillness of the Arabic world, "a ghost-world", which has been forgotten by its own fate: "fate has deserted us/ We live as wandering spirits/ with no memory/ no dreams, no longings, no hopes" (Al-Malā'ika 1987a: 4–6). This poem also speaks about the lack of passion of the Arabic life, as the poet experienced it: "the gray of a still lake, / like our silent brows, / pulseless, heatless, / denuded of poetry" (ibid. 8–11). The *silent brows* is a metaphor pertaining to Oriental terminology, which refers to the body parts that are uncovered by the veil. Here, the epithet *silent* complains about submissiveness, an Oriental value for women's submission, a gender-related terminology that was also identified in "Who Am I". Seeing the life in Iraq as pulseless triggers a reference to the absence of life, "no memory", which the poet clearly expresses in a later verse: "We wish to be dead, and refused by the graves" and "If only we could die like other people" (ibid. 17). The desire to be dead signals the fact that nothing can be sensed in this part of the world;

therefore, death is preferable to living a passionless life. Furthermore, the poet expresses her wish to live in excitement, to feel even the sadness of love or to have a national memory, hope or regret: "If only memory, or hope, or regret/ Could one day block our country from its path/ If only our lives could be disturbed by travel or shock, / or the sadness of an impossible love" (ibid. 22–27). All the elements mentioned here, memory, hope, regret, path, travel, shock, sadness or love, are in contrast with the Oriental stillness, express a desire to Deorient the Orient. The poet prefers to be dead than to feel nothing and go nowhere. Therefore, these elements that contrast with the Oriental lifestyle are terminologies that suggest Deorientalism.

The poet looks through many aspects of existence to express her dissatisfaction with living in her native country, such as fate, time, passion and excitement. Again, through her verses ("the gray of a still lake", respectively "denuded by poetry" (ibid. 4–6), Al-Malā'ika echoes Western beliefs, according to which the Orient is "frozen in time", and "not open to cultural dialogue" (Grosfoguel 2006: 19). Also, the fact that the poet separates herself and her people, collectively, from the rest of the world ("we are wanderers/ from a ghost-world, denied by man" (ibid. 1–2), signals her acknowledgment of the cultural distance between the Orient and the rest of the world. Hence, in her representation of the Orient, Al-Malā'ika reflects the same image of the Orient as the Westerners do.

Correspondingly, in *Love Song for Words*, the poet asks why we should fear words, which probably symbolises the silent oppression that people in the Arab culture have had to deal with on a daily basis, "We became still, fearing the secret might part our lips. /We thought that in/ words laid an unseen ghoul, /crouching, hidden by the letters from the ear of time" (Al-Malā'ika 1987b: 334), due to the rise of the Ba'ath Pay in Iraq. Using a number of similes, she exalts the necessity of words that to be borderless and help Arab culture to cross the boundaries into a culture of dialogue once again. It is clear that she accepts the Western view of the Oriental culture being closed as is expressed in this poem. As history bears witness, this inability to be able to express oneself freely among Arabs often leads to discrimination and suppression of certain people on the basis of religion, ethnicity, color and even gender if these unspoken rules of society are flouted. Even if she does not directly extol the Western culture or the Ba'ath Party in this poem, she feels as if the criticism that they have of the Oriental culture is valid and this is why she praises the necessity of words that is so crucial in every aspect and walk of Iraqi life.

As she describes the pleasure of using words, Al-Malā'ika also states that there is none in silence even though it has become the norm in Iraqi society "Why do we fear words/when among them are words like unseen bells, /whose echo announces in our troubled lives". In debunking the unnecessary fear that is attached to the use of words and the consequences that might arise if one is not careful or selective with their choice of words, she goes on to say that from these words one can enjoy smooth sweetness that can be likened to that of a cushion, referring a common practice in Arabic culture, where one lies back in a comfortable setting so as to enjoy some *sher shayri,* music in the form of ghazals, dance and wine apart. She seems surprised that people consider words to be a fearful thing instead of thinking of them as a way to express themselves, which is reflective of Western culture (ibid. 334).

In addition, she also considers words to be but an oud – a musical Arab instrument – or even bells – a Western musical instrument, since she believes that they are sweet to the ears as they have a life of their own in helping people express emotion or thought, while the combination of east and west in music is impressively Oriental and Deoriental. Now, of course, Iraqi society has been silenced, and even their desire to speak or lead a normal life has seemingly been crushed by the colonisation that they feel oppressed by. What is also evident is that this silence brings a kind of hopelessness that Al-Malā'ika wants to free the people from by reminding them of how beautiful words can be in a number of ways. It is why she says, "Tomorrow we will build ourselves a dream-nest of words", as she wants people to join her in the celebration of words so that they can express themselves freely and with joy (ibid.).

What is also interesting to note is how she ends this poem and where she talks about the necessity of words in prayer. One can only assume that most Arabs consider their religion, which is Islam, to be followed devoutly. While the initial stanzas of this poem celebrate the beauty of words, accepting the Western view of encouraging expression, the poet gives her reader a clear reason, assuming that they are Arabic, as to why words are definitely necessary. In saying that we also need words for prayer, she cements her poem, *Love Song for Words,* by telling her readers that it is also God's will to worship and pray to him using words. It is clear that she ends her poem this way so that she emphasises the message of the importance of words and dialogue in the hope that they will agree with her, given that they are a God-fearing society (Al-Malā'ika 2013).

Nāzik al-Malā'ika's poems *Who Am I, Revolt Against the Sun, New Year* and *Love Song for Words* present the construction of Orientalism as perceived by the Orient itself. Al-Malā'ika's work describes aspects pertaining to the Arab world, which makes her poems Oriental. However, the poet uses an elegiac tone and negative connotations for defining the Orient. Through this repellent attitude towards Orient and the expressed desire to live in a different world, described through words that contradict the Oriental terminology (*disowned, travel, resurrection, memory, hope, regret, love,* etc.) the poet engages in the process of Deorientalisation. Therefore, the poems are Oriental and Deoriental, one can see that while she laments the presence of the British in Iraq in colonial times in her poems, this changes to a surprising acceptance of the Western practice of using dialogue to affect change in society in *Love Song for Words.*

Conclusion

Arab poetry is framed in the Oriental literary style, primarily due to its geographical location, but also due to the national identity expressed in verses (Hafez 2004:76). Al-Malā'ika, an Iraqi poet, is therefore perceived as an Oriental poet, not only because she belongs to the Arabic Space, but also because of the themes that she explores in her poems. Nevertheless, as in her verses, she challenges the national identity, tradition, history, faith, or lifestyle of the Arabs, Al-Malā'ika's poetry can be interpreted as the reverse of Orientalism. The poetic works that have been developed by Al-Malā'ika represent an intersection between Orientalism and Deorientalism in the sense of reflecting a significant degree of intertextuality of the kind that indicates a crossroads between the Oriental and the Occidental worlds. It is apparent that the poet has incorporated a range of literary influences that help to generate a synthesis of poetic styles representing two great civilisations. Depending on perspective and intent, Nāzik al-Malā'ika's work could be interpreted as being Oriental, as being American, or as inhabiting a cultural borderland between the two. Having explored writers and theorists whose work and identity involve border crossing and cultural ambiguity between the Orient, the non-Orient, and a potential process of Deorientalisation, it is considered that Nāzik al-Malā'ika's poetry can be best understood as that of a writer who wishes to retain a primarily Arab identity. Perceptibly, Nāzik al-Malā'ika's poetry includes reference points and elements of identity from both traditional Arab culture and traditional Western culture; the hybridisation of these influences can be examined to ascertain which identity and influence can be understood as dominant. As it has been analysed earlier, her work seems to fit with a Deorientalist approach more closely than with an Orientalist approach. Alternatively, it could be considered and argued that neither traditional (Arab or Western) culture is dominant in the identity and poetry of

Nāzik al-Malā'ika as a writer. Her work may be understood as a true hybridisation of traditional Arab culture and traditional Western culture, creating a voice and a body of work that transcends or blurs borders and a binary way of viewing the Orient and the non-Orient.

Bibliography

Al-Azm, Sadik J. (2010). "Orientalism, Occidentalism, and Islamism: Keynote Address to 'Orientalism and Fundamentalism in Islamic and Judaic Critique: A Conference Honoring Sadik Al-Azm'". *Comparative Studies of South Asia, Africa and the Middle East* 30 (1): 6–13.

Al-Malā'ika, Nāzik (1965). "Literature and Cultural Invasion". *Al-Adab* 13.

—— (1974). "Who Am I". In: *Anthology of Modern Arabic Poetry.* Ed. Mounah Abdallah Khouri, Hamid Algar. California: University of California Press.

—— (1987a). "New Year". In: *Modern Poetry of the Arab World.* Ed. Abdullah Al-Udhari. London: Puffin.

—— (1987b). *Modern Arabic Poetry: An Anthology.* Ed. Salma Khadra Jayyusi. New York: Columbia UP.

—— (2013). "*Revolt against the sun* by Nazik al-Mala'ika". Transl. Emily Drumsta. *Jadaliyya,* Feb 28, 2013.

Abdul-Hai, Muhamad (1982). Tradition *and English and American Influence in Arabic Romantic Poetry.* London.

Appelrouth, Scott, Edles, Laura D. (2007). *Sociological Theory in the Contemporary Era: Text and Readings.* Thousand Oaks, CA: Pine Forge Press.

Balagangadhara, S. N. (1998). "The Future of the Present Thinking through Orientalism". *Cultural Dynamics* 10 (2): 101–121.

Biddick, Kathleen (2000). "Coming Out of Exile: Dante on the Orient(alism) Express", *The American Historical Review* 105 (4): 1234–1249.

Edwards, Holly (2000). *Noble Dreams, Wicked Pleasures: Orientalism in America, 1870–1930.* Princeton: Princeton University Press.

Grosfoguel, Ramon (2006). "The Multiple Faces of Islamophobia" *Human Architecture* 1(1).

Hafez, Sabry (2004). "Edward Said's Intellectual Legacy in the Arab World". *Journal of Palestine Studies* 33 (3).

Little, Douglas (2002). *American Orientalism: The United States and the Middle East Since 1945.* 3rd ed. Chapel Hill: University of North Carolina Press.

Lowe, Lisa (1992). *Critical Terrains: French and British Orientalisms.* Ithaca: Cornell University Press.

MacKenzie, John (1995). *Orientalism: History, Theory and the Arts.* Manchester: Manchester University Press.

Rotter, Andrew J. (2000). " Saidism without Said: Orientalism and U.S. Diplomatic History". *The American Historical Review* 105 (4): 1205–1217.

Chapter 2

An In-depth Comparative Study of Victor Hugo and Shahriar's Poetry

Mohammad Amin Mozaheb, *Imam Sadiq University/Iran*
Mostafa Shahiditabar, *Imam Sadiq University/Iran*
Mohammad-Javad Mohammadi, *University of Tehran/Iran*

Introduction

Various elements of religion are greatly represented by means of literature. Out of all the major world literature, the French and the Turkish literature are quite rich and important. The modern Azerbaijani-Turkish literature along with the diverse and rich French literature has given rise to several literary figures that have made their marks on world literature. Two of the most famous literary figures include Seyyed Mohammad Hossein Bahjat-Tabrizi, from the Turkish literature, and Victor Hugo, from French literature.

Seyyed Mohammad Hossein Bahjat-Tabrizi, an Iranian and Azerbaijani poet, commonly known as Shahriar, published poetry both in the Azerbaijani Turkish and the Persian languages. Shahriar was born in 1906, in a small town called Khoshgenab, in Tabriz. He became very popular due to his extremely well known nostalgic poem, called *Heydar Babaya Salam,* which was published in the year 1954. This legacy left by him has been admired in several ways, which includes placing his sculpture in Eynali (which is a mountainous range located north of Tabriz) and also placing his statue in the Tabriz Subway.

The French author Victor Hugo was a very popular and well-known writer in the whole of French literary history. He was born in the year 1802, and was a novelist, poet, and a dramatist, writing primarily about the Romantic Movement. During his younger days, Hugo supported the royalists; however, he became a Republican supporter later in life. The whole French history can be seen in his works. He has received many tributes and a lot of recognition, with his legacy being admired in several ways. In the current study, his major poems will be analysed.

The Significance of This Study

The literary figures under discussion, Shahriar, and Hugo, are very popular and effective in the Azerbaijani and the French languages, literature, arts, cultures, etc. The academic field which deals with the study of literary and cultural expressions all over the world, without any barriers regarding different languages, nations, or any other disciplinary boundaries, is known as comparative literature. This field of study resembles the International Relations study, but it deals with artistic and linguistic expressions and traditions. However, not many researchers have analysed the above-mentioned popular literary figures with a comparative literature viewpoint. In this study, we will take into consideration the discussion topic.

Review of Literature

There are several essays that have analysed Hugo's poems and Shahriar's poems separately i.e. Shahiditabar, Mehrpour and Mozaheb (2016: 24–26), Shahiditabar, Mozaheb and Monfared (2015: 519–521), Jafari (2013: 316–322), Qurat-ul-Ain, Dildaralvi and Baseer (2013: 116–123) as well as Mansoor (2009: 107–112), among others.

One study which has analysed Hugo and Shahriar's poems using a content-based analytical technique was carried out by Shahiditabar (2016: 521). According to this study, both the poets frequently used the word "God" in their poems. One of the most interesting facts that the authors observed after analysing the poems by the two poets was that while both the writers believed in God, Hugo believed that mankind would liberate itself from any type of religion to seek God. Furthermore, Shahriar only believed in the God described in Islam.

Another study conducted by Shahiditabar (2016: 455) observed that Shahriar's poems contained several Islamic themes. The authors noted that Shahriar often bridged the religious gaps and also highlighted the similarities between all people. According to Shahiditabar (2016: 520), Shahriar applied the Islamic and the Qur'an themes in the form of a collection of tools for transferring his many thoughts and ideologies.

Mansoor (2009: 107–112) has described the romantic experiences of Shahriar. The study observed that Shahriar often expressed his thoughts by using the feelings of excitement, love, romantic failures and even stress. The study also described the positive and the negative effects of these feelings on the poet.

The study conducted by Ahmad Qurat-ul-Ain analysed the poem *Les Miserables* written by Hugo. The authors used the textual analysis technique and concluded that all the double standards present in the society were created by man. The study also observed that economic equality and social impartiality were the best methods to resolve all the contradictory problems and abolish life's absurdity. The study also stated that class distinction which was the reason for persecution described in *Les Miserables* and in other societies was abandoned.

The complete literature review showed that no comparative study had been conducted based on the works having a religious theme, written by Hugo and by Shahriar. As stated earlier, Shahiditabar did observe the mention of the word "God" in several of their poems, and he also noted similar Islamic religious themes in many of the poems written by Shahriar. In this study, the researchers aim to observe similar religious themes present in Christianity and Islamic religions by analysing the Azerbaijani Turkish poetry by Shahriar and Hugo's French poetry by using a content-based analytical technique. In this study, the question which will be explored is: How did Hugo and Shahriar apply religious words and themes in their poems?

3. The Method

This is a qualitative analytical study which strives to analyse the poems written by Shahriar and Hugo in two different languages, i.e. Azerbaijani Turkish and the French language. A content-based analytical technique would be applied for answering the above-mentioned question.

3.1 Corpus

The major corpus in this study contains 30 different Shahriar's poems written in the Azerbaijani Turkish language, which has been obtained from Şəhriyar (2005; 2007) along with 30 different Hugo's poems written in French.

3.2 Procedure

All the poems written by both literary figures have been extensively studied in order to answer the research question. The study observed many religious themes by using the content-based analytical technique.

4. Results

Table 1: Religious Themes in Hugo's Poem

Religious Themes	Frequency	Percentage
God	40	19
Soul	18	8.6
Prayer	17	8.1
Pray	17	8.1
The Lord	13	6.2
Angel	10	4.8
Grave	7	3.3
Tomb	6	2.9
Divine	6	2.9
God	5	2.4
Sublime	5	2.4
Other words	66	31.4
Total	210	100

Table 1 depicts that Hugo's poems use "God" as the most common religious theme, thus implying that Hugo does believe in God. A similar observation was also made by the study conducted by Shahiditabar (2016: 521). The table also points out that the second most frequently used religious theme was the soul. Moreover, Hugo's poems frequently use the themes regarding pray and prayers.

Table 2. Frequency of Qur'anic Themes used in randomly-selected poems of Shahriar (extracted from Shahiditabar 2016: 519).

Religious themes	Frequency	Percentage
God and Faith	19	16.8

A similar context, namely, God and Faith have frequently been used as religious words in many of Shahriar's poems. His poetry also features Satan as the second most frequent theme, followed by Human. The important point to be noted is that Shahriar has used Satan as a warning in many of his poems, as described below:

> *"Aman Allah yenə şeytan gəlib iman apara,*
> *Qoruyun qoymayın imanızı şeytan apara."*
> Oh God, Satan has come again to take faith,
> Be careful; do not let Satan destroy your faith.

The above verses demonstrate that Shahriar has used Satan in his poem to warn people and that he has requested the people to turn towards Faith and God. The next frequently used theme, i.e., Human, can be further elaborated in this study based on the example below:

"Mənim insanlığımın gör nə hisari yavadır,
Ki günüz qul-i biyaban gəlir insan apara."
How weak are the restrictions of my humanity,
That the Dracula comes to take it in daytime.

Shahriar's poems also frequently feature the themes of The Holy Qur'an and the religion. This can be further explained by considering some poems written by Shahriar and Hugo in the following manner:

Shahriar

"Xəzan yeli yarpaqları tökəndə,
Bulud dağdan yenib kəndə çökəndə,
Şeyxülislam gözəl səsin çəkəndə,
Nisgilli söz ürəklərə dəyərdi,
Ağaclar da Allaha baş əyərdi."
When the cloud was turning and entering the village,
When Sheikhuleslam (i.e. a clergyman) was given his sermon,
The trees were praying as well.

The above verse showcases Shahriar's belief in the fact that the trees pray. A similar observation can be noted in Hugo's poetry described below:

"C'est Dieu qui remplit tout. Le monde, c'est son temple.
Œuvre vivante, où tout l'écoute et le contemple!
Tout lui parle et le chante. Il est seul, il est un.
Dans sa création tout est joie et sourire;
L'étoile qui regarde et la fleur qui respire,
Tout est flamme ou parfum!"
It is God who does all. The world is his temple.
Living work where all listen to Him and contemplate Him!
Everything talks to Him and sings Him. He is alone, it is One.
In His creation, all is joy and smile;
The star who looks and the flower that breathes,
Everything is a flame or perfume!

The piece of poetry quoted above shows that the poet believes that all living things can speak with God and sing about Him. Hugo also believes God to be exceptional and unique, and all His creation to be filled with smiles and joy. He has described the world to be God's beautiful creation. This perspective of Hugo and his manner of observing the world has also been noted in several Islamic texts, especially the Quran. An example is provided below:

وَلِلَّهِ الْمَشْرِقُ وَالْمَغْرِبُ فَأَيْنَمَا تُوَلُّوا فَثَمَّ وَجْهُ اللَّهِ إِنَّ اللَّهَ وَاسِعٌ عَلِيمٌ

> "And Allah's is the East and the West, therefore, whither you turn, thither is Allah's purpose; surely Allah is Ample giving, Knowing."
> (The Quran, Surah 2: 115)

It can also be stated that a similar belief has been voiced by many religious and Iranian poets, such as Baba Tahir, Sa'adi, and Mawlana. Hugo has observed the world as a living creation, wherein everyone listens to God.This was also seen in many of Malwana's poems.

With respect to the Holy Qur'an, the poet Shahriar states:

> *"Sübh oldu, hər tərəfdən ucaldı əzan səsi,*
> *Guya gəlir məlaikələrdən Quran səsi."*
> It is morning and the adhan can be heard from everywhere,
> Maybe the angles are reading the Qur'an.

The above verse creates a picture of the morning time of the day when the adhan (an Islamic call announcing Salah, which is a type of formal Islamic worship) is recited in several of the mosques by the muezzin in the mosques and is heard everywhere. He described this practice to be similar to reading the Qur'an. Shahriar also uses the concept of devotion towards God in his poems, as showcased in verse below:

> *"Yolum Allah səmtinədir, başqa bir yol tanımıram,*
> *Allah qismətimdən savay hər nətapsam, zay tapmışam."*
> My path is linked to God; I know no other path,
> Everything except what is given to me by God, found I waste.

The above verse describes the poet's feelings as he feels that his whole existence and his life revolves around God. He feels that other than the path linking him to God, he has no path. In the verse below, Shahriar also states that:

"Musa təngə gəldi xalqı əlindən,
Dağda vəhy eşitdi Allah dilindən.
İnsan hər bir şeyi biləbilməz tam,
Bircə Allah bilər hərşeyi tamam."
If a man knows nothing,
Then, just God knows everything.

Shahriar believes that humanity has no knowledge, whilst God possesses infinite amounts of knowledge. He also thinks that he knows nothing as compared to God's knowledge. A similar idea, with a variable point of view, can be seen as described by Hugo:

"C'est Dieu qui remplit tout. Le monde, c'est son temple.
Œuvre vivante, où tout l'écoute et le contemple!
Tout lui parle et le chante. Il est seul, il est un.
Dans sa création tout est joie et sourire;
L'étoile qui regarde et la fleur qui respire,
Tout est flamme ou parfum!"

It is God who does all. The world is his temple.
Living work where all listen to Him and contemplate Him!
Everything talks to Him and sings Him. He is alone, it is One.
In His creation, all is joy and smile;
The star who looks and the flower that breathes,
Everything is a flame or perfume!

"Ucaldar eşqimizi göyətanrı camalın,
Bu yollarda görərsən yorulmaz sarvan məni.
Belə söyləmişdir böyük Məhəmməd:
Ana ayağının altıdır Cənnət
Grand Prophet Muhammad (P.B.U.H.) has said that,
Heaven is under the feet of mothers."

In the above verse, Shahriar describes the very respectable and pious position of the mother in Islamic religion by reaffirming the statement by Prophet Muhammad (P.B.U.H.) according to which Heaven lies under a mother's feet.

Hugo

Similar to Shahriar, the poems of Hugo also contain many religious themes. In this study, the researchers analysed his poems for many religious themes, and the corpus contains his poems as below:

"Quoi! hauteur de nos tours, splendeur de nos palais,
Napoléon, César, Mahomet, Périclès,
Rien qui ne tombe et ne s'efface!
Mystérieux abîme où l'esprit se confond!
À quelques pieds sous terre un silence profond,
Et tant de bruit à la surface!"

What! The height of our towers, splendour of our palaces,
Napoleon, Caesar, Muhammed [P.B.U.H], Pericles,
Nothing that falls and disappears!
Mysterious abyss where mind is confused!
A few feet underground a deep silence,
And so much noise on the surface!

The above stanza names some popular figures, like Caesar, Napoleon, Pericles, and Prophet Muhammed (P.B.U.H). Hugo believes that everyone and everything will perish when he has written his work, *Rien qui ne tombe et ne s'efface*! In the stanza, Hugo wanted to name one important figure present in the Western society (i.e., Napoléon), one in the Roman society (i.e., César), one in the Eastern culture (i.e., Prophet Muhammad (P.B.U.H)) and another present in the Greek culture (i.e., Pericles). Thus, he described every person in the world, and he did not restrict himself to the French or the Christian community.

One important point made by Hugo in the stanza is that everyone is equal. He has put all the religious and the political figures he mentioned at similar levels and has also not considered the pious standing of Prophet Muhammad (P.B.U.H) in the Islamic culture. In his poems, Hugo considered only the political character of Prophet Muhammad (P.B.U.H).

His point of view can also be demonstrated in certain other stanzas as follows:

"Lorsque pour moi vers Dieu ta voix s'est envolée,
Je suis comme l'esclave, assis dans la vallée,
Qui dépose sa charge aux bornes du chemin;
Je me sens plus léger; car ce fardeau de peine,
De fautes et d'erreurs qu'en gémissant je traîne,
Ta prière en chantant l'emporte dans sa main!"
And when thy voice is raised to God for me,
I'm like the slave whom in the vale we see
Seated to rest, his heavy load laid by;
I feel refreshed—the load of faults and woe
Which, groaning, I drag with me as I go,

Thy winged prayer bears off rejoicingly!

The above stanza presents a very unusual picture when Hugo states that *I'm like the slave whom in the vale we see Seated to rest.*

There are other verses which describe impressive images of God, as written by Hugo, for example:

"Va donc prier pour moi!_Dis pour toute prière :
— Seigneur, Seigneur mon Dieu, vous êtes notre père,
Grâce, vous êtes bon! grâce, vous êtes grand! —
Laisse aller ta parole où ton âme l'envoie;
Ne t'inquiète pas, toute chose a sa voie,
Ne t'inquiète pas du chemin qu'elle prend!"

Then go, go pray for me! And as the prayer
Gushes in words, be this the form they bear:—
"Lord, Lord, our Father! God, my prayer attend;
Pardon! Thou art good! Pardon—Thou art great!"
Let them go freely forth, fear not their fate!
Where thy soul sends them, thitherward they tend.

The above stanza states that praying can have great influence on a person, which is as helpful for their souls, which can be depicted in Hugo's line: "Laissealler ta parole où ton âmel'envoie". A similar idea was presented by Imam Ali (P.B.U.H) in a Hadith: the best form of prayer can be described as the one that is sent towards God by a righteous person having a very pure heart.

خَيرُ الدُّعَاء مَا صَدَرَ عَنْ صَدْرٍ تَقِيٍ وَ قَلْبٍ نَقِيٍ (Hadith.net, 2016)

„Seigneur! préservez–moi, préservez ceux que j'aime,
Frères, parents, amis, et mes ennemis même
Dans le mal triomphants,
De jamais voir, Seigneur! l'été sans fleurs vermeilles,
La cage sans oiseaux, la ruche sans abeilles,
La maison sans enfants!"

Oh, God! Bless me and mine, and those I love,
And e'en my foes that still triumphant prove
Victors by force or guile;
A flowerless summer may we never see,
Or nest of bird bereft, or hive of bee,
Or home of infant's smile.

The above stanza presents the lines written by Hugo, which are *Seigneur! préservez–moi, préservez ceux que j'aime, Frères, parents, amis, et mes ennemis même.* It depicts God's kindness, and can also be observed in the Holy Qur'an.

One of the most important sources of Hugo's belief in God is his testament, which was written in two parts:

> *"Le 31 août 1881, il rédige son testament: « Dieu. L'âme. La responsabilité. Cette triple notion suffit à l'homme. Elle m'a suffi. »*
> *« C'est la religion vraie. J'ai vécu en elle. Je meurs en elle. Vérité, lumière, justice, conscience, c'est Dieu. Deus, Dies. Je vais fermer l'œil terrestre ; mais l'œil spirituel restera ouvert, plus grand que jamais. »"*

In his testament on 31 August 1881 Hugo wrote:

> "God,
> Soul,
> Responsibility,
> This threefold notion suffices for man. It was enough for me."
> "It is the true religion. I lived in it. I die in it.
> Truth, light, justice, conscience; these are God.
> I will close the earth's eye; But the spiritual eye will remain open, greater than ever."
>
> Le 2 août 1883, Hugo ajoute un codicille à ce testament : « Je donne 50 00 francs aux pauvres. Je désire être porté au cimetière dans leur corbillard. Je refuse l'oraison de toutes les églises. Je demande une prière à toutes les âmes. »
> « Je crois en Dieu. »"

On August 2, 1883, Hugo added a codicil to this testament:

> "I give 50 00 francs to the poor. I wish to be carried to the cemetery in their hearse. I refuse the prayer of all churches. I ask a prayer to all souls."
> "I believe in God."

As it is seen, Hugo's first and last words in his testament are God.

Also Hugo wrote is some of his poems:

> "Moi, je vais devant moi ; le poète en tout lieu
> Se sent chez lui, sentant qu'il est partout chez Dieu."
>
> I go straight,

Poet is everywhere,
Feeling in his heart that he is watched my God.

From the viewpoint of Hugo, liberty is the sign of God:

"Comment se figurer la face du profond,
Le contour du vivant sans borne, et l'attitude
De la toute-puissance et de la plénitude ?
Est-ce Allah, Brahma, Pan, Jésus que nous voyons ?
Ou Jéhovah ?"

How can one imagine the face of the deep,
The outline of the living without boundaries, and the attitude
Of omnipotence and fullness?
Is it Allah, Brahma, Pan, Jesus we see?
Or Jehovah?

As it is seen the God of Hugo is not the God of one specific religion; rather, he believed in a God that is not limited to just one religion.

Hugo asks a question about God since he did not believe in the Catholic God:

„Qui donc êtes-vous, Dieu superbe ?
D'où vient votre souffle terrible ?
Et quelle est la main invisible
Qui garde les clefs du tombeau ?"

Who are you, superb God?
Where does your terrible breath come from?
And what is the invisible hand
Who keeps the keys of the tomb?

Hugo believes that the human is surrounded by God.

Discussion

The data analysis shows that both the literary figures analysed in this study, i.e., Shahriar and Hugo, have used the word "God" most frequently in their works, thus indicating that they consider God to have a pious position. A similar observation was made by Shahiditabar (2016: 520).

Hugo believed in God and His signs in this world as mentioned in the previous section. He noted that "liberty is the sign of God." Moreover, he pointed out that "Is it Allah, Brahma, Pan, Jesus we see?". Besides, when he wanted to start his testament, Hugo writes God,

Soul, Responsibility. Additionally, he mentions that

> "I go straight,
> Poet is everywhere,
> Feeling in his heart that he is watched my God."

In a similar way, Hugo considered God Superb, saying that

> "Who are you, superb God?
> Where does your terrible breath come from?
> And what is the invisible hand
> Who keeps the keys of the tomb?
> The mentioned points all can be seen as proofs for Hugo's belief in God."

Hugo considered the popular characters of Napoleon, Caesar and Prophet Muhammad (P.B.U.H) to have been equal. This is one major point of distinction between the works of Shahriar and Hugo, where Shahriar believes that as Prophet Muhammad (P.B.U.H) was appointed as the last prophet by God, He could not be equated to any other influential person in the world.

One other point of difference between their works was that Hugo never focused on Christianity's canon laws, which form their basis on the Holy Bible but rather focused more on the spiritual features. Hugo thought that religion was one tool to escape the bitter problems in life. A similar point of view was described by several romantic poets. It is disputed that Hugo attained "neverland" using his religion. On the other hand, Shahriar always focused more on the Islamic teachings described in the Holy Qur'an.

Bibliography

Jafari, Nasrin (2013). "Shahryar Position In Persian Contemporary Poetry". *International Research Journal Of Applied And Basic Sciences* 7(5): 316–322.

Mansoor, Saeed (2009). "Love And Shahriyar". *History Of Literature* 59(3): 107–112.

Qurat-Ul-Ain, Ahmad, Dildaralvi, Sofia, Baseer, Abdul (2003). "Victor Hugo's Les Miserables: A Marxist Consciousness". *International Journal Of Contemporary Research In Business* 5(5): 116–123.

Şəhriyar, Mohammad (2005). *Türki Divani Kolliyyat-I, Heydərbabaya Salam Mənzuməsiilə*, Tehran: Negah Nəşriyyatı.

—— (2007). *Seçilmiş Əsərləri*, Bakı: Avrasiya Press.

Shahiditabar, Mostafa, Mehrpour, Hamed, Mozaheb Mohammad Amin (2016). *Representation Of God In The Poetry Of Victor Hugo Versus Shahriar*, Proceedings Of The Ires 26th International Conference, Paris, France, 30th January 2016.

Shahiditabar, Mostafa, Mozaheb, Mohammad Amin, Monfared, Abbas (2015). "Islamic Themes Found through Content-based Analysis of Shahriar's Azerbaijani Turkish Poems". *The English Literature Journal* 2(6): 519–521.

Chapter 3

Crossing Borders in the Opposite Direction. An Influence of Western Elements in Contemporary Chinese Poetry*

Daniela Zhang Cziráková, *Slovak Academy of Sciences/Slovakia*

The influence of the Orient in the Western literature is a well-known topic. However, the borders have often been crossed also from the opposite side by Chinese artists, writers, poets, since Chinese students started to study at European and American universities in the first half of the 20th century. Chinese poetry has been deeply influenced by Western poetics since starting of using contemporary Chinese (*baihua*) instead of classic Chinese (*guwen*).

The May 4th movement brought different opinions on using the Chinese language in the literature, and we can speak about the revolution on using modern language since that period. While in prose and scholarly texts the modern Chinese was enforced relatively easily, poetry tended to be closely connected with classical language, from the usage of words to the topics, phraseology, which caused even a lot of reformers to refuse it as the language not very suitable for subtle nuances of poetry.

Since the beginning the modern poetry written in contemporary Chinese was strongly influenced by Western poetics, it can be even said that all modern and contemporary Chinese literature written in modern Chinese not using ancient Chinese is based on Western influence[1]. Although the situation

* The article was published within a grant VEGA 2/0102/16: *Reflexia kozmologických predstáv v duchovnej a materiálnej kultúre Ďalekého Východu, južnej Ázie a Oceánie.*

has changed later, and modern and contemporary Chinese literature started to search the inspiration in the Eastern tradition, too, Western elements can be easily found in the contemporary Chinese poetry. If would be hardly possible to analyse all influence of the Western poetry in Chinese modern and contemporary poetry, whose birth and growth was strongly influenced much more by Western poetic tradition than traditional Chinese poetry, as they tried to define themselves as both contemporary and Chinese. In wider meaning, the whole contemporary poetry written in China is based on the Western literary tradition. We can find similar tendencies in contemporary Chinese painting, especially in the oil painting which had grown up without any traditional background and despite the lack of background in tradition, it was able to establish typical features that defined and distinguished it from Western art.

Most intellectual poets acknowledge that Western poetry serves as an important inspirational source for their works, but few would agree that they write merely "to pay tribute to Western masters". They describe whatever Western traces that occur in their writings as evidence of complex intertextuality (Li 2008: 198).

Contemporary Chinese poets do not have the same celebrated place in society as their forebears had in that long and glorious tradition. This is thus a more grievous relative anonymity that could make the Chinese tradition seem less relevant to contemporary Chinese poets and obscure the ways in which transcendence might embellish the poetic life (Weaver 2008: xiii).

In my paper, there will be discussed the influence of Western elements in the poems of four contemporary Chinese poets, whose works I have translated recently for the international festival of poetry *Ars Poetica*, which was held in 17.–21. November 2015, Bratislava: Chen Dongdong, Song Lin, Tang Xiaodu and Zhao Si. The reason for choosing them is very simple, as a translator I had to work with and analyse their texts, communicate with the authors in order to be sure about the meaning of their works for them to be translated correctly. This has given me a lot of opportunities to read their poems, to consider all

---

[1] I am using the terms of modern and contemporary literature not according to Ezra Pound's understanding of modern era (since 1900 to about 1950), but as Chinese sources are used to, especially in the Mainland China. Modern (xiandai) literature usually refers to the period 1919–1949, contemporary literature refers to the period after 1949. The May 4th movement is important since than Chinese started to use contemporary Chinese more often than before, but the issues of poetry are rather different, as there are still authors using classical Chinese in their poetry.

possible meanings and the connotations of the text. During my work, I realised that the Western influence is transparent not only in the structure of language, in the way of using metaphors, but sometimes even in using specific names of geographical places or names of people. Some of their poems bear stronger features of the West, visible in using Western localities, as, e.g. the Powązki Cemetery in Poland in the poem *Rose Garden* by Zhao Si, the Boulogne Forest in the poem "In the Boulogne Forest" of Song Lin. The crossing of Western and Eastern influences is a typical feature of the contemporary Chinese poetry. On the one hand, authors are playing with the elements typical for Chinese poetry in the last centuries, trying to find a way how to combine modernism and original Chinese tradition, how to be both Chinese and contemporary. Of course, the poetry selected here does not include the entire spectrum of contemporary Chinese poetry, as there are avant-garde poets writing on the Internet, as well as rural poets, poet-migrants, etc., the list is long. Thus, my study represents only some of them, but, as I believe, it is enough to give us an approximate reflection of Western elements in contemporary Chinese poetry after *Misty Poetry*, one of the most important movement in contemporary Chinese poetry in Mainland China after Cultural revolution, which has formed as a movement at the beginning of the 1980s of the 20th century.[2]

All of the above-mentioned authors belong to generation after *Misty poetry*, which was one of the strongest poetic movements after the Cultural Revolution. They can be considered the poets of the Third generation of Chinese poets (maybe with the exception of the youngest of them, Zhao Si), defining themselves as more contemporary than the poets of *Misty poetry* were. The poets mentioned here are all well educated, inheriting the intellectual, literary tradition of Chinese literature, unlike rural poets who started to become involved in the poetry recently.

I prepared poems that introduced some of the most obvious Western elements in their works, as well as lack of the first-plane Western elements, using elements typical of Chinese poems, such as pavilions, annotations on the old poem, Chinese philosophy instead, or, on the contrary, the use of modern language and avoidance of direct cultural references to both cultures in their works. As to translations, in all cases, I used translations provided by authors to the festival *Ars Poetica*, conscious of the particular semantic shifts in translation. The aim of this article is to the present poets with reference to the greater or lesser intensity of Western elements in their work, and by doing so,

---

[2] For more about Misty poetry, see for example: Hong 1999: 297.

consider these translations sufficient. I am not analysing their poetry from the linguistic point of view, I consider it is necessary to also take into account the artistic value of translation, as English is not my mother tongue and my translations would hardly be able even to have the ambition to overcome the translators selected and approved by authors.

Firstly, I would like to mention the poem by the contemporary poet Song Lin 宋琳 (born 1959 in Xiamen, Fujian province). In 1983 he graduated from the Shanghai Normal University, the faculty of Chinese language. In 1991, he moved to France and pursued graduate work in the Department of Far Eastern Studies at Paris 7 University. After graduation, he lived in Singapore and Argentina. He has been teaching at various universities in China since 2003, as a lot of other overseas Chinese citizens, attracted by the policy of Chinese government trying to persuade successful and highly educated Chinese to come back to their home country. He has published several books of poetry; one of them, *The City Wall and the Setting Sun* was published in France, by the publishing house Charecteres, Paris, 2007.[3] He is involved in writing and painting for full time now. His poetry collections include *City Dwellers* (Collected Works, 1987), *Vestibule* (2000), *Fragments and Farewell Songs* (2006), *Visiting Mr. Dai on Snowy Nights* (2015), *Oral Message* (2015). His essay collections include *Continuous Approaches to Moving Icebergs*, and *Orpheus Looks Back* (2014). He edited the poetry anthologies *Blank Etudes* (with Zhang Zao, 2002). He is also working as poetry editor for the literary journal *Today*, and an editor for *Reading Poetry*. He is on the editorial board for *Contemporary International Poetry*. He is a recipient of *Rotterdam International Poetry Award*, *Shanghai Literature Magazine Award*, and *Dong Dangzi Poetry Award* (Ars Poetica 2015: 179).

As we can see, Song Lin spent a considerable time of his life in France, therefore a strong presence of French elements is visible at first sight, or better said, from the titles of some of his poems, as is, for example, *In the Boulogne Forest*[4]. He plays with evocations that can bring readers the feeling of visiting Paris, as a big circus, full of images, colours, impressions. Like most of his poems, this one is in free verse, in style evoking French surrealist poetry from the first half of the 20th century, as is, f. e. poetic style of Guillaume Apollinaire. In the poem selected here, I am using the translation of Jami Proctor-Xu, provided by the author to the festival *Ars Poetica*.

---

[3] Chinese poetry website, http://www.zgshige.com/c/2016-03-08/568195.shtml#srzy_srjj, [accessed: 21.03. 2017]

[4] Chinese original see Ars Poetica 2015: 191, English translation: Ars Poetica 2015: 197.

At the beginning of the poem, we can observe short description of the atmosphere of Paris. After a few poetic images - engaging first impression becomes more personal. Lin is using the metaphor of "wind counting grey hair" which can be understood as a feeling of personal life experience, as well as a reference to the elapsed time, which is a frequently mentioned element of the Chinese literary tradition. The phenomena of floating time can be observed in a lot of famous poems and literary works as a whole, from Tang, Song dynasties, until later periods. Floating time and ephemerality of human existence is very often mentioned not only in Chinese culture but also in Japanese culture, as the observation of blossoming flowers reminds us of the same feeling the boundedness of human life and all living beings. Images of an old clock beating against death row memories are enhanced by the atmosphere of sadness, melancholy, perhaps indicating the grief for author's homeland or simply awareness of the tragedy of human fate.

布洛涅林中	**In the Boulogne Forest**
湖水的碎银，在巴黎的左侧 狮子座越过火圈。	Broken silver on the lake surface; on Paris' Left Bank, Leo passes through a ring of fire
松针，你的仪式道具。	Pine needles, ceremonial props
风数你变灰的头发， 睫毛，影子凌乱的狂草。	The wind counts your grey hairs, your eyelashes, wild grasses with shadows in disarray
桨，沉默之臂划过蓝天 兜着圈子，干燥像孩童挖掘的沙井 在梦之岸坍塌下来。 呼吸与风交替着 串串水珠的松林夕照 挂上隐居者的阁楼。	The oar, the silent arm, paddles across the blue sky moving in rings, dry as the wells children dig in sand that collapse into the banks of dreams Breath alternates with the wind The pine forest at sunset with strings of dewdrops hanging from hermits' attics
巨人头颅，无人授受 磨亮渡口的老钟远在西岱岛， 敲打死囚的回忆。	No one accepts the giant's skull The old clock at the bright ferry crossing is far away on the Ile de Cite beating against death row memories
火鹤，你渴慕的竖琴， 弹拨湖心。 彩虹里盲目的金子挥霍着， 覆盆子的受难日， 林妖现身于马戏团，	Flamingo, the harp for which you thirst, plucks at the lake's heart The blind gold in the rainbow is being squandered The Good Friday of raspberries The forest monsters appear in the circus

爻辞之梅酸涩， 没有归期。	The sourness of the trigram's plums has no return date.
从水圈到水圈， 星的王冠被夜叉击碎。	The crown of stars is smashed by Yaksha from hydrosphere to hydrosphere
铁塔下边走来一个亡命者。	A fugitive walks over beneath the iron tower

The influence of Western elements is visible in the poetry of Zhao Si 赵四 (b. 1972), a poet, essayist, translator, poetics scholar, editor. She received her PhD degree from the CASS (Chinese Academy of Social Sciences) in 2007, afterwards, she started to study post-doctoral studies in the field of contemporary Western poetry at Beijing Normal University.[5] She is the author or translator of several books, including *White Crow* (Poems, 2005), *Gold-in-sand Picker* (Prose Poems, 2005), *Disappearing, Recalling* (2009–2014), *New Selected Poems* (2016), which won the "2014 Major Support Project" of the China Writers Association, two poetry books of Tomaž Šalamun: *Light-blue-pillow Tower* (2014) and *The Enormous Boiling Mouths of the Sun* (2016) Edmond Jabes (co-translation, forthcoming, 2017), and selected works by others: Hart Crane (US), Ted Hughes (UK), Vladimir Holan (Czech), and others. Some of her poems have been translated into 15 languages and published worldwide. She is a frequent guest at different poetry festivals held in Europe. She works for the *Poetry Periodical*, which is the top poetry magazine in China and is the Executive Editor-in-Chief of the prestigious poetry translation series *Contemporary International Poetry*. She was awarded the Polish Maria Konopnicka Prize in 2012. She lives in Beijing.[6] Like many other contemporary poets, she has strong knowledge of Western poetry, she often travels to Western countries, which makes her poems more international. She admitted that some of her poems are strongly influenced by scientific research, some of them by her personal experiences from traveling.[7]

I picked up one of her poems for introducing here, *Rose Garden*, strongly connected with Poland, which was also the reason for choosing especially this one of her poems. In the poem, she describes her feelings when she visited Powązki cemetery in Warsaw. This is the only poem mentioned here which

[5] *Zhao Si shiren jienjie ji zuopin* 诗人赵四简介及作品, published: 2016-10-28 editor: Shen Shuwen 沈舒文 http://www.yuwenmi.com/shici/shiren/19730.html, [accessed: March 21, 2017]

[6] For more of her credentials, email from author, March 24, 2017 12:38:45 AM.

[7] Interview with Zhao Si, Peking Foreign language university, April 8. 2016.

was not included in the selection of *Ars Poetica* in 2015, as publishers of the festival *Ars Poetica* asked me to translate more of her poetry, and it will be published as a book in Slovakia soon. Zhao Si chooses to use words that concern statues of angels, children, everything is disappearing in nothingness, which is another way to express the ephemerality, disappearing in time. Regarding the title of the poem, where she is using rose as a flower frequently used in Western literature, I would like to mention the different connotation of the rose in China, different to the West. While rose in the Western countries is regarded as the flower of love, queen of flowers in Western culture, the understanding of roses in terms of its symbolic meaning in Chinese culture is quite different. Beautiful women are usually compared to peonies or other flowers. Perhaps this may be one of the reasons why the author decided to call the cemetery rose garden. In Chinese minds, as is visible in the poem, too, rose evokes thorns, pain, bitterness associated with this flower, the sadness of death. As a translator, Zhao Si is aware of both possible symbolic meanings of this flower, as well as most of her readers, educated in Western poetry, and she is playing with the double symbolic meaning of the rose. The third meaning of the rose is a quote from Umberto Eco's well-known novel bearing the same name, in which we can find a parallel with the cemetery. There are books destroyed in a fire, representing transience, forgetting, disappearing. Here we can see in one simple example the usage of all possible cross-cultural annotations in Zhao Si's poetry.

玫瑰园

雨洗着一块块墓石，
漫长时光，不再磨碎成分秒，
小时，年月，亦不再被使用。
墓园浸在秋雨的无底洞里，
树叶落尽的枝丫露出夜的筋络
墓上天使、儿童、衣瓮、花饰
在应许的空无里连年增进凝合
变成同一个名字——死亡
也依然拥有玫瑰的名字

墓园曲折，道路无尽，雨落
在完整静谧世界的激情象征花园里
一页页墓碑的纪念册

Rose Garden

It drizzles over each headstone,
and long time is no more ground into minutes, seconds,
nor are hours, months, years entitled to use.
The cemetery immersed in the bottomless pit of autumn rain,
leafless branches featuring veins of night;
stone sculptures of angels, children, urns, festoons...
increase and blend in the promised land of nothingness
turning into one common name: death
which is also a sort of *Il nome della rosa*

Winding graveyard, endless path, it rains
in the passionate symbol garden of entire tranquil world.

将徜徉其间的探访者
亦翻看成一个个静谧溢出的字符
脱离了世界性石质语言的统一语境
掉出两个世界的象征符号们
哀悼回不去的家园

Browsing among tombstone pages of this memorial book
wandering visitors are also visioned as
every letter spilled over from the tranquility;
detached from the world's unified context of stone language,
symbols falling off two separate worlds
lament the homeland with no way to return.

在波翁兹公墓，我小心翼翼地
向那板结的虚无禁区靠近了一步，
便被什么东西整个儿拉了进去！
想得过于深刻的完整大地
看见了庞大黑暗的玫瑰园

In Powazki Cemetery, I made one cautious step
closer to the hardened forbidden zone of nihility,
when plunged in fully by something unknown!
The entire intact earth out of so much meditation
seizes the view of a colossal dark rose garden.

Chen Dongdong 陈东东 (1961–) is a well known contemporary poet. He was born in Shanghai. He started to write poetry in the 1980s, shortly after he begun to study at the Shanghai Normal University. During his studies at the second year of the university, he started to publish a journal "Works", of which he has published about 20 numbers. He is an important participant of the contemporary Chinese poetry, and considered to be one of the leading poets of the "third generation". His publications include a book of long poems, *Book of Summer – unamended Title* (2011), a collection of short poems, *Guide Map* (2013) and a volume of hybrid writing, *Flowing Water* (1998) (Ars Poetica 2015: 315). He was mentioned as a member of the New-born Generation of poets (or the Third Generation), who started to publish their works after Misty poetry (Hong 1999: 313). Chen was a frequent contributor to unofficial poetry journals throughout China during the 1980s, and he was one of the chief editors of "Tendencies" (1988–1991) and "South Poetry Magazine 南方诗志" (1992–1993). The first officially published collection of poetry did not appear until the early 1990s, although Chen's poetry often appeared in officially published literary journals and overseas Chinese language literary journals throughout the 1990s. In 1996, Chen was awarded the New York based Hellman-Hammett Prize, and he spent a few months in the USA as a result (Li 2008: 187).

He is regarded as the more traditional of contemporary poets, as we can see from the way how he uses words, from his verses, his poetic language is deeply influenced by traditional Chinese poetry. We can find a strong feeling of music and rhythm in his works; he does not only rewrite eternal topics mentioned in traditional Chinese poems in using the language of contemporary

Chinese but often features strong elements of Chinese tradition in his works. We can see that his poetry is the most traditional of all poets mentioned here and the influence of Western literature is maybe the weakest in his case. The way of using metaphors and that some expressions remind us of ancient Chinese poetry, especially visible in this poem, as we can already see from its title, which clearly admits strong inspiration by ancient poetry.

Links to ancient poems can be found in Chen's descriptions of nature, in describing Zaijiu pavilion, where the mere mention of the pavilion evokes ancient Chinese poetry[8]. The mention of Song poetry is a clear allusion to Chinese historical and cultural legacy, but traces of the old poets can also be found in the specific description, as for example, the motifs of fog on the river, flowers fallen with autumn's wind, silent mountains, moon over the mountains, which was a frequently used image in ancient Chinese poetry. But from the structure of verses, the use of more or less free verses, although some syllabic structures still remind us of ancient poetry, from modern ways of establishing poetics, we can realise that it is a poem written by a contemporary author deeply involved in Chinese poetic tradition. The elements of direct Western poetic influence are not visible.

独坐载酒亭。我们该怎样去读古诗
Sitting Alone at Zaijiu Pavilion: How Should We Read Ancient Poetry

江面上雾锁孤帆。清晨入寺	Fog on the river locks a sail. Dawn enters a temple
红色的大石头潮湿而饱满	Red rocks, damp but plump
像秋染霜叶，风吹花落	Like frosted leaves tinted with autumn, flowers fall with wind
像知更鸟停进阴影之手	Like robins stopped in shadow hands
这些都可能是他的诗句 在宋朝：海落见山石 一个枯水季节，尘昏市楼	These are perhaps his verses from the Sung era: tides ebb, mountain rocks emerge a dry season, dust and dusk upon city buildings
而我经历了一夜大雨	I've gone through a night of downpour
红石块上，绿叶像无数垂死的 鱼，被天气浸泡得又肥又鲜	On red rocks, green leaves look like countless dying fish, soaked fat and fresh by the weather
树皮这时候依然粗糙 漂在池上，什么也不像	The tree bark is still jagged drifting on the pond, resembling nothing

[8] Original see *Ars Poetica* 2015: 322–323; English translation see ibid.: 329–330

隔江望过去 ，中午的载酒亭	Gazing across the river, Zaijiu Pavilion at midday
依山静坐，我在其中	sits quietly against the mountain, as I
见江心有一群撕咬的猛禽	see at the heart of the river a flock of raptors tearing
翼翅如刀	their wings like knives
我们也得有	We must also possess
刀一样的想法。在载酒亭	thoughts like knives. At Zaijiu Pavilion
他的诗句差不多失效	his verses have lost their charm
独坐里，我们也得用	Sitting alone, we must also use
自己的眼睛，看山高月小	our eyes to see high mountains, and the moon small

(1985)

The last poet mentioned here is the poet and literary theorist Tang Xiaodu 唐晓渡 (b. 1954). He was born in the Jiangsu province. After finishing secondary school he served in the army for three years, and then worked as a worker. In January 1982 he graduated the Nanjing University faculty of literature, in February of the same year, he went to the editorial department of the Chinese Writers' Association, where he worked as editor of the journal "Poetry". In February 1998 he started to work as the editor at the Publishing House of Chinese Writers' Association. He is a member of the Chinese Writers Association, director of the Chinese New Poetry Society, researcher of the New Poetry Research Centre at Peking University. He started to write poetry during his studies at the university, since 1981 he has been publishing his works. He published seven critical collections of essays, including articles on literary criticism, as, for example, *Starting Points Anew Constantly, Antology of Tang Xiaodu´s Poetic essays,* he translated studies on poetry from Milan Kundera, selected works of Sylvia Plath, Václav Havel, Czeslaw Milosz, Zbigniew Herbert, Miroslav Holub and other poets and writers, and a number of books on history of poetry. In 2004 his book *Once uncertain adventure of language* won the award Contemporary Writers Review Outstanding Critics[9].

He published a lot of books of poetry as well as books on research of Chinese literature. His poetry is quite modern, without very obvious traces of either Western and Chinese elements as was the case with the poetry of abovementioned authors. In the poem chosen here, *I cry out your name*[10], there can be seen feelings of a modern man, unrestrained by time, or country of origin. His language is contemporary, we do not see there references to classical Chinese poetry that the previous author makes or direct allusions to

[9] Available at: http://www.chinawriter.com.cn/fwzj/writer/292.shtml [accessed: 10.04.2017], see also *Ars Poetica 2015*: 187.

[10] Original see *Ars Poetica* 2015: 296–297; English translation see *Ars Poetica* 2015: 302.

Western culture or places he visited. The only connection with China is the mention of silkworms. Instead, we can admire the language of poetry, repeating a game with the central motif *cry out your name*, which is repeatedly used throughout the whole poem.

叫出你的名字

叫出你的名字
就是召唤月亮、星辰和大地
光流尽荒漠
桑田无边涌起
一只蚕蛹咬破茧壳
我叫出你的名字

叫出你的名字
就是召唤根、鲜花和果实
麦芒刺痛天空
云烟横布心事
一叶利刃滑过咽喉
我叫出你的名字

叫出你的名字
就是召唤风、波涛和神迹
落日挽紧帆篷
群鸟飞进海市
一块石头滚下山坡
我叫出你的名字

叫出你的名字
就是召唤我自己
帷幔次第拉开
玻璃澄清墙壁
唯一的钥匙折断锁孔
我只好沉默。只好让沉默

叫出
叫出你的名字

I cry out your name

crying out your name
invoking moon stars and earth
the light exhausts the wilderness
the cultivated field rises, endless
an immature silkworm bites through the cocoon
I cry out your name

crying out your name
invoking roots flowers and fruits
the ear of wheat pricks the sky
the bank of cloud permeates my knowing
a sharp blade strokes the throat
I cry out your name

crying out your name
invoking winds waves and miracles
the setting sun draws sails into an embrace
the flock of birds flies into a mirage
one rock rolls down the slope
I cry out your name

crying out your name
invoking myself
the velvet curtain opens fold upon fold
the panes make the wall transparent
one unique key breaks the lock
I have to be silent. Let the silence

cry out
cry out your name

In conclusion it is necessary to admit that although Western poetry had deeply influenced Chinese poetry since 1919, we cannot find direct traces of Western influence in the most literary sense, as speaking of the names of historic places, buildings, in the poems of all poets mentioned here. Instead, in the works of poets selected here, we can see the whole spectrum of contemporary Chinese poetry. From the poetry of the youngest author, Zhao Si, whose works bear strong influence of Western culture, through Song Lin's works, deeply influenced both by Western and Eastern literary tradition, Chen Dongdong's poetry, mostly involved in Chinese traditional elements, to the contemporary poetry of Tang Xiaodu, rather modern without strong traces of either. The approach of each of the poets is different, and we can observe the modern narrative language of Tang Xiaodu in comparison to using symbols and metaphors in the case of Song Lin and Zhao Si.

As seen from the above samples, the authors use different starting points and different literary techniques to express themselves. Of course, a few selected poems by four poets mentioned here us fail to cover the full range of contemporary Chinese poetry, which includes avant-garde poetry, underground poetry published mostly on the Internet, as well as the creation of contemporary traditional-oriented writers who are even now writing poems in the traditional style. It can be said that the current Chinese poetry, through all the pitfalls, caused the paradoxically long literary tradition from which it separates, slowly get out of initial isolation and begins to be accepted by broader layers of intellectuals, who are often stressing the fact that they, first of all, accept the beauty and traditional forms of ancient Chinese poetry.

Bibliography

Ars Poetica 2015 International poetry festival, November 17.–21. (2015). Ed. Solotruk, Martin. Bratislava: Ars Poetica o.z.

Chinese poetry website, http://www.zgshige.com/c/2016-03-08/568195.shtml#srzy_srjj [accessed: March 21, 2017]

Hong Zicheng洪子诚 (1999). Zhongguo dangdai wenxue shi中国当代文学史. Beijing: Beijing Daxue chubanshe

http://leiden.dachs-archive.org/poetry/MD/Chen_Dongdong_trans.pdf, [accessed: April 12. 2017]

http://www.chinawriter.com.cn/fwzj/writer/292.shtml [accessed: April 10. 2017]

Li Dian (2008). "Poetic debate in Contemporary China". In: *New Perspectives on Contemporary Chinese Poetry.* Ed. Christopher Lupke. New York: Palgrave Macmillan

Weaver, Afaa Michael (2008). "Muddy Rivers and Canada Geese". In: *New Perspectives on Contemporary Chinese Poetry.* Ed. Christopher Lupke. New York: Palgrave Macmillan

Zhao Si shiren jienjie ji zuopin,诗人赵四简介及作品, published: 2016-10-28 editor: Shen Shuwen沈舒文
http://www.yuwenmi.com/shici/shiren/19730.html, [accessed: March 21, 2017]

II

Literary Boundaries — Ethical Limitations: Classical Literatures of the Orient

Chapter 4

Borderlines of Morality: Exploring the Ethos of the *Mu'allaqa*

Zane Šteinmane, *University of Latvia/Latvia*

The *Mu'allaqa*, also known as "The Seven Long Poems" is the name attributed to an anthology of poetry from the pre-Islamic times (*al-ǧāhiliyya*). The poems included are considered to be the most highly praised poems of the time. The anthology is believed to have been fully constructed sometime around the 8th century by the collector Ḥammād ar-Rāwī, although opinions about the true author of the first collection vary. The name – *mu'allaqa* – usually is translated as "The suspended ones", interpreted as a derivation of the verb *'alaqa* "to hang". A popular legend would have it that the best poems of seven authors were written on strips of linen in golden ink and hanged on the walls of Ka'aba in Mecca. The remains of these relics have not been found, nor is there any reliable evidence of their existence, since no such tradition of golden inking has ever been mentioned anywhere in the early literature or the Qur'an (Beeston 1983: 111).

The poems were collected and written down about two centuries after their composition, and the name is not likely a contemporary with the poems themselves (Nicholson 1907: 102). A debate exists on the authenticity as well as the collector's faithfulness to the original,[1] and, due to the inconsistency of tradition and the existence of various versions of the anthology, the poets included in *mu'allaqa* also vary in different editions. The most well-known

[1] Al-Mufaḍḍal al-Ḍabbī is reported to have said: "Ḥammad is a man skilled in the language and poesy of the Arabs and in the styles and ideas of the poets, and he is always making verses in imitation of some one and introducing them into genuine compositions by the same author, so that the copy passes everywhere for part of the original, and cannot be distinguished from it except by critical scholars – and where are such to be found?" (Nicholson, 1907: 133).

compilation includes the following authors: Imru' al-Qays, Ṭarafa, 'Antara, Zuhayr, Labīd, 'Amr Ibn Kalṯūm, Ḥāriṯ Ibn Ḥilliza.[2]

Ethos and Ethics. Values and Morality

Ethos is a Greek concept that is translated as "character", and is largely used to describe the character of a nation or a community that shares beliefs and ideals. The Cambridge dictionary defines *ethos* as "the set of beliefs, ideas, etc. about the social behaviour and relationships of a person or group" (Cambridge Advanced Learner's Dictionary 2008: 479). The word *ethos* forms the root of Greek *ethikos,* meaning "moral, showing moral character". In *Nicomachean Ethics,* Aristotle claims that "moral virtue comes about as a result of habit, whence also its name (*ēthikē*) is one that is formed by a slight variation from the word *ethos* (habit)" (Aristotle 2009: 23). *Ethos* is also closely related to the English word *ethics,* the study of morality and concepts of right and wrong. "Values" describe individual or personal standards of what is valuable or important, while "ethics" describes a generally accepted set of moral principles, and "morality" describes the right or wrong of actions.

Considering literature, ethos and ethics correlate with the personality of the individual as a character: the personality of the character is also the means through which the character of an epoch can be read – namely, ethos. The characters through which the author speaks deliver the ideas and observations of their society, often innately passing the judgement on what is right and wrong, as well as on the environment they reside in – reconstructing the ethos of their time and place. Therefore, ethics can be seen as embedded in the ethos of a definite group of people.

The society of ancient Arabia was built on certain moral ideas even before the appearance of Islam. Even though a specific law did not exist, the compelling rules of traditional custom were enforced by the public opinion (Nicholson 1907: 82). These moral and social customs, political and cultural realities have been preserved in pre-Islamic Arabic poetry (Rippin 2010: 266). Poetry served as the record of the Arabs, and through these poems, we may attempt to unveil the identity of the pre-Islamic Arab desert dwellers – their values, judgment and traditions, their morals and history (Johnson Faizullabhai 1893: vii).

---

[2] The other authors that have sometimes been mentioned amongst the seven are An-Nābiġa az-Ẕubyānī, Al- A'šā and 'Abīd Ibn al-Abraṣ. The works of these poets will not be considered in the research of this paper.

The works of scholars exploring *mu'allaqa* mostly mention and proceed to analyse the values expressed by the poems, focusing on the Bedouin concepts of honor. References to said concepts can be found in the written literary histories of Arabs, studies of the Bedouin societies, etc. The poems of *mu'allaqa* can hardly be viewed as moral treatises, but, on a certain level, judgment about the ethics of the epoch can be passed. The classical Arabic literature is described by its didactic character, as the word *adab* itself has educational and moralistic connotations (Meisami 2010: 193). Meir Jacob Kister's theory on the collection of *mu'allaqa* also suggests that the poems were collected to educate Mu'awiya's son, suggesting a didactic value to the texts.

Exploring the Ethos and Ethics of *Mu'allaqa*

In order to evaluate the ethical principles represented in the *mu'allaqa*, a close reading of the poems must be conducted, focusing on (1) the values and traits of personality praised by the poets, especially the contradictory statements, to reveal any possible differences between idealistic perceptions that might differ completely from the moral standards of a functioning society, (2) the conflicts described, in order to understand how they are resolved, (3) personal relationships that could provide insight into behavior considered moral or immoral, actions perceived right and wrong.

Since most of the knowledge about pre-Islamic society comes from the pre-Islamic literature itself, no objective information about it is there to be found. In a paper, Jonathan A. C. Brown reports on his case study method of reading the *mu'allaqa*, comparing some of the values praised by the ancient poets with the values of the Bedouin tribes who are still adhering on some level to the nomadic lifestyle.[3] Although the idea that these Bedouins would still live by the same values as the 6th-century poets is controversial, some of his findings in the comparisons are noteworthy and will be mentioned in the following part of the paper.

(1) The Cherished Values

Although many values could be mentioned, the most prominent ones are honor, generosity, and hospitality.

---

[3] Brown mentions the following societies: the Bedouin of the Negev and Syrian deserts, the Bedouin of Cyrenaica and their cousins in the Northwestern Desert of Egypt, the *Šammār*, *Rwala* and *'Anaza* tribes in Northern *Naǧd*, and the Ogaden nomads of the south-eastern Somali highlands. (Brown 2003: 34)

The **honor** of a pre-Islamic Bedouin is inseparable from the honor of his family. Defending the family and the tribe, both individually and collectively, was regarded as a sacred duty of all the men. This sentiment is also evident in the poems, alluding to the importance of family relations:

> "Let me be summoned in a serious fix, and I'm there to defend,
> Or let your enemies come against you sternly, I'm stern to help;"
> (Arberry 1957: 87)

Putting the necessities of the tribe over the needs of the whims of the individual is shown to be of utmost importance. If help was demanded by someone in the tribe, doubt was out of the question. Self-sacrifice and devotion on behalf of the kinsfolk, therefore, was held up as an ideal. The idea of loyalty in the Arab tribe meant a faithful loyalty to one's equals.

But the individuals also needed to earn their respect. We clearly see that honor could be lost, and, when the status and moral integrity of an individual was in question, as we can see in Ṭarafa's *mu'allaqa,* where he depicts cold and scolding treatment from his cousin Malik, the help and protection of the family could also be denied, and ultimately he declares:.

> "Truly, the tyranny of kinsfolk inflicts sharper anguish
> Upon a man the blow of a trenchant Indian sabre." (Arberry 1957: 88)

Ṭarafa lost his possessions living an extravagant life, and then also squandered whatever possessions his relatives had. Then, when he went on to work for his cousin, he lost the herd of camels entrusted to him and fell into disgrace. Autonomy and self-governance were amongst the things that substantiated a man's position in the society (Abu-Lughod 2016: 85–86.). Eventually, his tribe and relatives turned away from him – a grave consequence in the aforementioned context. But Ṭarafa's actions could not be seen as ethical in the first place. Understandably, a conflict of interests is depicted in the poem, and the morality of the decision making is hard to judge.

Generosity and hospitality are amongst the most exalted values as well, often mentioned among the traits that define the greatness of a person or of their tribe (Brown, 2003: 42), as they are also correlated with helping people in need. Food sharing is of utmost importance for the nomadic people. The imagery of killing a camel to feed the tribespeople or friends is used by Imru' al-Qays, Ṭarafa, Labīd, and in his elocution of virtues, Zuhayr declares:

> "Whoever, being in abundance, grudges to give of his abundance
> To his own folk, shall be dispensed with and reviled." (Arberry, 1957: 117)

But, as we read the poems of *mu'allaqa*, a very different, distinctive character of generosity can be separated: on the one hand, there is the aforementioned generosity as willingness to help the people in need, for example, the members of the more powerful tribes protecting the people whose tribe lacks the martial prowess and who cannot defend themselves against raids and pillages, or who are suffering from famine. As Amr Ibn Kulthūm declares::

> "[...] in every scant year we are the protectors,
> We the bountiful givers to them that beg of us,
> We the defenders of those near us." (Arberry 1957: 208)

But on the other hand, there is a selfish, hedonistic generosity that is present in the poems as well. The poets boast their generous demeanour, buying wine for their companions, giving gifts and living a lavish life, without regard for the sustainability of resources.

> "And whenever I have drunk, recklessly I squander
> [...] And whenever I have sobered up, I diminish not my bounty."
> (Arberry 1957: 181)

Often the poets offer a drink and company to their enemies or offenders, thus seemingly boasting their magnanimity. Thus, we observe that these two kinds of generosity coexist in the Bedouin ethos. The morality of the society would praise the selfless generosity of the first kind, but the ego of the individual – the poet – delights in the hedonistic lifestyle.

(2) Conflicts in the *Mu'allaqa*

The feuds represented by the poems of *mu'allaqa* can be divided into two large groups: (1) personal conflicts and (2) war. And in the context of morality, the second issue deserves critical attention.

War usually deals with intertribal conflicts that are often held to be one of the signature entities of the pre-Islamic times: wars are portrayed in *Ayyam al-Arab*, in the poetry, certainly in the *mu'allaqa* as well. Moreover, the literature attests the Bedouins in particular for their fighting skills, bravery, and even bloodthirst. The poets often talk in-depth about the battle, mentioning details that may seem borderline macabre to the reader. They boastfully illustrate their successes at killing, in the name of creating an intimidating reputation for themselves and their tribe members, going as far as comparing battle to children's games:

> "We hack their heads off without compassion [...]
> It is as though our swords, flailing between us,
> were bladders buffeted by playing children." (Arberry 1957: 206)

Clearly, war plays an important role in the creation and maintenance of the pre-Islamic Bedouin self-image. However, contradictory opinions can be seen in the poems as well. Zuhayr, whose *mu'allaqa* comes close to being a didactic ode, condemns war and useless bloodshed, praising peaceful solutions that don't harm people.

> "War is nothing else but what you've known and yourselves tasted,
> [...] it grinds you as a millstone grinds on its cushion."
> (Arberry 1957: 116)

In terms of survival in the harsh circumstances of pre-Islamic nomadic life, the tribes must have depended on cooperation. Brown's study of the Bedouins also suggests that the Bedouins "find cooperation indispensable, because excessive violence threatens access to shared pastures and resources essential to survival, and may also endanger important social institutions" (Brown, 2003: 38); for example, marriage is also mentioned in Al-Hārit's *mu'allaqa* as a means of bringing about a benevolent relationship between peoples:

> "In near kinship, after the marriage-gift came to us;
> Such a kinship brings out loyalty in people,
> A boundless vista of unending benevolence." (Arberry 1957: 227)

Thus, we may judge that perhaps, despite the popular Bedouin self-image of a distinguished warrior, morality (as avoiding the causing of suffering to others) did play a part in their solving conflicts, and the people strived to resolve feuds in a diplomatic way, for example, war could be avoided by paying the so-called "blood money". Such resolution is depicted in the poem of Al-Ḥāriṯ, which mentions mending a rift of prolonged bloodshed between two tribes by a gift of hundreds of camels:

> "The wounds were healed by that offering of hundreds of beasts
> [...] And they shed not between them so much as a cupper's glass of blood."(Arberry 1957: 115)

(3) Morality and Interpersonal Relationships

Firstly, love, the most exalted theme must be considered. Most of the *mu'allaqas* speak on a loved one in the prelude to their poem. They mention a girl who is unreachable to the poet and is the cause of the poet's grief.

The Bedouin woman's honor was embedded in her chastity (Bouhdiba 2013: 110). And the chastity of a woman was to be protected at all costs because this kind of honor could not be regained – the men of the tribe were willing to protect the honor of a woman with a fierce passion. But then – in the very first *mu'allaqa* – Imru' al-Qays boasts about his sexual adventures, not only chasing his beloved but pursuing other women as well.

> "Many's the pregnant woman like you, aye, and the nursing mother
> I've visited [...]
> Many's the fair veiled lady, whose tent few would think of seeking,
> I've enjoyed sporting with."
> (Arberry 1957: 62)

Similar sentiments are found in some of the other poems as well. The moral integrity of these lines is questionable, incompatible even with the moral code of protecting a woman's honor. Even the poet himself alludes to the understanding that his actions might become the cause of his death, yet he still boasts of it as an accomplishment.

Secondly, a common theme is friendship, which goes together with the glorification of the use of alcohol: the so-called "boon brothers". A similar episode of wine-drinking appears in Ṭarafa, 'Antara, and 'Amr:

> "And if you hunt me in the taverns there you'll catch me.
> Come to me when you will, I'll pour you a flowing cup."
> (Arberry 1957: 85)

The poet sits and drinks with his friends, generously spending his possessions on wine and amusement. This motif is significant because through this setting excessive use of alcohol is romanticised, Tarafa even compares his friends, with whom he spends his nights drinking, to the stars. (Arberry 1957: 85)

The drinking of wine is not portrayed as a mere means of entertainment, more so it can be read as a means of self-destruction. The motif is connected with squandering treasure, being reckless and earning condemnation of the family and tribe. The poet is aware of the message that is conveyed, and still, he is proud, boasting of his actions as if proclaiming that it serves as a way to gain most out of life:

> "So permit me to drench my head while there's still life in it,
> [...] You'll know tomorrow, when we're dead, which of us is the thirsty one." (Arberry, 1957: 86)

Even though the poets justify the misuse of wine through apologetic verses, it is not likely that such actions, even though idolised in poetry, could have been considered moral.

Conclusion

Following the concise report on the afore mentioned phenomena, several conclusions can be made: firstly, the pre-Islamic Arabic poetry is inclined towards hyperbole, boasting, and idealisation. The traits glorified in the poems are likely to have made it to the poems because they are exciting, and the people enjoy such tales, rather than day-to-day life occurrences. Secondly, it follows that we must be critical when assuming the ancient poems depict the actual social context of the pre-Islamic society, simply because the accounts of the poems are most likely exaggerated and partly fictional. Therefore, thirdly, even though the ethos portrayed by the poems might not fully depict the ethics of the Bedouin society, it is likely that such an impression is only due to the poets' storytelling.

Bibliography

Abu-Lughod, Lila. (2016). *Veiled Sentiments: Honor and Poetry in a Bedouin Society.* University of California Press.

Arberry, Arthur John (1957). *The Seven Odes: The First Chapter in Arabic Literature.* R.&R. Clark.

Aristotle (2009). *The Nicomachean Ethics.* Transl. David Ross. Oxford University Press.

Beeston, Alfred Felix Landon (1983). *Arabic Literature to the End of the Umayyad Period.* Cambridge University Press.

Bouhdiba, Abdelwahab. (2013). *Sexuality in Islam.* London: Routledge.

Brown, Jonathan Andrew Cleveland (2003.) "The Social Context of Pre-Islamic Poetry: Poetic Imagery and Social Reality in the Mu'allaqa." *Arab Studies Quarterly* 25(3): 29–50.

Cambridge Advanced Learner's Dictionary (2008). Ed. Elizabeth Walter. Cambridge: Cambridge University Press.

Meisami, Julie Scott, Starkey, Paul. (2010) *The Routledge Encyclopedia of Arabic Literature.* Abingdon: Routledge.

Nicholson, Reynold Alleyne (1907). *A Literary History of The Arabs.* New York, Charles Scribner's Sons.

The Islamic World (2010). Ed. Andrew Rippin. Routledge: Taylor & Francis Group.

The Seven Poems Suspended in the Temple at Mecca (1893). Ed. Shaikh Faizullabhai. Transl. Francis. E. Johnson. Education Society's Steam Press.

Chapter 5

Formation of Plot Canon in Arabic Literature: The Case of Love Stories About Poets of Bedouins

Arzu Sadykhova, *Adam Mickiewicz University/Poland*

An Introduction to the Problem

Romantic stories in Arabic literature are numerous, thus, we remember fine love stories among the Arabian Nights, other folklore tales and anthologies, but the stories about poets of Bedouins are special. Due to the true and devoted love described there, they became very popular all over the Arab and Muslim world and were even introduced into European literature: for instance, the outstanding German poet Johann Wolfgang von Goethe was inspired by Persian and Arabic poetry to a great extent and composed his famous *West–Eastern Diwan* (1819), where motifs of these stories are presented.

The studying of the poetry of these poets in Europe began a long time ago with studying of Arabic literature in general and particularly the Umayyad period. In the nineteenth century some translations of the poems into European languages appeared, then the scholars introduced these romantic stories into the books devoted to the history of Arabic literature (Nicholson 1907: 238; Huart 1903: 47–48, 53; Filshtinsky 1985: 219–242); particularly notable was Carl Brockelmann (1909: 65–66; 1937: 78–83), who paid special attention to the biographies of the poets and folklore nature of the novels. Usually, the poetry of the poets of Bedouins is studied by those scholars who are interested in the appearance and development of the ġazal genre (Meisami 1998, Blachère 1991, etc.). Besides, these stories were studied by scholars in order to get to know the biographies of the poets and to find out their historicity (ʿAbbās 1986; Bauer 2000; Gabrieli 1986; Gabrieli 1991; Pellat 1986). However, no one has studied these stories as independent literary novels with regard to the plot, as far as I know. Therefore, nowadays there is a good deal of research on the poetry and biographies of those poets and in general on love lyrics of the Umayyad period, but the prosaic elements of all stories have not been thoroughly analysed.

These love stories obviously appeared after the death of the poets as the commentaries to their verses; thus, every story consists of a series of episodes with the verses attached to each episode. The love stories about poets of Bedouins are numerous in Arabic literature (Ibn an-Nadīm: 425–426), but the most popular are the following pairs: 'Urwa Ibn Ḥizām (d. 30/650) and his beloved 'Afrā', Tawba Ibn al-Ḥumayyir (d. 55/674) and his beloved Laylà al-Aḫyaliyya (d. ca. 80/704), who was also a talented poetess, Qays Ibn Ḏarīḥ (d. 60/680) and Lubnà, Qays Ibn al-Mulawwaḥ (Maǧnūn, the madman of the tribe of Banī 'Āmir,) (d. ca. 68/688) and Laylà, Ǧamīl Ibn Ma'mar (d. 82/701), and Buṯayna, Kuṯayyir (d. 105/723) and 'Azza.

At first sight all these stories are very similar: they are about unhappy love and failed lovers with a sad end. That is what we know from the works on the history of Medieval Arabic literature. But how, when and why all these stories appeared? Have they been changed in the course of time or not? If yes, to what extent and how exactly did this process happen? It should be noted especially that this research does not aim to reveal the historicity of the poets and the certainty of facts of their biographies, it focuses only on the formation and development of the plot of the stories as literary works.

It is well known that medieval literary works were usually composed in accordance with certain canons, and thus the romantic love stories about the poets of Bedouins had to have their own rules of narration as well. "It is therefore appropriate to think that the appearance of such stories as that of al-Majnun, though based on an already existent tradition, started a fashion for a genre of love literature that proved to be enormously popular," pointed out Salma K. Jayyusi (1983: 421) and this statement shows the importance of that problem. Therefore, the aim of this research is to study the prosaic parts of the stories as original narratives in order to reveal how and when the canon of these romantic stories has appeared. The text sources of the research are the following anthologies:

1. *Ṭabaqāt aš-šu'arā'* of Muḥammad Ibn Sallām al-Ǧumaḥī (d. 231–232/845–846)
2. *Diwān al-ḥamāsa* of Abū Tammām (d. 231–232/845–846)
3. *Kitāb aš-ši'r wa-š-šu'arā'* of Ibn Qutayba (d. 276/889)
4. *Kitāb al-aġhānī* of Abū al-Faraǧ al-Iṣfahānī (d. 356/967)
5. *Maṣāri' al-'uššāq* of Ǧa'far Ibn as-Sarrāǧ (d. 500/1106)
6. *Tazyīn al-aswāq bi-tafṣīl ašwāq al-'uššāq* of Dā'ūd al-Anṭākī (d. 1008/1599)

These anthologies cover an extended period of time; each of them presents the literary tastes of its own epoch. Hence, a detailed investigation of the stories in every book and then a comparison between them can help us to answer the questions mentioned above, besides, we will see the dynamics and the character of stories changing over the course of time. The research was carried out on the base of structural, functional and comparative analysis of the parts of the stories, taking into consideration methodology elaborated by Vladimir Propp (1969).

Love Stories in the Earliest Anthologies

A textual analysis of the first and the second books has demonstrated that in the 1st part of the ninth century AD these romantic stories were not so popular as they became later, or probably even had been not composed yet, at least not all the poets mentioned above were included into these anthologies. Al-Ǧumaḥī, the author of the earliest preserved literary anthology reported some information about two poets and cited their verses (they are Ǧamīl and Kuṯayyir) (Al-Ǧumaḥī 2001: 165, 167, 186, 190) and mentioned one female poet, Laylà al-Aḫyaliyya, but without her beloved Tawba (Al-Ǧumaḥī 2001: 53). There is no any romantic stories or prosaic episodes related to these poets in the *Ṭabaqāt aš-šu'arā'*, except the information that these poets were talented in the ġazal genre and presentation of the poetry of Ǧamīl and Kuṯayyir with the remark that the latter was the transmitter (that is *ar-rāwī*) of the former (Al-Ǧumaḥī 2001: 168).

As for Abū Tammām's anthology, it was used as an auxiliary source, because it contains only poetic fragments of various poets who were very popular by the middle of the ninth century AD and whose poetry was considered to be classical, so, undoubtedly this book indicates the literary tastes of that time. In contrast to al-Ǧumaḥī, who was a scholar of the Basra school, Abū Tammām, who was a talented poet, collected the verses of 4 poets: Tawba Ibn al-Ḥumayyir (Abū Tammām 1998: 251, 264), Qays Ibn Ḏarīḥ (Abū Tammām 1998: 236, 260), Ǧamīl Ibn Ma'mar (Abū Tammām 1998: 263, 272, 282) and Kuṯayyir (Abū Tammām 1998: 245, 513).

Thus, we see that the popularity of the poets was different over the course of time and naturally depended on the taste of the author of the anthology. At any case, it may be observed that by the middle of the ninth century AD the romantic stories about these poets have not been composed yet as the literary romances because they are not mentioned in the early anthologies. Moreover, this circumstance proves the fact that these love stories really have grown later as a result of making commentaries to the verses of the poets.

Therefore, it is safe to say that the first half of the ninth century AD is an initial period of the stories' formation, and it is very likely that it is in this period that the stories about the poets still existed in oral form, though there were some attempts to write down several poems of those poets. In other words, the first half of the ninth century AD could also be considered a transitional stage for these stories, from the oral form to the written one.

Love Stories in the *Kitāb aš-šiʿr wa-š-šuʿarāʾ* of Ibn Qutayba

Studying biographies and poetry of the poets of the fifth to ninth century AD, the researchers usually take information from the famous *Kitāb al-aġānī* (*the Book of Songs*) of al-Iṣfahānī, whereas another popular anthology, the *Kitāb aš-šiʿr wa-š-šuʿarāʾ* (*The Book of Poetry and Poets*) of Ibn Qutayba is rarely used because of the absence of detailed references to the transmitters (that is *isnāds*) and sources in the majority of cases. However, I suppose that the *Book of Poetry and the Poets* can help in the revealing the process of the emergence of the canon of love stories. Thus, appreciating these two anthologies with regard to the history of the romance about Maǧnūn and Laylà, the academic Ignaty Krachkovsky notes that among all sources devoted to Maǧnūn, these two anthologies are the most important (Krachkovsky 1941:8). An outstanding scholar, Ibn Qutayba was probably the first author in medieval Arabic literature who tried to compose a coherent narration for the reader, which is why his anthology is of particular interest for the researcher because it undoubtedly can shed light upon the formation of plotted stories (Ibn Qotaiba 1904).

Therefore, a thorough analysis of the text of the *Kitāb aš-šiʿr wa-š-šuʿarāʾ* of Ibn Qutayba demonstrated that: firstly, the source includes all stories about six poets and secondly, these tales have already had a certain structure in it. Every story begins with the genealogy of the poet and his beloved, then the author refers whole romantic story, which consists of certain prosaic episodes and the verses of the poet attached to them. Although the plot of all stories is similar in general, every story differs with regard to details (for example, there are some versions of one event[1]). All stories[2] have unhappy endings: being far from each other, poor lovers suffer and die.

---

[1] Thus, the most variable episodes are those that deal with the first meeting of the heroes and their secret rendezvous in spite of the prohibition of their parents.

[2] Except one: the story about Qays Ibn Ḏariḥ and his beloved Lubnà has no ending in the book of Ibn Qutayba.

The longest stories are the following two in the anthology: the novels devoted to Maǧnūn (Ibn Qotaiba 1904: 355–364) and Ǧamīl (Ibn Qotaiba 1904: 260–268) – the former consists of 11 episodes, the latter includes 14. The shortest novels are another two examples: the story devoted to Tawba, which has 4 episodes (Ibn Qotaiba 1904: 269–274) and the tale about Qays Ibn Ḏariḥ, composed of only 1 episode (Ibn Qotaiba 1904: 399–400); the stories about 'Urwa (Ibn Qotaiba 1904: 394–399) and Kuṯayyir (Ibn Qotaiba 1904: 316–329) with 10 episodes in everyone take the average position. The correlation of verses and prose is unique in every story and sometimes unequal. For instance, the prosaic part of the novel about Kuṯayyir and 'Azza is the smallest among all stories, while its poetic part is the longest, so, the verses predominate over the prose in it. For its part, in the longest story, devoted to Maǧnūn, the prosaic part prevails over the poetic one, although the story about Ǧamīl has approximately equal shares of prose and verses. But only one novel has the best and orderly composition with predomination of prose over verses, and it is the story about 'Urwa Ibn Ḥizām and 'Afrā', while other stories are presented in a less coherent manner. In other words, it is the prosaic part of this story that looks like a complete novel about the poor lovers.

Here is the full structure of the novel about 'Urwa Ibn Ḥizām and his beloved 'Afrā': the poet grew up with his lover to-be 'Afrā' (she was his cousin); later they fell in love, but their parents prevented them, because 'Urwa dedicated verses to her[3]; then 'Urwa asked her parents for permission to marry 'Afrā', but they refused; the lovers were meeting secretly and, in order to stop these meetings, the parents of the girl gave her in marriage to another man who lived far from her tribe; when away from each other, the lovers suffered and finally died. It is also very interesting to note that at the beginning of the story Ibn Qutayba wrote: "This is one of the Arab lovers who was killed by love" (Ibn Qotaiba 1904: 394). It is quite possible that this remarkable appreciation awarded by the author of the anthology to the poet demonstrates the high popularity of that novel by the time of composing of the book, i. e. by the end of the ninth century AD.

Other stories have different structures, and some of them look like incomplete and imperfect novels. For example, the plot of the story about Maǧnūn, the most popular poet of the Bedouins, has the following peculiarities regarding to the plot. There are several versions of the romance, and according to one of them the poet grew up with his cousin Laylà, then he fell in love with

[3] According to the ancient Bedouin tradition the dedicating of the verses to a woman was prohibited because it could influence negatively her reputation.

her, very soon became mad because of this love, which is why he lived in the forest with the wild animals. Such an episode is unique; there is nothing like this in other stories. There are no episodes dealing with the poet asking to marry Laylà or her marriage to another man. It is a surprising fact that only this poet has three different versions of genealogy and this is to say that already at that time Maǧnūn was indeed a collective character. But the main distinguishing feature of this story consists in its emotional and artistic qualities. Its characters Maǧnūn and Laylà are nearly real persons, so it seems to the reader that Ibn Qutayba is interested in presenting the feelings of the heroes to a greater extent than in narrating the events.

Overall, based on the analysis of all stories it is possible to conclude that most likely the plot of the story devoted to 'Urwa and 'Afrā' was the earliest one that came into being and probably became a model for other romantic novels while they were at their formative stage. In any case, everything will become clear after analysing the stories from later anthologies, particularly, the famous *Kitāb al-aġānī*.

In the *Kitāb al-aġānī* of al-Iṣfahānī

The next anthology, the *Kitāb al-aġānī*, of course, includes all six stories with a highly developed plot, which demonstrates how and to what extent these tales were changed in comparison with the early anthologies and the *Kitāb aš-ši'r wa-š-šu'arā'* of Ibn Qutayba during the period about 100 years. All these stories are about unfortunate, poor lovers who were separated forcibly, and about their tragic death. Every tale has a similar, rigid composition: it consists of the chain of episodes which sometimes are not connected logically, but every episode includes the *isnād* (that is the reference to the transmitters) and the *ḫabar* (that is the information about the event) with the verses of the poet attached to it. The set of episodes is approximately the same, so it is possible to classify them into 11 groups or components, which are:

1. The genealogy of the poet himself and of his beloved
2. The first meeting of the heroes, which means the beginning of their love
3. The poet asks the beloved's parents to marry her, but they refuse
4. The parents of the beloved give her in marriage to another man
5. The meetings of lovers in spite of obstacles
6. The parents of the beloved complain to the local ruler about the poet's behaviour and the ruler outlaws the hero

7. The poet is obsessed by his love (In the story devoted to Maǧnūn, obsession transforms into madness, that is to say, an extreme form of the obsession)
8. The poet has to wander and suffer because of unhappy love
9. Unsuccessful attempts of relatives to heal the poet from his love
10. The death of the unfortunate heroes
11. Auxiliary episodes that do not play a role in the development of the plot of a story. This group consists of information about the popularity of the poet, his appearance, description of his beloved, appreciations of poet's verses and his poetic mastery.

It should be pointed out that the last group of events was not analysed, however, the quantity of such episodes in every story certainly indicates the level of popularity of the poet and the story itself by the middle of the tenth century AD. At the same time, the episodes listed above present the common structure of the love story or its compositional canon.

The remaining ten groups present several more or less detailed versions of one event, and after analysing all the episodes, it has become clear that the most variable and numerous are the second and the fifth components. The preliminary quantitative analysis of all episodes of the novels has demonstrated that firstly, not all the stories have the complete set of groups or components (for example, in the novel devoted to Kuṯayyir and 'Azza the 3rd, 6th, 7th and 9th components are omitted) and, secondly, the versions of one group are to be found among the episodes of any other group. In other words, the manner of narration of almost all stories is inconsistent in the *Book of Songs.*

Here are the samples of the second group variations, that is, how the heroes met and fell in love. There are several versions of the heroes' meeting in every story, but I have chosen the best passage from each romance.

'Urwa grew up with 'Afrā' and fell in love with her when they were children (al-Iṣfahānī 2008, 24: 80); Ǧamīl was impressed and charmed by the wit of Buṯayna when she scolded him (Al-Iṣfahānī 2008, 8: 71); when he was thirsty, Qays Ibn Ḏarīḥ asked to drink, and it was Lubnà who gave him water (Al-Iṣfahānī 2008, 9: 134); Maǧnūn passed by a group of women and saw Laylà (Al-Iṣfahānī 2008, 2:11); Kuṯayyir was fascinated by 'Azza when she chaffered a ram (Al-Iṣfahānī 2008, 9: 20). Only the story devoted to Tawba and Laylà al-Aḫyaliyya does not have any version of the first meeting of lovers, however, such a "defect" of the story was compensated in the course of time and the appropriate episode was invented later and, therefore, it is to be found in the later anthology. According to al-Anṭākī, Tawba saw Laylà al-Aḫyaliyya among the women who met him with other soldiers after the victory over another tribe (Al-Anṭākī 1901: 96). This example presents the formation of the plot canon of love story according to the literary tastes of Arab society of the ninth-tenth century AD. Just as a pre-Islamic poet began his long poem (*qasīda*) with *aṭlāl* (that is asking his friends to stop and stand by the ruins of the camp of his beloved's tribe), but every poet did it in his individual manner, so the storyteller began his romantic story with the meeting of heroes, but in his own manner.

The romantic story about Mağnūn and Laylà is the longest among all love novels presented in the *Book of Songs*, the most elaborate and complicated in comparison with the others. This novel consists of all the components listed above and includes many various scenes of the lovers' meeting and of the suffering of the hero. Certainly, this fact indicates that the tale had become the most popular only by the first part of the tenth century AD due to the efforts of numerous storytellers, transmitters and scholars and that confirms the opinion of I. Krachkovsky about the later popularity of Mağnūn (Krachkovsky 1941: 16, Pellat 1986:1102). All components with numerous versions can be found in the story devoted to Ğamīl and Lubnà; as has already been mentioned, the story about Kuṯayyir consists of the fewest of the components. The novel about Qays Ibn Ḏariḥ comprises of all the components, although almost without variations; nevertheless, its plot is the most complicated because of the addition of an episodes dealing with the marriage of the lovers, then their divorce on the parents' insistence, the suffering of the heroes and two versions of the ending – a happy and an unhappy one. This is a quite remarkable fact. It is most likely, therefore, that at the beginning that story had a happy end. But in the course of time with the formation of the love story canon in medieval Arabic literature, this tale was provided with the invented sad ending in order to be in harmony with the rigid rules of the canon and literary tastes of that time[4].

The novel devoted to 'Urwa and 'Afrā' is particular, because of its perfect, complete plot with a very simple and elegant composition about poor lovers who died at one day. There are very few different versions of episodes dedicated to one event in the novel. Mentioning the name of 'Urwa in the verses of other poets of the Umayyad period is another fact indicating that this story was a forerunner of all romantic tales. This circumstance proves again that

---

[4] The detailed results of the research on the peculiarities of the stories about Qays – Lubnà and Tawba – Laylà were presented in June 2017 on the 10th All Polish conference "Arab World in History, Language and Culture".

this story has already been well known among the Arabs by the beginning of the eighth century AD. The other five stories have highly elaborate and incoherent structure with many versions of one event, which indicates the formation of plot canon by inventing additional episodes provided alongside real events in order to transform the real facts into familiar canon.

In Later Anthologies

The 4th source, the anthology of Ǧa'far Ibn as-Sarrāǧ, composed at the end of the eleventh century AD, is very close to the 5th one, that is the anthology of al-Anṭākī, who composed his work on the basis of the former text. There is a very slight difference between the two sources, so, it is possible to present here the combined results.

Of course, the stories were changed a little bit in comparison with the *Book of Songs*, but each of them in its own way, obviously depending on the popularity of the poets and in accordance with the literary tastes of the epoch. Generally, the plot of the stories did not change by the sixteenth century AD, and the set of components of a love story is the same, however, there were some peculiarities. Two stories have the simplest plot with few variations of each component, and these are the romances about 'Urwa and 'Afrā' and Tawba and Laylà. In contrast, one story has the most complicated plot (the romance about Qays b. Ḏarīḥ and Lubnà) with not many versions of some components. Two stories (Maǧnūn–Laylà, and Ǧamīl–Buṯayna) have an average position as regards the plot, but they are the leaders in the diversity of versions and variations of episodes. Therefore, these two stories are the longest of all. And here we can conclude that the plot composition of every story was dependent on the popularity of the poet. The more popular the poet is, the more complicated the plot of the story is and the more different versions of each component it has. It is important to point out that almost all new episodes added to the stories after composing the *Kitāb al-aġānī* deal with the details of an event or introduce real historical persons into the story (caliphs, local rulers, judges or certain popular poets) in order to stress the reality of events and the historicity of the poet himself. Here are the examples of such episodes which were invented later and attached to the story about Maǧnūn: Kutayyir cited the poem of Maǧnūn to the caliph and inform the ruler about the meeting with the poet (As-Sarrāǧ 2:62); Maǧnūn secretly came to the camp of Laylà's tribe and a woman Su'ād helped him (al-Anṭākī 1901: 55).

The earliest and simplest stories ('Urwa–'Afra' and Tawba–Laylà) were created at the time when the plot canon in Arabic literature was at its formative stage, and the rules of canonicity were not so rigid; later, in accordance with the tradition, the plot canon was developed and fulfilled in other stories, whose composition was changed according to new literary tastes. The theme of love, passion, and obsession was an integral part of such stories, and it was "improved" to its extreme level – to the madness in the story about Mağnūn. This is probably one of the reasons for such unbelievable popularity of this poet in the Muslim world: it is this story that presents a highly extreme form of the canon realisation.

Conclusion

This research on the prosaic parts of the love stories conducted on the basis of different medieval anthologies has revealed that the process of composition of the love story canon was long and that finally it had been formed no earlier than by the end of the ninth century AD. That is clear from the *Kitāb aš-ši'r wa-š-šu'arā'* of Ibn Qutayba, where the canon of love story is in its formative stage and the famous *Kitāb al-aġānī* of Abū al-Farağ al-Iṣfahānī, where the same canon is finally completed. The story devoted to 'Urwa and 'Afrā' is the earliest one and, therefore, it seems to be a pattern for other medieval stories about unfortunate lovers in Arabic literature. Moreover, it has become clear that, over the course of the canon formation, a division of functions occurred in the stories: the prosaic elements have a plot function, while the verses have an emotional function. According to the plot canon, all stories have a rather rigid structure with a set of certain components which have been discussed in the text. Over the course of time, the prosaic parts transformed from disconnected comments to the verses of the poets into a completed story about the given poet's life and his love.

The variety of versions of one story undoubtedly proves that it must have been circulating in the oral form for a long time.

Two stories have certain peculiarities. The story of Qays and Lubnà is atypical and unique because it survived in two versions – an unhappy and a happy one. A detailed comparative analysis of numerous prosaic elements of this story contained in different literary anthologies has revealed that originally there was a happy ending in it; the sad ending was invented and added to the story later, in order to provide it with the "clothing" of canon. Another unusual story about Laylà al-Aḫyaliyya and Tawba b. Ḥumayyir is interesting due to its "overturned plot": the central hero is a woman, who is also a poet, which was not in harmony with Islamic ethics; that is why the plot of this story did not develop much. These two atypical stories demonstrate some freedom in the composing of folklore tales in spite of the rigid frames of canon.

Bibliography

'Abbās, Iḥsān (1986). *Kuṯhayyir b. 'Abd ar-Raḥmān*. Encyclopeadia of Islam. Vol. V. Leiden: E.J. Brill. Pp. 551–553.

Abū Tammām, Ḥabīb (1998). *Diwān al-ḥamāsa*. Bayrūt: Dār al-Kutub al-'Ilmiyya.

Al-Anṭākī, Dā'ūd (1901). *Tazyīn al-Aswāq bi-tafṣīl ašwaq al-'uššāq*. Al-Qāhira: al-Maṭba' al-Azhariyya.

Al-Ǧumaḥī, Ibn Sallām (2001). *Ṭabaqāt aš-šu'arā'*. Bayrūt: Dār al-Kutub al-'Ilmiyya.

Al-Iṣfahānī, Abū Al-Faraǧ (2008). *Kitāb Al-Aġānī*. Bayrūt: Dār Ṣādir. Vol. 1 – 25.

As-Sarrāǧ, Ǧa'far (No Date). *Maṣāri' Al-'Uššāq*. Vol 1 – 2. Bayrūt: Dār Ṣādir.

Bauer, Thomas (2000). *'Urwa b. Ḥizām*. Encyclopeadia of Islam. Vol. X. Leiden: E.J. Brill. Pp. 908–909.

Blachère, Régis (1991). *Ghazal. I – The Ghazal In Arabic Poetry*. Encyclopeadia of Islam. Vol. II. Leiden: E.J. Brill. Pp. 1028-1033.

Brockelmann, Carl (1909). *Geschichte der arabischen Literatur*. Leipzig: C. F. Amelangs Verlag.

—— (1937). *Geschichte der arabischen Literatur*. Erster Supplementband. Leiden: E. J. Brill.

Filshtinsky, Isaak (1985). *Istoria arabskoy literatury. V – nachalo X veka*. Moskva: Nauka.

Gabrieli, Francesco (1986). *Laylā al-Akẖyaliyya*. Encyclopeadia of Islam. Vol. V. Leiden: E.J. Brill. P. 710.

—— (1991). *Djamīl*. Encyclopeadia of Islam. Vol. II. Leiden: E.J. Brill, P.427–428.

Huart, Clément (1903). *A History of Arabic Literature*. New York: D. Appleton and Company.

Ibn An-Nadīm, Abū Al-Faraǧ (No Date). *Al-Fihrist*. Bayrūt: Dār Al-Ma'Rifa.

Ibn Qotaiba, Abū Muḥammad (1904). *Liber Poësis Et Poëtarum*. Ed. M. J. De Goeje. Lugduni-Batavorum (Leiden): E.J. Brill.

Jayyusi, Salma (1983). „Umayyad Poetry". In: *Arabic Literature to the End of the Umayyad Period*. The Cambridge History of Arabic Literature. London: Cambridge University Press.

Krachkovsky, Ignaty (1941). „Ranniaya istoria povesti o Majnune i Leyle v arabskoy literature". *Izvestia Akademii Nauk Soyuza SSR* (*Bulletin de l'Académie des Sciences de L'URSS*) 2: 7 – 21.

Meisami, Julie Scott (1998). *Ghazal*. Encyclopedia of Arabic Literature. P. 249 – 250.

Nicholson, Reynold A. (1907). *A Literary History of the Arabs*. London: T. Fisher Unwin.

Pellat, Charl (1986). *Maḏjnūn Laylā* (I). Encyclopeadia of Islam. Vol. V. Leiden: E. J. Brill. Pp. 1102-1103.

Propp, Vladimir (1969). *Morfologia Skazki.* Moskva: Izdatelstvo Nauka. II Izdanie.

Chapter 6

Poetic Souvenirs: The Meaning of *Ise Monogatari* in Sōkyū's *Miyako no Tsuto*

Adam Bednarczyk, *Nicolaus Copernicus University/Poland*

Foreword

"Writing and travel have always been intimately connected. The traveller's tale is as old as fiction itself [...]" (The Cambridge Companion 2002: 2) – such ascertainment is quite well reflected in ancient Japanese literature. Already the oldest work of travel writing, Ki no Tsurayuki's *Tosa Nikki* (Tosa Journal), the recognised antecedent of the form, partly uses fictional elements of prose as well as a poetic convention of travel account, which dictated that "the narrator's predominant feelings should be sadness, loneliness, homesickness, fatigue, discomfort, and uneasiness" (Classical Japanese Prose 1990: 23). This remarkable genre of the Japanese early-medieval and medieval self-reflective literature, represented by *Tosa Nikki,* has been called travel diary (*kikō* 紀行), that generally means a short work in prose and poetry, describing somebody's one-way more often than round-trip journey. Written as records of travel experience, *kikō* adhere both to the traditions of Japanese poetry and religion. As Donald Keene reads, travel diaries are mainly a phenomenon of the Japanese middle ages, when places visited by the writers had either – in the form of a pilgrimage or a hermit life – a sacred character or familiar because of frequent mentions in poetry (Keene 1999a: 114). A special reason for travel was the separation of government between the site of the imperial court and the shogunate, which – especially during the Kamakura period – forced many people to travel a long distance from Kyōto (Nakazato 1972: 49–53).

Among the most influential works of travel literature (*kikō bungaku*) of the first half of the Northern and Southern Courts period is a short account of a journey titled *Miyako no Tsuto* 都のつと[1] (Souvenir for the Capital, c. 1352) by

[1] The word つと can be written with following characters: 苞 or, uncommonly, 土産, both meaning 'local produce', 'souvenir', 'present', 'gift'.

priest Sōkyū 宗久[2] who "seems to have had an incurable urge to roam, not only to places of religious importance but to utamakura, the sites mentioned in the poetry of the past" (Keene 1999a:183). His records describe a journey made from Kyūshū, through Kyōto to Matsushima in northeastern provinces. All noted places that Sōkyū could see during his journey have appeared in well-known phrases, have been evoked in names of poets or poems included in several imperial anthologies and other works from many centuries. The paper discusses references to these works, especially to the most important one, *Ise Monogatari* 伊勢物語 (Tales of Ise)[3], and focuses on the role and significance of intertextual references to ancient works in order to show (un)changing the perception of *utamakura*. Moreover, it also attempts to answer the question whether *Miyako no Tsuto* can be regarded as an exemplification of a thematised work or if it takes up new topics as well.

1. Poetry as Description of Two Worlds

If we can believe the postscript of *Miyako no Tsuto* written by Nijō Yoshimoto 二条良基 (1320–1388) in 1367, the author of the text was the priest Sōkyū, who was also known as a poet and his four poems were included in imperial anthologies[4]. Yoshimoto describes Sōkyū in the following way:

> 心を一枝の花に染め、思ひを八重の風にかけて、蓬生の跡定むる所なく、浮き草の露誘ふ水にまかせてなんまどひ歩き侍りけり。［…］三十一字の風情尋ねぬかたもなし。［…］墨染の袖のうちには、とこしなへに大き硯を放たず。昔の杖のほとりには又短き筆をなむ取り添へ侍りける。剡溪の暁の雪を望まざれども、数寄の友を尋ねては、そこ

[2] Sōkyū 宗久 (?-d. after 1380) – a poet and priest (*hōshi*) of Nanbokuchō period; probably a member of Ōtomo clan (大友氏 Ōtomoshi). Men of the clan were granted the function of constable (*shugo*) of Bungo豊後, Buzen 豊前 and Chikugo 筑後 provinces in Kyūshū. One of the most famous members of the clan was Ōtomo no Kuronushi 大友黒主, a Japanese poet and one of the Rokkasen 六歌仙 (lit. 'six poetry immortals') described in the *Kokinwakashū*. Cf. Inada 1995: 1–13.

[3] Early Heian collection of 125 poem-tales (*utamonogatari*), involving 209 poems. Its authorship is unknown and plural, however the center character is suggested to be Ariwara no Narihira (825–880). More on this work see The Ise Stories 2010: 1–12.

[4] *Shinshūi Wakashū* 新拾遺和歌集 (New Waka Collection of Gleanings, 1364), *Shingosen Wakashū* 新後撰和歌集 (New Later Collection of Waka, 1303), *Shinshoku Kokinwakashū* 新続古今和歌集 (New Collection of Early and Modern Poetry Continued, 1439), cf. Inada 1995: 1–2.

はかとなくあくがれ、　盧山の夜の雨を聴かざれども、沈昧の腸をくだきて、心ざしを述べずといふことなし［…］(Inada 1995: 4–6)
"He was a man of exquisite taste, giving the heart to the blossoms, and dedicating his thoughts to the eight-fold winds. There was no place in the vast land that he desired to settle down in, and he wandered about aimlessly like the dew on a floating weed drawn by the currents. [...] Everywhere he sought to express his feelings in the thirty-one syllables. [...] He always kept a small inkstone under his black priest's robe, and along with old walking stick that he had long cherished, he carried a short writing brush. Although he did not yearn for the snow at dawn at Yen Ch'i River[5], he liked nothing more than to visit old friends who loved poetry. He did not hear the rain during the night at Lu Shan, but he never failed to express his feelings about things that moved his heart to sadness [...]." (Four Japanese Travel Diaries 1984: 74)[6]

In Yoshimoto's opinion, the author of *Miyako no Tsuto* was a wanderer of "exquisite taste" who, because of his love to poetry everywhere, "sought to express his feelings in the thirty-one syllables". His penchant for the quest of new inspirations during his travels resulted from the fact that "there was no place in the vast land that he desired to settle down in" as well as an excellent understanding of nature's complexity. But how does it translate into his poems?

Donald Keene claims that Sōkyū was not a distinguished poet and his records are of only moderate intrinsic interest (Keene 1999a:184). Most of the twenty-two poems included in his diary are tightly coupled with the places he visited, and only a few of them allude to earlier works. Sōkyū's poems also suggest the freedom from worldly bonds that a typical hermit enjoys. It is evident in *Miyako no Tsuto* that its author enjoyed traveling freely, with no special aim, schedule or destination, from one place of poetic interest to another. Moreover, as we read in the epilogue by Yoshimoto, Sōkyū "liked nothing more than to visit old friends who loved poetry", which indicates that Sōkyū appreciated a company of people of similar status and interest.

---

[5] The name indicates Shanxi River, the upper reach of Cao'er River in Zhejiang Province 浙江省.

[6] Full title: *Four Japanese Travel Diaries of the Middle Ages* (henceforth FJTD).

His poems mirror his freeing from reality and describe the world he wanted to live in. As he explains at the very beginning of his diary: みづから銀山鉄壁を徹る心ざしなしといへども、樹下石上を占めし跡を慕ひて (Sōkyū 1990: 348) "I did not have an iron will which could enable me to run through walls; yet I had yearned for many years to live under the trees and on the rocks" (FJTD 1984: 61). His both literally and lyrically understood escape from what is called "run through walls" suggests a type of self-identification, probably used to avoid the impression that he was writing an official travel diary. "His work shows more freedom in style and content than official diaries, a liberty a hermit, who has little or no connection with the official life at the court, can allow himself to take" (FJTD 1984:13).

When Sōkyū states that he cannot "run through walls", he also explains that: いづくもつゐの住みかならねばと思ひなしつゝ、しらぬひの筑紫を立ち出でしより、こゝかしこまよひありき侍し程に (Sōkyū 1990: 348) "With the thought that there is no place where one can stay forever, I left Tsukushi [Kyūshū] and wandered around without destination" (FJTD 1984:62). The way of thinking that Sōkyū presents is closely connected with the perception of *mujōkan* 無常感, the evanescence of life or sense of the vanity of life. Although he is aware of that truth, he could understand it deeply when one day during his journey he passed by Shiga Bay as the sun rose. He watched Lake Biwa and in one moment saw boats moving far away on the water. The view of the wake of the rowboats changed his mind. Sōkyū recorded,

> かの満誓沙弥が「何に譬へん」と詠じんける風情も、心に浮び侍り。叡山楞厳の先徳、和歌は化論の翫びなりとて停められけるが、[…] この歌を詠吟しけるを聞き給て、観念の助縁と成ぬべかりけりとて (Sōkyū 1990: 348–349)
> "I remembered the poem, "What should the world be compared to?" which the famous Mansei Shami composed. The head priest of the Ryōgon-in [Temple] of Eizan [Enryaku-ji Temple at Mt. Hiei] had prohibited poetry, saying that it is just a transient pleasure [...] It is said that when he heard someone recite this poem, he felt that poetry can help attain a state of enlightenment." (FJTD 1984: 62–63)

The celebrated poem composed by Sami no Manzei, a poet of the early Nara period and one of the greatest poets of Tsukushi, was included in *Man'yōshū* (III, 351):

世間乎　何物尓將𧬂　旦開　榜去師船之　跡無如
世間を何に譬へむ朝びらき漕ぎ去にし船の跡なきごと
(Man'yōshū 1957: 178–179)
"To what shall I compare/ This world of ours?/ It is like the wake/
Disappearing behind a boat/ That is rowed away at dawn"
(Keene 1999a: 114)

"The effectiveness for the High Priest of this *waka* was that it both portrayed a landscape he knew well and suggested the implications of this scene for all of human life; it persuaded him that poetry could help people to attain a state of enlightenment" (Keene 1999a: 114). Thus, the one scene in Sōkyū's life complemented his comprehension of the world and pointed the way he should follow.

However, it must be remembered that even though priest Sōkyū fixed no destination of his journey, he clearly states in the text that his journey toward the east was "to undergo Buddhist discipline", *shugyō* 修行 (in Sanskrit *dhūta*). As Plutschow explains, "*Shugyō* (also *gyō*) means certain hardships acolytes willingly undergo as an act of Buddhist discipline. Such hardships could go to extremes (*aragyō*) such as dwelling in caves, standing under waterfall or climbing or dwelling in the mountains. In travel diary literature, *shugyō* usually means travel, either travel to sacred places or wandering without a fixed destination. *Shugyō* as a purpose of travel was undertaken – as Priest Sōkyū tells us in his *Miyako no Tsuto* – in order to attain Buddha-hood (bodaishin)" (FJTD 1984: 62–63).

2. Charm of Famous Places

The text of *Miyako no Tsuto*, like many other accounts of the journey, refers to all noted places Sōkyū just passed or could visit. The practice of referring, paraphrasing or alluding to well-known phrases, names of poets, places from poems included in imperial anthologies and other works has been continued for many centuries. Particularly place names or the names of features associated with them, cultivating allusion and intertextuality between individual poems and within the tradition called *utamakura* 歌枕 (literally 'poem pillow')[7] in Sōkyū's work are meant to be of great importance. Because of many

---

[7] Five or seven syllables long; (1) originally, words, phrases and images codified for poetic use referring to seasons, flora, fauna, and other details such as the legendary or human customs associated with the annual observances, as well as famous places (*meisho*); (2) more particular and dominant later usage is restricted to names of famous places (cf. The Princeton Companion 1988: 433–441).

references to early medieval works *Miyako no Tsuto* can be regarded not only as an account of a journey or guidebook for travelers but also – to some degree – as a kind of itinerary of *utamakura*.

Attentive readers of Sōkyū's diary would be able to list most places mentioned by the author: Kiyomizu Temple, Kitano Shrine, Mount Ōsaka, Ishiyama Temple, Mount Kagami, Fuwa Barrier, Narumi Beach, Mount Utsu, etc. They are named explicitly and let the reader easily trace the route of Sōkyū's journey. But which places in the text were especially emphasised by the author?

The first poem included in *Miyako no Tsuto* was composed when priest Sōkyū reached famous Kagami Mountain, an *utamakura* of Ōmi 近江 province, at present the Shiga prefecture. The author describes that episode as follows:

> 鏡山を過ぐるとても、墨染に改むるわが面影も憚りある心地して、「いざ立ち寄りて」とも覚え侍らず。
>
> 立寄りて見つと語るな鏡山に留めん影も憂ければ (Sōkyū 1990: 349)
>
> "While passing by Mt. Kagami [Mirror Mountain], I felt shy in my new priest's dress, and did not feel quite the same as the poet who said, "Let us [stop and] have a look [at Mirror Mountain]." I wrote:
>
> Do not say that I came
> And looked at you,
> Mt. Mirror,
> For I do not like my image
> Nor making a name for myself
> In this world" (FJTD 1984: 63)

In this poem, Sōkyū does not even pretend that he remembered the words of a certain poet. However, looking at Mt. Kagami Sōkyū "did not feel quite the same" as that poet felt. The source of the mentioned poem by an anonymous person is *Kokinwakashū* (Collection of Early and Modern Poems, 905)[8]. Aside from *Shūi Wakashū* (Collection of Gleanings of Japanese Poems, 1005), *Goshūi Wakashū* (Later Collection of Gleanings of Japanese Poems, 1086), *Shinkokinwakashū* (New Collection of Poems Ancient and Modern, 1205) Sōkyū refers to this anthology quite frequently. Thus, when he passed over Mt. Utsu in Suruga 駿河 province (at present the Shizuoka prefecture), another

---

8 Poem no. 899:「鏡山いざたちよりてみてゆかん年へぬる身はおいやしぬると」(cf. *Kokinwakashū* 1965: 282); translation: "Let us stop/ And have a look/ At Mt. Kagami (Mirror Mountain)/ To see/ How old I became" (FJTD 1984: 106).

famous place of poetry often related to ivy, he came eventually to Kiyomigaseki (Kiyomi Barrier), now Seikenji. He recorded his visit in that place adding one poem again:

> 清見が関にとゞまりて、まだ夜深く出侍るとて、思ひ続け侍りし。
> 　清見潟波のとざしも明けて行月をばいかに夜判の関守
> 立たぬ日もありと聞きし田子の浦波にも、旅の衣手はいつとなく潮垂れがちなり。(Sōkyū 1990: 350)
> "I stayed overnight at Kiyomi Barrier, and when I left the next morning before dawn, I continued my musing:
> 　When at Kiyomi Beach
> 　The sea is opening its gate
> 　For daylight to enter
> 　How can you see [and let pass]
> 　The traveling moon,
> 　Guard of the Barrier?
> The sleeves of my dress became soaked with sea water [not that I could tell when they did] by the waves of the Bay of Tago – about which I have heard that on certain days its waves do not rise." (FJTD 1984: 64)

In this case, although Kiyomi Barrier was used as the main topic of the poem, reference to earlier works was marked in the last part of the quoted passage. Sōkyū mentioned that he had heard about the Bay of Tago where there are no waves on certain days. His recollection is, in fact, an allusion to a love poem from *Kokinwakashū*.[9]

Besides Kiyomi Barrier there was another famous barrier in Shirakawa. The author of *Miyako no Tsuto* described his stay in this place referring to the Heian period poet Nōin 能因 (988–ca.1055).

> またこの秋の末にこの関を越え侍しかば、古曽部の沙弥能因が「都をば霞とともに立しかど秋風ぞ吹く白川の関」と詠じけるはまこと也けりと、思ひ合はせられ侍り。(Sōkyū 1990:354)
> "[...] it was the end of autumn now as I crossed this Barrier [Shirakawa]; therefore, I felt convinced that it must have been true that Nōin,

[9] Poem no. 489: 「するがなるたごのうら浪たゝぬ日はあれども君をこひぬ日はなし」 cf. *Kokinwakashū* 1965: 204; transl.: "Though there may be a day/ When the waves rise not/ At Tago Bay in Suruga/ Yet no day passes/ Without my love for you" cf. FJTD 1984:107.

> the acolyte of Kosobe wrote: "I left the capital/ Together with the [spring] mist/ But now/ The autumn wind is blowing/ At Shirakawa Barrier." (FJTD 1984:67–68)

Established in the Nara period, the barrier of Shirakawa in Ōshū 奥州 (Tōhoku region) became famous in poetry through the poems of the tenth-century poet Taira no Kanemori 平兼盛 and Nōin as well. The poem quoted here by Sōkyū was included in *Goshūishū.*

All three above discussed excerpts from Sōkyū's travel account show quite similar technique of reference to earlier works. Firstly, the author could use only a few-word citation or, on the contrary, a quotation of the whole text of a poem. Secondly, a reference to the main topic could proceed in conjunction with another *utamakura.*

In his essay *Intertextual poetics: tradition and perspectives* Ryszard Nycz explains that "the awareness of disappearing or effective contestation of ability which enables elaboration of a new and original work, among other things, led – in the field of literature – to emphasising and evident thematisation of the sphere of relations between texts" (Nycz 2012: 154). Did the medieval Japanese travel literature, because of its extremely frequent references to already existing works, undergo a similar thematisation? In my opinion, the problem of selecting particular topics as themes of discourse or as themes of sentences seems quite congruent with Nycz's interpretation. Though almost all *utamakura* derive from the ancient times, the most famous places that are mentioned in travel diaries, of course, also in Sōkyū's work result in the work, in a certain sense, becoming a recapture of words well-known from other texts. That would mean that the possibility of creating an original account of the journey without referring to *utamakura* would be rather inconceivable.

There is, however, another question, namely, can we ascertain any changes in perception of *utamakura*? Since most of them were known from many earlier works, we could not answer positively. But *Miyako no tsuto* shows that in this text we can find both new topics for poetical compositions or occasion for discussion on visited places. First of all, the Sōkyū's diary possesses a special interest in that it seems to anticipate Matsuo Basho's 松尾芭蕉 (1644–1694) famous *Oku no Hosomichi* おくのほそ道 (The Narrow Road to the Deep North, 17th c.)[10]. "Comparing the two diaries is unkind to Sōkyū, but parallel passages will suggest the closeness of the resemblances" (Keene 1999a: 184). References to *utamakura* of Ōshū: the already mentioned Shirakawa Barrier,

---

[10] For a recent study discussing this subject matter see Muramatsu 2001.

but also Shiogama-Matsushima Bay or Matoara were known and recalled in poems since ancient times. In one passage, Sōkyū mentions three place names that we can find in Basho's diary:

> さて、陸奥国多賀の国府にもなりぬ。それより奥の細道といふ方を南ざまに、末の松山へ尋ね行きて、松原越しにはる／〵と見渡せば、げに波越すやう也。(Sōkyū 1990: 350)
> "I reached Taga, the capital of Michinoku Province, and from there I went on the Oku no Hosomichi Road southward to visit Sue no Matsuyama. Looking over the pine forest in the distance, it seemed indeed [as the poem says] that the waves spill over the pines." (FJTD 1984: 71)

The names Taga, the Narow Road of Oku, and Sue no Matsuyama are very significant in Bashō's travel diary, but while reading Sōkyū's account one may notice that "even Matsushima failed to excite Sōkyū, thought Bashō's evocation of the pine-covered islands rising from the sea" (Keene 1999a: 185).

3. *Ise Monogatari* and *Miyako no Tsuto*

Sōkyū, who drew on literary experiences of his predecessors, also alludes to *Ise Monogatari*, the famous tenth-century Japanese *uta monogatari*, or collection of *waka* poems and associated narratives. *Ise Monogatari*, called by Nakazato "a poetic anthology of travel accounts" (*kikōteki kashū* 紀行的歌集) (Nakazato 1972: 54), seems to have a particular meaning in *Miyako no tsuto*[11], although there are only a few references to the work included in Sōkyū's account.

The first allusion to the *Ise Monogatari* appeared when the priest reached the Suruga province. As he then wrote:

> やがて駿河国、宇津の山を越ゆ。蔦の下道もいまだ若菜の程にて、紅葉の秋思ひやられ侍り。
> 　紅葉せば夢とやならん宇津の山うつゝに見つる蔦の青葉も
> (Sōkyū 1990: 350)
> "Then I passed over Mt. Utsu in Suruga Province. The road was covered with ivy decked in young leaves, and I imagined the beauty of its crimson [leaves] in autumn:
> When they turn crimson in autumn
> They must be as lovely as in a dream –
> These young ivy leaves

[11] For references of *Ise Monogatari* to Sōkyū's work cf. Nakada 1971: 38–44.

That I now see in reality
At Mt. Utsu" (FJTD 1984: 63–64)

Scenery similar to this depicted by Sōkyū can be found in the ninth story of *Ise Monogatari*:

ゆき／＼て。するがの國ゝいたりぬ。うつの山にいたりて。わがゆくゑのみちは。いとくらくほそきに。つたかづらはしげりて。もの心ぼそう。すゞろなるめを見ることとおもふに。す行者あひたり。かゝるみちは。いかでかおはすといふに。見れば見し人なりけり。京にその人のもとにとて。文かきてつく。
するかなるうつの山への現にも夢にも人にあはぬなりけり
(Ise Monogatari 1946: 124)
"On they journeyed to the province of Suruga. At Mount Utsu, the road ahead was dark, narrow and overgrown with ivy and maples. They were eyeing it, filled with dismissal forebodings when a wandering ascetic came into view. "What are you doing on a road like this?" he asked. Recognizing him as someone he had known in the old days, the man gave him a message for a woman in the capital:
Beside Mount Utsu
In Suruga Province,
I can see you
Neither when I am awake
Nor, alas, even in my dreams."
(Classical Japanese Prose 1990: 42)

The next famous place, after Mount Utsu and Kiyomi Barrier, that Sōkyū could see during his journey was Mt. Fuji. He described his first impressions as follows:

富士の山も見渡せば、いと深く霞込めて、時知らぬ山とも更に見えず。朝日の影に高嶺の雪なをあざやかに見えて、鏡をかけたるやう也。筆も及びがたし。
時知らぬ名をさへこめて霞む不尽の高嶺の曙
富士の嶺の煙の末は絶えにしを降りける雪や消えせざるらん
(Sōkyū 1990: 350)
"Looking over toward Mt. Fuji, I saw it through a deep mist, so that I could not agree that it knows of seasons. One could clearly see the snow lying on the high peak, reflecting the morning sun, and it looked like a mirror suspended in the sky. It was beyond description.

Covered with mist
The high cone of Mt. Fuji
Is said to know no season.
How marvelous it looks
On this early morning in spring.

Because the smoke has ceased completely
To rise above
The peak of Mt. Fuji,
The snow that fell on it
Will never vanish." (FJTD 1984: 64)

Mt. Fuji mentioned in *Ise Monogatari* just after the account relating to Mt. Utsu was depicted in the same manner as by Sōkyū. The author of the ninth story noted that even though it was the end of the fifth month, pure white snow had fallen on Mt. Fuji. It is exactly the poem added to the account in *Ise Monogatari* where it is said that Fuji is a peak indifferent to the season.

In terms of significance of the whole text of *Miyako no Tsuto,* undoubtedly the last sentence of the diary is a meaningful one. The passage is considered not only an explanation of the diary's title, but it also suggests what the probable objective of writing the work was. Sōkyū recorded as follows:

> 一夜の旅の宿にて、老の眼を醒して、壁に向へるの灯を挑げそへて、道すがらの名高き所／＼の心に残しを、忘れぬさきにとて、思ひ出るまゝに、前後の次第を言はずこれを記しつけて、都のつとにとて持上りぬ。(Sōkyū 1990: 350)
> "One day, when I awoke from an old man's sleep at a travel inn, I faced the wall and wrote down by the last flickering of my oil lamp, in order not to forget, my impressions of the famous places I had seen on my way just as they came into my mind, and I brought these notes with me to the capital as a souvenir of my journeys."
> (FJTD 1984: 64)

The quoted passage includes a phrase that served Sōkyū as the title of his work. This expression, however, was not coined by the priest but borrowed from the poem added to the fourteenth tale of *Ise Monogatari.* The story talks about a certain man who came to Michinoku in the course of his wanderings, and about a provincial girl, who, probably unaccustomed to meeting travelers from the capital, became infatuated with him. The man had to return to Kyōto, but sent a poem to the girl:

栗原やあねはの松の人ならは都のつとにいさといはまし
(Ise Monogatari 1946: 126)
"If the pine of Aneha at Kurihara
Were but a person
Long awaited,
I would say «Come with me as a souvenir
To the Capital»"[12]

The girl was overjoyed by the letter and thought that the man was in love with her as well.

As we read in the epilogue by Nijō Yoshimoto, although Sōkyū was not the author of the poem "The pine of Anehara", "he wrote down his travel notes and entitled them *Miyako no Tsuto* (Souvenir for the Capital). One may say that his notes are a foolish pleasure, but why could they not serve as a lesson on how one should express one's feelings?" (FJTD 1984: 75) This question may be open, but the last sentence of Sōkyū's diary gives the reader many hints to better understanding the sense of the work.

Conclusion

Miyako no Tsuto is one of the first poetic diaries that describe the Michinoku (Ōshū) province, contemporary the Tōhoku region. Numerous references and allusions to various works from ancient and medieval Japanese but also to Chinese literature show that Sōkyū was an educated and skilful poet. Like *Ise Monogatari*'s male protagonist identified with Ariwara no Narihira, a famous poet and legendary lover, who "convinced that he could serve no useful function if he remained in the capital, [...] decided to set out for the East in search of a suitable place to live in that region", and eventually "discovered a world of his own of true miyabi and of mono no aware, a sensitivity to things" (Keene 1999b: 455), Sōkyū was convinced that poetry could help people to attain a state of enlightenment, so he followed the tradition of earlier diarists in composing poems at each famous place he passed on his journey toward north-eastern provinces. On the one hand, because of the frequent referring to *utamakura*, his work in a certain sense became a recapture of other well-known texts. And on the other hand, Sōkyū's diary-like many other similar

[12] McCullogh's translation: "Were it but human – / the pine tree of Aneha / at Kurikara – / I would tell it, "Come and be / my keepsake in the city." According to McCullogh, "the man implies that he would like to take the girl home with him", however, there could be another interpretation of the poem. It can also mean: "I consider you scarcely human. Naturally, I won't take you with me." (cf. Classical Japanese Prose 1990: 46).

works displays coherence and permanence of Japanese poetry tradition. The author of *Miyako no Tsuto* was aware of the sense of composing poetry. His "Souvenir for the Capital" could not be written down only as a foolish pleasure. To the contrary, I believe that he was thinking about his next life, and composing poetry was only one of the ways to get there.

Bibliography

Classical Japanese Prose. An Anthology (1990) Ed. Helen Craig McCullough. Stanford: Stanford University Press.

Four Japanese Travel Diaries of the Middle Ages (1984). Ed. Herbert Plutschow, Hideichi Fukuda. "Cornell University East Asia Papers" no. 25. Ithaca-New York: Cornell University.

Inada Toshinori (1995). "Sōkyū ron: «Miyako no tsuto» no sakusha" 宗久論：「都のつと」の作者 (An essay on Sōkyū: The author of «Miyako no tsuto»). *Okayama daigaku kyōiku gakubu kenkyū shūroku* 岡山大学教育学部研究集録 (Bulletin of School of Education, Okayama University) 99: 1–13.

Ise Monogatari 伊勢物語 (1946). "Gunshruijū" 群書類従, vol. XVII/307. Ed. Hanawa Hokiichi. Tokyo: Taiyō shuppan kabushikigaisha.

Keene, Donald (1999a). *Travelers of the Hundred Ages.* New York: Columbia University Press.

Keene, Donald (1999b). *Seeds in the Heart. Japanese Literature from Earliest Times to the Late Sixteenth Century.* New York: Columbia University Press.

Kokinwakashū 古今和歌集 (1965). Ed. Saeki Umetomo 佐伯梅友. "Nihon koten bungaku taikei" 8. Tokyo: Iwanami shoten.

Man'yōshū 万葉集 (1957). Ed. Takagi Ichinosuke 高木市之助 et al. Vol. 1. "Nihon koten bungaku taikei" 日本古典文学大系 4. Tokyo: Iwanami shoten.

Muramatsu Tomotsugu 村松友次 (2001). *«Oku no hosomichi» no sōzōryoku: chūei kikō «Miyako no tsuto» to no ruiji* 「おくのほそ道」の想像力：中世紀行「都のつと」との類似. Tokio: Kasama shoin.

Nakada Takeshi 中田武司 (1971). "«Ise monogatari» kyōju to «Miyako no tsuto»" 伊勢物語享受と「都のつと」. *Gakuen* 学苑 380: 38–44.

Nakazato Jūkichi 中里重吉 (1972). "Kamakura jidai kikō bungaku no kōsatsu – «Kaidōki», «Tōkan kikō», «Izayoi nikki» ni tsuite" 鎌倉時代紀行文学の考察ー海道記・東関紀行・十六夜日記についてー (A study on the literature of travelling in Kamakura age: On «Kaidōki», «Tōkan kikō», and «Izayoi nikki»). *Chūō gakuin daigaku ronsō: Ippan kyōiku kankei* 中央学院大学論叢：一般教育関係 7(2).

Nycz, Ryszard (2012). *Poetyka intertekstualna: tradycje i perspektywy* [Intertextual poetics: tradition and perspectives]. In: *Kulturowa teoria literatury. Główne pojęcia i problemy.* Ed. Michał P. Markowski, R. Nycz. Kraków: Universitas.

Sōkyū, *Miyako no tsuto* 都のつと (1990). In: *Chūsei nikki kikō shū* 中世日記紀行集. Ed. Fukuda Hideichi 福田秀一 et al. "Shin nihon koten bungaku taikei" 新日本古典文学大系 51. Tokio: Iwanami shoten.

The Cambridge Companion to Travel Writing (2002). Ed. Peter Hulme, Tim Youngs. Cambridge University Press: Cambridge.

The Ise Stories (2010). Ed. Joshua S. Mostow, Royall Tyler. Honolulu: University of Hawai'i Press.

The Princeton Companion to Classical Japanese Literature (1998). Ed. Earl R. Miner, Robert E. Morrell and Hiroko Odagiri. Princeton: Princeton University Press.

III

Orient-Occident Historical and Social Borders in Literature

Chapter 7

The "East-West" Dichotomy in the English Modernist Novel: An Imagological Perspective

Tetiana Derezhytska, *Ivan Franko National University of Lviv/Ukraine*

The aim of the paper is to show the functional revelation of the textual and contextual aspects of discursive constructions of auto- and hetero-images in the novels of Leonard Woolf and Edward Forster.

There was a long-standing interest, especially in the Western cultures, in the relations between different countries and nations. Many scientists tried to discover the peculiarities of various treatments of certain nations and draw necessary and relevant inferences from their own investigations. Thus, it was even argued that cultural differences should be viewed in terms of mutual attitudes and perceptions rather than notions and essences. It seemed that humankind tended to form particular images towards different nations, similar or dissimilar to them, either friends or enemies, neighbors or people living far away.

Literature played an extremely important role in implementing these constructed images, making them come true throughout the world. It constituted a vital element of the world policy since with its help it was almost always more possible to propagate certain ideas.

After the epoch of Modernism, when globalisation started to penetrate into all the spheres of life, when the British Empire was coming apart, when colonialism came to its end, and post-colonial migration began to spread worldwide, a new kind of studies took force, namely Imagology. It is a comparative literary approach which explores intercultural relations in terms of mutual perceptions, images, and self-images in fiction.

Thus, according to Amel Chiheb, studying the images or the representations of the others makes the object of Imagology. The image "is born as an ensemble of beliefs, requests, attitudes, opinions, hypothesis, mentalities, preconceived ideas, experiences, assumptions, illusions that belong to groups of individuals, to communities, to institutions or to other types of phenomena or objects. The images are framework interpretations resulted from representations which, in their turn, incorporate interpretations of large complexity" (Chiheb 2014:128).

Amel Chiheb also points out that Imagology, a young and perspective branch of studies, has its right to existence nowadays since variables, sometimes even vacillations between extreme appreciation or depreciation have become to attract the attention of numerous literary critics at present. It is in this comparatist aspect that imagology holds out a challenge and a promise for future research (Chiheb 2014:88).

The turning point in the imagological studies is the recent emergence of Studia Imagologica, Amsterdam Studies on Cultural Identity, and especially of its two brightest representatives – Hugo Dyserinck and Joep Leerssen.

The study of national images is a comparative enterprise: it addresses cross-national relations rather than national identities. Likewise, patterns of national characterisation will stand out most clearly when studied supranationally as a multinational phenomenon. This indicates that national characterisations are often specific instances and combinations of generic moral polarities and that our way of thinking in terms of national characters boils down to an ethnic-political distribution of role patterns in an imagined anthropological landscape. It is in this comparatist aspect that imagology holds out a challenge and a promise for future research.

Constructed images are ethnocentric, and their contraction is intertwined with a process of Othering. Images are constructed for the purpose of defining the unknown Other. What is unknown is dangerous. To define it is to have control over it and to dominate it. The image is an efficient way to dominate the unknown Other because once built and established, images stick and could not be easily removed. Literature and art are means of constructing images. An example is the image that Orientalist artists and writers built about the Orient. They wanted to define the unknown Orient to have control over it. They built a faulty stereotypical image (the exotic, the barbaric) which was accepted and interiorised by the Orient and turned into its reality. What used to be an image in the mind of the West about the East became the reality of that East.

In his doctoral thesis, written in Finnish and entitled *Imagology. Some Theories of the Public Image Presented, Analyzed and Criticized,* Karvonen Erkki states that: "To revise that image, the East should employ the same strategy and adhere to the philosophy of 'define yourself, or you are defined' " (Karvonen 1997: 185). It is through literature and art that this image was constructed and it is through literature and art that it should be revised.

1. Hybridity As a Result of Colonialism

The problem of interconnection between culture and supremacy has become well explored by many researchers. The close relationship between British imperialism and culture has become well investigated, in particular, by American–Palestinian literary theorist, critic Edward Said, the forefather of the postcolonial theory. His *Orientalism* (1978), representing the Middle East, according to Firdous Azim: "heralded a revolution in the field of literary studies. It shows how no form of intellectual or cultural activity is innocent of power hierarchies, highlighting the collusion between literary representation and colonial power" (Hewitt 1988: 237–238).

Edward Said basically describes the concept of Orientalism as "a Western style for dominating, restructuring, and having authority over the Orient". From the late eighteenth century, Western colonialist and imperialist powers, especially England and France created "an identity of Other" and named it as "the Orient" to complete their own identity construction. These powers, positioning themselves as "the center of the world and civilisation," constructed "a West and East dichotomy". Accordingly; unfavourable, negative adjectives or qualities such as "irrational, barbaric, backward, inferior, weak and periphery" were related to "the Orient". On the other hand, "The West" was constructed as "rational, civilized-modern, sophisticated, superior and omnipotent".

The British presence in Africa and Asia led to an enormous growing body of English literature set in the colonies. Literature thus produced what is known as colonial or colonialist literature, which often shows colonization as the legalistic undertaking of land for the process of the civilisation of its natives. This is exemplified by Rudyard Kipling's statement that white men had the burden and responsibility of bringing the blessings of their superior civilisation to the savages of the non-European world. Furthermore, their literature presents "natives" as weak, incomprehensible, illogical, and irrational and the White men as the exact opposite of it. The arbitrary nature of imperial justice, the exploitation rather than nurture of Ceylon's population, and the inability to improve the lives of those living in Britain's foreign possessions all raised doubts about the empire (Boehmer 2005: 23).

Literature became the main way to propagate imperial colonial thriving and justify its policy. Thomas Babington Macaulay approved of colonisation and displayed the superior qualities of the English people – "the greatest and most highly civilized people that ever the world saw" (Beyond Culture 1997: 918).

The English modernist novels under discussion try to clarify the issue of Imagology as they throw the light on various spheres of usage of different types of images between English and Indian/Ceylonese and also their functional characteristics.

Moreover, the novels raise the issue of Colonisation as a chief factor of grounds for the British domination, its right to do whatever they want. Therefore, the problems of British justification of its colonial mission and the loss of identity in the East are raised most vividly in the works of these two Modernist authors. The writers both show the endeavor of colonisers to bring the rudiments of civilisation to the illiterate and uneducated nations of the Third world, to maintain law and order there. However, this innocent and "beneficial" task turns out to be a total disaster for both sides, since it causes devastation and explicit as well as implicit feuds. The production of such intermixture of cultures is a "hybrid with perverted thinking" unable to fulfill self-realization, find one's place in the world and the essence of existence.

Later post-colonial theorist Homi Bhabha considers colonisation to be "a process of subject formation". According to him, "the old binaries – master/slave, colonizer/ colonized or European/other – are broken down, and a new 'hybrid' identity is seen to emerge". Thus, he declares explicitly that: "The image of the post-Enlightenment man is tethered to, not confronted by, his dark reflection, the shadow of colonized man, that splits his presence, distorts his outline, breaches his boundaries, repeats his action at a distance, disturbs and divides the very time of his being" (Ganguly 1992: 44).

Bhabha opposes Said's binary and denotes the close interrelationship between coloniser and colonised. What is more, "The new colonial subjectivity that emerges then becomes a strange amalgam – a hybrid, born out of mimicry of colonial forms" (Nilsen 2011: 114). Bryan Turner critiques Said's work saying there were a multiplicity of forms and traditions of Orientalism. He is therefore critical of Said's attempt to try to place them all under the framework of the Orientalist tradition.

The issue of mixed or unidentified identity is raised from time to time in Edward Forster's novel, focusing reader's attention on the drastic results of Colonialism: "Then you are an Oriental" (Forster 2006:13) or "The long and the short of it is Heaslop's a sahib; he's the type we want, he's one of us" (Forster 2006:15).

Besides, a feeling of total dissatisfaction with life penetrates into the text since: "What does unhappiness matter when we are all unhappy together?"(Forster 2006: 71). Colonial domination resulted in the feeling of being lonely, forgotten, exiled and far away from the native state. This point caused the sense of hybrid identity, lost "self" and frustration: "Her manner had grown more distant since she had discovered that some of the group was Westernized, and might apply her own standards to her"[8] and "When English and Indians were both present, he grew self-conscious, because he did not know to whom he belonged. For a little he was vexed by opposite currents in his blood, then they blended, and he belonged to no one but himself" (Forster 2006: 27).

The issue of lost identity and indefiniteness is very vivid in the novel: "To slink through India unlabelled was his aim. Henceforward he would be called 'anti-British', 'seditious' – terms that bored him, and diminished his utility. He foresaw that besides being a tragedy, there would be a muddle; already he saw several tiresome little knots, and each time his eye returned to them, they were larger. Born in freedom, he was not afraid of the muddle, but he recognized its existence". (Forster 2006: 95)· Moreover, this issue is often foregrounded in the text: "We are both of us slaves", (Forster 2006: 64) and "It's inevitable. I can't avoid the label. What I do hope to avoid is the mentality". (Forster 2006: 125) The reason is quite clear: "Such affability is seldom seen. But what can we offer to detain them? You can make India in England apparently, just as you can make England in India" and, in addition: "The East had returned to the East via the suburbs of England, and had become ridiculous during the detour" (Forster 2006: 162).

Thus, the feeling of loneliness, despair, lost dreams and expectations is quite visible and sensible even in the colonisers. These dismal tokens are results of colonisation, and even the English can be viewed as prey of that process.

2. Hetero Images › Auto-images

The Village in the Jungle by Leonard Woolf

Leonard Woolf, who lived in the early XX century, is recognised as the best creative writer in English on Ceylon. His Diaries in Ceylon, 1908–1911, Records of a Colonial Administrator (Assistant Government Agent in Ceylon) provide a remarkable account of the day-to-day workings of one small corner of the British Empire in the first decade of the twentieth century. Despite the compassion he felt for the suffering villagers, Woolf never criticised the bureaucratic regulations in his diaries nor went out of the way to glorify the past of the subjugated race as some earlier diarists have done. Despite the apparent concerns about the disciplinary nature of colonial rule, he remained committed to the efficacy of British law, arguing in Ceylon, "If one has a bad law, I believe it is almost better to enforce it than to leave it unenforced" (Woolf 1983: 198).

First of all, it should be mentioned that the story is given through the narrator's eyes or, in other words, the author's own experience of living somewhere over there in Sri Lanka. Thus, it is possible to distinguish his attitude towards natives, their lifestyle, and beliefs, creed and mentality.

Throughout the novel, the theme of the British authority in Ceylon is very clear-cut and definite. The writer clearly demonstrates the superiority, might and immense power of the coloniser. Thus, the British auto-image is very well described and even, at some moments, justified.

The power and might of colonisers is in the air everywhere in the story, it is pending over the inferior race: "And Babehami was a quiet, cunning man in the village: he never threatened, and rarely talked of his loans to his debtors, but there were few in the village who dared to cross him, and who did not feel hanging over them the power of the little man" (Woolf 1931: 19).

Mutual recognition of power is the factor which stimulates and simplifies the ruling of the conqueror, giving him an opportunity to control and possess: "The villagers were completely in his hands, and both sides were fully aware of it. The whole transaction, certainly, so far as the headman was concerned, was illegal". Besides, "To the villagers Fernando was, owing to his dress and habits, a Mahatmaya. He did not treat them as his equals, and they– being in his debt– treated him as a superior" (Woolf 1931: 63).

The doomed existence of the colonised nation is foregrounded and intensified through many statements and facts provided in the text: "The villagers owned no jungle themselves; it belonged to the Crown, and no one might fell a tree or clear a chena in it without a permit from the Government. It was through these permits that the headman had his hold upon the villagers. Application for one had to be made through him; it was he who reported if a clearing had been made without one, or if a man, having been given one, cleared more jungle than it allowed him to clear" (Woolf 1931: 20).

Anglo-Indians argue that natives are ignorant, thus the former's hetero-images of Indians coincide with the latter's auto-images: "It's very difficult, sir. They live far away in these little villages. Many of them are good men and help the villagers. But they are ignorant, too" (Woolf 1931: 107) vs. "I do not know what I was saying, I am a poor man, Arachchi, very ignorant, a little mad. But I am a quiet man; I have given no trouble in the village" (Woolf 1931: 97). In addition to this, the natives speak up about themselves without being deceitful or sly: "We are poor men, aiya, and ignorant". (Woolf 1931: 64) And, once again, "Why come and trouble us? We are poor and ignorant, and you have wealth, and women in the town as you told us. Leave us in peace, aiya, leave us in peace" (Woolf 1931: 75).

Quite often some hetero-images pass into auto-images, e.g., "I am afraid of everything, Arachchi; the jungle, the devils, the darkness. But, above all, of being hunted" (Woolf 1931: 99).

"The Village in the Jungle" has long inspired and sustained curiosity about what happens in the meeting of cultures; about the question of the mutual dependence of cultures; about what we need to do to understand such a cultural encounter and its implications.

"The Village in the Jungle" also reminds us that in the end what we suffer from is a kind of cultural vertigo. The novel is also the hallmark of such a cultural encounter and what occurs in the meeting of minds. What Woolf succeeded in accomplishing with his writing of this book was extraordinary. He demonstrated how to creatively and ethically intervene into the colonial project.

The novel does not preach, but it does speak indirectly of Woolf's disillusionment with the role of the white-colonial tin god and with the pretensions of imperialism. The story raises the question whether it is possible to be anywhere, go anywhere, without colonising, without touching and being touched by the colonial project?

Succeeding the works of Rudyard Kipling and preceding those of Joseph Conrad and E.M. Forster, "The Village in the Jungle" occupies an important place in the history of the English colonial literature.

A Passage to India by Edward Forster

Forster is among those novelists whose works pay special attention to the colonial territories. However, in *A Passage to India*, he turns into an objective voice and narrates what he has experienced personally during two travels to India. Forster was critical towards the Indian people in his previous recordings. In some of his works, his European nature dominates, and he introduces Indians as inferior and unequal to Europeans. When he traveled to India, he reported the country as an uncivilized, miserable place which suffers villainies and chaos (Siber 2012: 210).

As a result of traveling to India, he encounters the real state, removes his presuppositions, and writes the novel based on his own observations and becomes a critic of stereotypical representation of Indians. In this way, he is among the novelists who see India through the lenses of a man who has neither imperial tendencies to despise the country nor is fond of India to support it. In this way, his attitude towards India separates him from his contemporaries who have extremist ideas against Indians and wish to Orientalise them.

A Passage to India examines the racial misunderstandings and cultural hypocrisies that characterised the complex interactions between the Indians and the English toward the end of the British occupation of India. Moreover, the novel traces the products of the Colonisation process which are inevitable results of such a fierce campaign. It characterises the whole state of affairs beyond the British zone of comfort, far away in India. Thus, it is possible to evaluate the relationships between both the coloniser and the colonised and their imagological tendencies.

A Passage to India begins and ends by posing the question of whether it is possible for an Englishman and an Indian to ever be friends, at least within the context of British colonialism. Forster uses this question as a framework to explore the general issue of Britain's political control of India on a more personal level, through the friendship between the characters Aziz and Fielding: "They were discussing as to whether or not it is possible to be friends with an Englishman" (Forster 2006: 3).

Forster's final vision of the possibility of English-Indian friendship is a pessimistic one, yet it is qualified by the possibility of friendship on English soil, or after the liberation of India. As the landscape itself seems to imply at the end of the novel, such friendship may be possible eventually, but "not yet."

Besides, the big and inevitable difference between Anglo-Indians and natives is foregrounded everywhere in the text: "He had discovered that it is possible to keep in with Indians and Englishmen, but that he who would also keep in with Englishwomen must drop the Indians. The two wouldn't combine" (Forster 2006: 45)

However, slight traces of modified treatment of his own English race can also be traced in the text: "Here is a native who has actually behaved like a gentleman; if it were not for his black face, we would almost allow him to join our club. The approval of your compatriots no longer interests me, I have become anti-British, and ought to have done so sooner, it would have saved me numerous misfortunes" (Forster 2006: 182).

The author's perception of India itself is rather dubious, he either denounces it or justifies its subjugated position: "It matters so little to the majority of living beings what the minority, that calls itself human, desires or decides. Most of the inhabitants of India do not mind how India is governed. Nor are the lower animals of England concerned about England, but in the tropics, the indifference is more prominent, the inarticulate world is closer at hand and readier to resume control as soon as men are" (Forster 2006: 80).

The sense of disaster, decay, and ruin is traced both subtly and overtly in the author's vision: "But men try to be harmonious all the year round, and the results are occasionally disastrous. The triumphant machine of civilisation may suddenly hitch and be immobilized into a car of stone, and at such moments the destiny of the English seems to resemble their predecessors', who also entered the country with intent to refashion it, but were, in the end, worked into its pattern and covered with its dust" (Forster 2006: 152).

Moreover, "It was, in a new form, the old, old trouble that eats the heart out of every civilisation: snobbery, the desire for possessions, creditable appendages; and it is to escape this rather than the lusts of the flesh that saints retreat into the Himalayas" (Forster 2006: 175).

The British mission or so-called "The White man's burden" has the right to its existence in the novel since it is always justified: "We're not out here for the purpose of behaving pleasantly! We're out here to do justice and keep the peace. India isn't a drawing room. [...] There's no point in all this. Here we are, and we're going to stop, and the country's got to put up with us, gods or no gods" (Forster 2006: 33).

The Englishman highlights his mission with inexorable force: "I am out here to work, mind, to hold this wretched country by force. I'm not a missionary or a Labour Member or a vague sentimental sympathetic literary man. I'm just a servant of the Government; it's the profession you wanted me to choose myself, and that's that. We're not pleasant in India, and we don't intend to be pleasant. We've something more important to do" (Forster 2006: 33).

The racial difference is often depicted as a pivotal factor in relations between nations, the one which constructs barriers between them: "Don't worry me so, you blacks and whites. Here I am, stuck in dam India same as you, and you got to fit me in better than this" (Forster 2006: 63). And what makes the matter even worse is the revelation: "But he had forgotten his back collar-stud, and there you have the Indian all over: inattention to detail; the fundamental slackness that reveals the race" (Forster 2006: 56).

The important thing about imagological aspects is that very often they get distorted, falsified and forged, utterly without the grain of the truth. The reason is that stereotypes interfere with the right and relevant mutual look at each other: "The remark suggested that he, an obscure Indian, had no right to have heard of Post Impressionism—a privilege reserved for the Ruling Race", (Forster 2006: 45) or "Indeed, he was sensitive rather than responsive. In every remark, he found meaning, but not always the true meaning, and his life though vivid was largely a dream". And what is the most important is that: "Ronny was tempted to retort; he knew the type; he knew all the types, and this was the spoilt Westernized" (Forster 2006: 53).

The feeling of sadness, despair and gloominess is transparent in the story as a result of a lost purpose in life: "After forty years' experience, he had learnt to manage his life and make the best of it on advanced European lines, had developed his personality, explored his limitations, controlled his passions—and he had done it all without becoming either pedantic or worldly. A creditable achievement, but as the moment passed, he felt he ought to have been working at something else the whole time, — he didn't know at what, never would know, never could know, and that was why he felt sad" (Forster 2006: 138).

As a writer, Forster has his own Orientation towards the colonial situation that is inevitably reflected in his novel. Besides, the author's perception of India reflects his attitude toward a completely different country, strange and peculiar: "No one can even begin to think of knowing this country until he has been in it twenty years" (Forster 2006: 17). The narrator concludes: "India isn't home" (Forster 2006: 21).

Although Forster is sympathetic to India and Indians in the novel, his overwhelming depiction of India as a muddle matches the manner in which many Western writers of his day treated the East in their works: "All invitations must proceed from heaven perhaps; perhaps it is futile for men to initiate their own unity, they do but widen the gulfs between them by the attempt" (Forster 2006: 23).

At one point, the fairy tale of wonderful India vanishes and falls into oblivion: "The wonderful India of her opening weeks, with its cool nights and acceptable hints of infinity, had vanished", (Forster 2006: 113) since, as the Englishman claims, "You don't happen to know this poisonous country as well as I do" (Forster 2006: 123). Moreover, "You can't run with the hare and hunt with the hounds, at least not in this country" (Forster 2006: 135). A kind of epiphany strikes one of the characters: "You mean that my bothers are mixed up with India?" (Forster 2006: 69).

As far as the true Indian identity is concerned, it is never easy to define it, it slips unnoticed, ambiguous and indistinct: "India — hundred Indias — whispered outside beneath the indifferent moon, but for the time India seemed one and their own, and they regained their departed greatness by hearing its departure lamented, they felt young again because reminded that youth must fly" (Forster 2006: 7). Moreover, "But nothing in India is identifiable, the mere asking of a question causes it to disappear or to merge in something else. That's India all over... how like us... there we are..." (Forster 2006: 70).

Acclaimed as his masterpiece. *A Passage to India* is a picture of society in India under the British Raj, of the clash between the East and the West, and of the prejudiced misunderstandings that foredoomed goodwill. Criticised at first for its anti-British and possibly inaccurate bias, it has been praised as a superb character study of people of one race by a writer of another. However, as an Englishman, Forster is inevitably influenced by English social and cultural circumstances. In this dramatic story, Forster depicts, with sympathy and discernment, the complicated Oriental reaction to the British rule in India, and reveals the conflict of temperament and tradition involved in that relationship (Mermoune 2010: 69).

The narrator describes the Oriental country as being "The Scented East of tradition" (Forster 2006: 167), and he even makes such an interesting comparison: "To regard an Indian as if he were an Italian is not, for instance, a common error, nor perhaps a fatal one, and Fielding often attempted analogies between this peninsula and that other, smaller and more exquisitely shaped, that stretches into the classic waters of the Mediterranean" (Forster 2006: 41).

Besides, the difference between them is all the time only widened: "They listened delighted, for they took the public view of poetry, not the private which obtains in England", (Forster 2006: 7) and "There was a curious uncertainty about their gestures, as if they sought for a new formula which neither East nor West could provide" (Forster 2006: 27).

Moreover, the striking verisimilitude between two poles, two edges of the Earth is highlighted in the text: "In our Father's house are many mansions, they taught, and there alone will the incompatible multitudes of mankind be welcomed and soothed. Not one shall be turned away by the servants on that verandah, be he black or white, not one shall be kept standing who approaches with a loving heart. And why should the divine hospitality cease here?" (Forster 2006: 24).

Such a difference is often compared to the gulf: "He did succeed with his pupils, but the gulf between himself and his countrymen, which he had noticed in the train, widened distressingly", (Forster 2006: 41) because, according to the narrator, "Experiences, not character, divided them; they were not dissimilar, as humans go; indeed, when compared with the people who stood nearest to them in point of space they became practically identical" (Forster 2006: 59). And, finally, an ironic statement sums up that in case of Britain and India: "The twentieth century took over from the sixteenth" (Forster 2006: 115).

However, the aspiration to unite the East and the West, to link them in order to recreate the harmony is present in the story: "His whole appearance suggested harmony — as if he had reconciled the products of East and West, mental as well as physical, and could never be discomposed", (Forster 2006: 49) and "With humorous appreciation of the East, where the friends of friends are a reality, where everything gets done some time, and sooner or later everyone gets his share of happiness" (Forster 2006: 99).

In *A Passage to India*, Forster gives an unbiased representation of the Indian. In his India, everything is happening silently. Britain is exerting its imperial power on the natives through social and political domination without any resistance from the natives. Using stereotypes as the determiners in interacting with people leads to the "colonization of [the natives'] minds", in which the natives' minds automatically consider the British as superior to themselves. Such imperial objectives are in accordance to Orientalising the Orientals; i.e., the natives are treated as suppressed, invisible, and trivial objects to be controlled: "Fancy inviting guests and not treating them properly!" (Forster 2006: 29) and "The Englishmen had intended to play up better but had been prevented from doing so by their womenfolk, whom they had to attend, provide with tea, advise about dogs, etc. When tennis began, the barrier grew impenetrable. It had been hoped to have some sets between East and West, but this was forgotten, and the courts were monopolized by the usual club couples" (Forster 2006: 30).

Forster spent time with both Englishmen and Indians during his visit, and he quickly found that he preferred the company of the latter. He was troubled by the racial oppression and deep cultural misunderstandings that divided the Indian people and the British colonists, or, as they are called in *A Passage to India*, Anglo-Indians. The prevailing attitude among the British in India was that the colonists were assuming the "white man's burden" – novelist Rudyard Kipling's phrase – of governing the country, because the Indians could not handle the responsibility themselves (Forster 2006: 145).

It is no surprise, then, that Forster felt sympathetic toward the Indian side of the colonial argument. Indeed, Forster became a lifelong advocate for tolerance and understanding among people of different social classes, races, and backgrounds.

Nowadays the issue of imagological aspect in the English modernist novels is of great importance. The analysed works of L. Woolf and E. Forster prove that the consequence of the European superiority is mainly their loss of identity in the Eastern surroundings. They demonstrate that colonial policy and insatiable greed for personal power are the chief causes of the conflict which leads to self-destruction. Thus, the tragic outcome of this trouble is turning from the Lord to the Captive, unable to identify oneself and constantly searching for one's place in the world. Besides, the novels demonstrate that hetero-images of each other turn into auto-images. Critical reception of the French comparative literature by the Aachen Program (H. Dyserinck) resulted in the insight of the impossibility of separating the image of the other (hetero-image) from the image of the self (auto-image), as well as of the constructional/representational character of these images. Thus, it is fair to argue that mutual perceptions and attitudes of both Eastern and Western populations have a drastic effect upon the formulation of national Image.

What is more, Leonard Woolf and Edward Forster, two modernist writers managed to outline the emergence of such an important science nowadays as Imagology. They had predicted its course of development long before it actually happened. And nowadays we can trace its evidence in as far back as these early modernist literary works.

Bibliography

Beyond Culture: Space, Identity, and the Politics of Difference (1997). Ed. Gupta, Akhil and Ferguson, James. Durham: Duke University Press.

Boehmer, Elleke (2005). *Colonial And Postcolonial Literature.* 2nd Ed. Oxford: Oxford University Press.

Chiheb, Amel (2014). *Imagology.* On-Line Publication Available At: Http://Compalit.Blogspot.Com/2014/02/Imagology.Html [Accessed: March 4, 2017].

Forster, Edward (2006). *Passage to India.* London: Longman.

Ganguly, Keya (1992). Migrant Identities: Personal Memory And The Construction Of Selfhood". *Cultural Studies,* 6, 1.

Hewitt, Douglas (1988). *English Fiction Of The Early Modern Period.* London And New York: Longman.

Karvonen, Erkki (1997). *Imagology. Some Theories Of The Public Image Presented, Analysed And Criticized.* Doctoral Thesis, Written In Finnish. Tampere: University of Tampere, Department of Journalism And Mass Communication.

Mermoune, Amina (2010). *The Impacts Of Imperialism On Human-Relations In Edward Morgan Forster's "A Passage To India"*Diss. Constantine: Mentouri University.

Nilsen, Sarah Rhoads (2011). *Power, Distance, And Stereotyping Between Colonizer And Colonized And Men And Women In A Passage To India.* Diss. Oslo: University of Oslo.

Siber, Mouloud (2012). *Rudyard Kipling, Edward Morgan Forster, William Somerset Maugham And Joseph Conrad: The British Imperial Tradition And The Individual Talent.* Diss. Tizi-Ouzou: Mouloud Mammeri University of Tizi-Ouzou.

Woolf, Leonard (1931). *The Village In The Jungle.* London: Hogarth Press.

—— (1983). *Diaries in Ceylon, 1908-1911, Records of a colonial administrator.* Shri Lanka: Tisara Press.

Chapter 8

Between Literature and Ideology. *Ad-da'wa Al-Islāmiyya* in the novels by Nağīb Al-Kaylānī

Magdalena Kubarek, *Nicolaus Copernicus University/Poland*

Introduction

Propaganda is not a modern phenomenon. It has accompanied humankind since the rise of the civilisation, when different groups needed collective support for their own interests and goals. Both in ancient culture and in pre-Islamic Arabia, the oratorical art was highly valued, and poets took the floor creating occasional poems, aimed at convincing listeners to their arguments (or their patron's reasons). In Europe, the origins of the institutionalised propaganda, associated with the court of the emperor, are attributed to the Roman period. In the Middle Ages propaganda also "celebrated its triumphs" and by using the "living word" it was able to induce thousands of people to take part in the crusades (Hołda 2008: 19–20). In the Arab world, the institutionalisation of propaganda came after the rise of Islam and the caliphate. At the time various fractions and parties started to struggle for power. One of the earliest and "most refined" propaganda campaigns involves the Abbasids taking power from the Umayyads by attacking their moral character and administration (Hitti 1970: 283).

Propaganda and mission

The term "propaganda" comes from the Latin *propagare, propago,* which means "skillful cutting of the grapevine", so that it can best flourish. The concept of "propaganda" (*propagation, extension*) was introduced into public life in the first half of the 17th century (Mirek 1948: 335). The Catholic Church used it in this sense when Pope Gregory XV established the Sacred Congregation for Propagation of the Faith (Propaganda Fide) in 1622. Its purpose was to promote the Catholic faith in a world still lacking in evangelisation and to eradicate heresy in the doctrine of the Church (Jacques Ellul, quoted in Zwoliński 2003: 238). Thus, the original meaning of the word "propaganda" was the religiously motivated desire to shape human attitudes. It was a form of evangelisation referring to the traditions of medieval Catholic monasteries. Moreover, it constituted the basis of the concept of the mission (Nieć 2011: 228–229). Therefore, in the religious sense, the meaning of the term "propaganda" was close to teaching and upbringing. Over time, the concept of propaganda has changed. It has moved from the religious and Church domain to the secular, ideological and political ones (Zwoliński 2003: 238).

The changing of the connotations of the term "propaganda" can be observed in the 20th century. Already in the pre-war period, Władysław Baliński defined propaganda as influencing public opinion by introducing individual judgments about certain phenomena into the world of collective judgments. This process applies intangible methods, appeals to intellect and emotion and often refers to public affairs or great ideas. The researcher presented such understanding of propaganda in opposition to the advertisement, which is linked to the private interest and to agitation which contains the element of coercion and can take a violent course (Baliński, quoted in Hołda 2008: 19–20). Today, in the Western world propaganda refers to electoral struggles, ideologies and mass truths. This is where manipulation in the transmission of persuasive messages, which evoke expected attitudes and behaviors, moves to the forefront (Nieć 2011: 230).

In the Arab world, the equivalent of the term "propaganda" relating to the spread of the faith, exhorting to truth and giving a good example is the *ad-da'wa* – a verbal noun from the verb to "invocate/ invite/ pray". In Arabic dictionaries, it is defined as: "invitation, prayer, persuasion, mission" (Dusūqī 'Alī 2011: 9). The Arabic-English Wehr dictionary lists a spectrum of meanings, including: "call, appeal, bidding, invitation, missionary work, propaganda" (Wehr 1993: 327). The word is mentioned in many verses of the Quran (e.g., II:195, XIII:14, XXX:25, XL:43). In the following ages, the concept of mission was developed in the *Sunna* of the Prophet (Islamic tradition). It became the object of the studies of *ulema* also in the aspect of the obligation of missionary duty of every Muslim. Nowadays, the noun *ad-da'wa* is used with the adjective "Islamic" (*al-islāmiyya*) to describe the propagation of the message of Islam (*risālat al-islām*), understood as continuous efforts to familiarise others with Muslim doctrine and practice and to encourage them to convert. However, these efforts should be undertaken by people with appropriate moral qualifications (Ḏikrā, quoted in Dusūkī 'Alī 2011: 10).

On the other hand, the Arabic equivalent of the term "propaganda" in the contemporary Western sense is *ad-di'āya*. The noun is derived from the same roots as the word *ad-da'wa*. The Wehr dictionary provides only two meanings of this word, namely: "propaganda" and "advertising" (Wehr 1993:327). Arabic dictionaries[1] define *ad-di'āya* as oral or written agitation (*ad-da'wa*) on behalf of ideology/ religion (*maḏhab*) or view. These sources also mention the example of using this world by the Prophet Muhammad in the letter to Heraclius: "Ad'ūka bi-di'āya al-islām" (I bid you obey the divine call) which is preserved in the *Sunna*[2].

Many of today's fundamentalist Muslim apologists of the significant role of *ad-da'wa* refer to the views of the conservative theologian Ibn Taymiyya (1263–1328), valued for his participation in the battles with the Mongols, but eventually slaughtered by the Mamluk sultans due to his threatening radicalism[3]. It is worthwhile to mention that this scholar was active in the time of enormous mobilisation of religious propaganda, not only on the Christian side but also on the side of Mamluks preparing for the final confrontation with the infidels under the banners of Islam.

Literature in the service of ad-da'wa

Ḥasan al-Bannā, (1906–1949), who founded the Muslim Brothers in 1928 in Egypt (Mrozek-Dumanowska 2010: 62; Grabowski 2013: 32–38), was also the one to re-formulate the traditional understanding of mission (*ad-da'wa*): "the term has gained the meaning of active missionary activity based on religious propaganda" (Mrozek-Dumanowska 2010: 60.)

The subsequent leaders of this movement, with its main ideologue Sayyid Quṭb (1906–1966)[4] and his brother Muḥammad (1919–2014), began propagat-

---

[1] E.g. *Al-Mu'ğam al-Wasīṭ*. See also: http://www.almaany.com.

[2] E.g. *Saḥīḥ al-Buḫārī* (The Book of Jihad: 2782).

[3] Though Ibn Taymiyya had numerous religious and political adversaries in his own time, he has strongly influenced the modern Islam for the last two centuries. He is the source of the Wahhābiyyah, a strictly traditionist movement founded by Muḥammad Ibn 'Abd al-Wahhāb (d. 1792). Ibn Taymiyya also influenced various reform movements that have posed the problem of reformulating traditional ideologies by a return to the roots. See: https://www.britannica.com/biography/Ibn-Taymiyyah.

[4] Sayyid Quṭb's most important works are the six-volume commentary on the Qur'an: *Fī Ẓilal al-Qur'ān* (In the Shade of the Quran) and *Ma'ālim fī aṭ-Ṭarīq* (Signposts on the Road/ Milestones). The Islamic League has published two works by Sayyid Quṭb in

ing the idea of using art, including literature, as an efficient tool of missionary work (Kubarek 2016: 55). However, we can speak of deliberate propagation of Islamic literature (*al-adab al-islāmī*) since the 1980s, when the International League of Islamic Literature (*Rābiṭat al-Adab al-Islāmī al-'Ālamiyya*) was founded by writers and critics close to Muslim Brothers[5]. On the League's website (http://adabislami.org/intro.html) its founders explain the reasons for the foundation of this of organization as a kind of *ad-da'wa*:

> "It was indeed the duty of *ad-da'wa* to God Almighty through the authentic and engaged words as well as the eagerness of the promotion of Islamic literature and prevention of the spread of false literature in the Arab and Islamic world, which encouraged some Islamic writers to think about establishing an association that gathers their ranks".

The new kind of literature aimed to defend Islamic values from economic, political and ideological Western interference and shape the synthesis of virtues for a perfect modern Muslim. Nowadays, the term "Islamic literature" which relates to all genres: poetry, prose, and drama, is used by critics and writers not only in the Arab and Muslim world but also in the circles of Muslim minorities in Europe and the USA as well. The distinctive feature of this literature is its didactic, moral or utilitarian function. Thus, Islamic literature is engaged literature (*al-adab al-multazim/ al-adab al-mas'ūl*) and denies the slogans of art for art's sake – *l'art pour l'art*. The novel has become its most popular genre, which has happened as a result of the activity of the League. This particular kind of fiction, which propagates Muslim values, is known as *ar-riwāya al-islāmiyya* (Islamic novel). In the recent years, it has gained a wider readership, as well as become an object of literary studies (Dziekan 2009: 15–25; Kubarek 2014: 39–53; Kubarek 2016a).

Nağīb al-Kaylānī and his literary creation

Nağīb al-Kaylānī, considered the father or pioneer of the Islamic novel, was the first who started to create this kind of literature. He was also the one to formulate theoretical assumptions for the new genre. Undoubtedly, his theories – and he was an active and engaged member of Muslim Brothers – were influenced by the ideas of Quṭbs' brothers. Al-Kaylānī included his concepts

---

Polish: *Islam* and *Islam. The Religion of the Future.* Both withdrawn, allegedly due to errors in the text. (See more: Berger 2011: 64)

[5] The organization was founded in 1984, initially located in India's Lucknow, now being relocated to the capital of Saudi Arabia.

in the following works: *Islamic character and literary schools* (Al-Islāmiyya wa-l-Maḏāhib al-Adabiyya), *Introduction to Islamic literature* (Madḫal ilā l-Adab al-Islāmī), *Iqbal, a Revolutionary Poet* ('Iqbāl aš-Šā'ir aṯ-Ṯā'ir), *Horizons of Muslim literature* (Āfāq al-Adab al-Islāmī) (Kubarek 2014a: 170–172).

Twenty years after his death, Al-Kaylānī – the author of over thirty novels – remains a role model for successive generations of writers and the best-known representative of Islamic prose. His books are so popular that some of them have been published in over ten editions. Apart from the novels, he is also an author of several collections of short stories, poetry collections, and dramas. He also received state awards for some of his novels, among others, the Award of the Egyptian Ministry of Education.

Al-Kaylānī mentions in his autobiography that he did not know the theory of Islamic literature when he was creating his first novels. He simply wrote from the perspective of a man attached to the traditional values of Islam (Al-Kaylānī 2006). However, it is obvious that Al-Kaylānī's creativity in that period was greatly influenced by his rural origin. The plot of the novels, published before 1970, often takes place in the Egyptian province (Barīġiš 1994: 38). Through the history of rural families, the author shows the three main problems affecting Egyptian society: ignorance, poverty, and disease (Kubarek 2014a: 173).

In later periods Al-Kaylānī's works cover current issues from the angle of the foregone times, starting with the rise of Islam – *Hamza's Killer* (Qātil Ḥamza), *The Light of God* (Nūr Allāh) – through the epoch of the Crusades and the Mamluks – *Promised Day* (Al-Yaum al-Maw'ūd), to the period of Napoleon's expedition to Egypt – *The Parade of Free People* (Mawākib al-Aḥrār) and the Revolution against the British in 1919 *The Eternal Call* (An-Nidā' al-Ḫālid).

The series *Contemporary Islamic Novels* (Ar-Riwāya al-Islāmiyya al-Mu'āṣira) forms a separate chapter in Al-Kaylānī's works, which brought him fame in the Muslim world. All of these novels take place in the 20th century in various Arab and Muslim countries, the societies of which must heroically face a threat posed by hostile ideologies: imperialism, communism, and Zionism. This cycle includes, among others*: The Nights of Turkestan* (Layālī Turkistān) – taking place in Communist-led Turkestan after 1918, Virgin of Jakarta ('Azrā' Jākartā) – regarding the Communist Uprising in Indonesia in 1965, or *Giants of the North* ('Amāliqat aš-Šamāl) – depicting Nigeria in the years of the coup in the years 1965-70. Sometimes Al-Kaylānī focuses on lesser-known events such as in the novel *Black Shadow* (Aẓ-Ẓill al-Aswad), whose hero Lij Iyasu, the ruler of Ethiopia from 1913 to 1916 was removed from power due to his favorable treatment of Muslims.

Since the Israeli uprising in 1948, the conflict over occupied Palestine has undoubtedly had the greatest impact on Arab literature. Motifs and themes related to Palestine appear regardless of ideological options in the writings of many Arab writers and poets who express their views and emotions giving them the form of artistic expression. The Palestinian problem also makes it way to Al-Kaylānī's work. The issues of "the catastrophe" (*an-naqba*), as the Arabs call the events of 1948, appear in the novel *The Land of the Prophets* (Arḍ an-Anbiyā'), the plot of which takes place in Haifa. In the novel *Umar Appears in Jerusalem* (Umar Yaẓharu fī al-Quds) Al-Kaylānī touches upon the reasons for the defeat of Arab armies in the Six-Day War. In turn, in the novel *Ramadan, My Beloved* (Ramaḍān Ḥabībī) the author deals with the subject of the 1973 Arab-Israeli War (the Battle of Ramadan 10th – October 6th).

Nationalism *vs.* pan-Islamism

At the turn of the 19th and 20th century, three ideologies came to life in response to Western economic and political domination in Egypt. These were: pan-Islamism, Egyptian nationalism, and pan-Arabism. The conviction of the Egyptian Modernists, led by Muḥammad 'Abduh (1849–1905), that all the followers of Islam form a single community, the division of which into smaller regional or national m units is unnatural, became the foundation of the Muslim Brothers' ideology, although it was rejected by both pan-Arabism and nationalism supporters.

Al-Bannā himself was against the idea of nationalism. However, nationalist sympathies were reflected in the process of crystallising the ideology of the Muslim Brothers. He perceived it primarily as an invention of the West which is alien to the Muslim community. To assert the rightness of his judgments, he referred to the distortions of Italian fascism and German Nazism. (Zdanowski 1986: 52–57). Sayyid Quṭb after initial fluctuations also rejected nationalism, believing that religious identity rather than the identity of the nation was the one Muhammad chose for his followers (Danecki 2002: 132–133). At the same time, he combined the notion of nationalism with the notion of tyrant, which was a clear allusion to Naser's then-dominant power (Sivan 1990: 16–49; Zdanowski 2009: 65–68) In this ideological context it is not surprising that the issues surrounding power as well as the motifs of the righteous ruler and the tyrant are frequent in all of Al-Kaylānī's novels.

Al-Kaylānī's works show a gradual evolution in the author's views. Initially, he devotes considerable attention to issues related to the fight for freedom and the formation of the national consciousness of the Egyptian people. Therefore, in many novels, such as *Promised Day* or *Parade of Free People*, he focuses on the people of Egypt and the of national identity that was often forged as a result of the clash with foreign powers, e.g. the Sixth Crusade of Louis IX, King of France, or Napoleon's expedition to Egypt (1798–1801). He also recalls historical figures such as Ḥāǧǧ Muṣṭafā al-Baštīlī, who decided to fight against the mighty Napoleon without looking at the consequences and lack of support of the Mamluks and Ottomans.

Although religious background naturally appears in the early works, their text is not as permeated by religious rhetoric as his later works. The author uses such terms as freedom (*al-ḥurriyya*), liberation (*at-taḥrīr*) or homeland (*al-waṭan*). He also refers to the problems of social inequality and discrimination against women. He depicts the class stratification of Egyptian society, and it often turns out that real heroism is not represented by the elites but by the plebeians, not by professional soldiers, but by enslaved women. Thus, it does not come as a surprise that Al-Kaylānī was criticised by some theorists of Islamic literature because of his vividly clear nationalist inclinations. 'Abdallāh al-'Arīnī, the author of the monograph on Al-Kaylānī's life and works, faults the writer for presenting the history of Egypt in a nationalist perspective and giving priority to the issues of homeland instead of religion (Al-'Arīnī 2005: 45). Muḥammad Ḥasan Barīġiš (1942–2003), the Syrian writer and theorist of Islamic literature, criticises Al-Kaylānī's condemnation of the Mamluk dynasty in Egypt and the Sultans of Ottomans (Barīġiš 1994: 77–78).

The idea of pan-Islamism comes to full prominence in the cycle of *Contemporary Islamic Novels,* in which the author clearly promotes the idea of unity within the community and to the concept of *at-tawḥīd (monotheism, conjunction, consolidation*) in the interpretation of Sayyid Quṭb. Quṭb recognised the social and historical significance of the *at-tawḥīd,* which also includes the unification of people of different national, ethnic and racial groups under the banner of Islam. It also means equality between a woman and a man, at least in theory, as well as between representatives of different social classes. In Quṭb's conception, those who wish for another system are the enemies of humanity. Only through the combination of the diversity that they have received from the Creator are people able to achieve lasting peace on Earth (Toth 2013: 104). In other words, what Quṭb means is that all mankind should become Muslim in order to create an ideal global society.

In his previously mentioned book Al-'Arīnī quotes the writer's explanation of his motivations for creating the series *Contemporary Islamic Novels:* "I wanted to encourage the average reader to understand the problems of the Muslim world, while dealing with a story where he would find all his longings and which, at the same time, would relate to some important issue" (Al-'Arīnī

2005: 256). Another aim of the author was to "de-arabise" Islam, by moving the center of gravity from the problems of the Arab world to the problems of the Muslim world, as well as by giving the voice to black Africans and inhabitants of Asia. The consolidation and integration of this world were undoubtedly determined by the persistence of a sense of threat and the conviction of the existence of a common enemy who continually, in one way or another, emphasised his presence. Thus, Al-Kaylānī locates certain phenomena and historical processes taking place in the world of Islam in a universal perspective, making them independent of the socio-political circumstances.

In the novels devoted to the Palestinian question the analogies in terms and symbols used by both Muslim fundamentalists and Al-Kaylānī are difficult to overlook: the religious significance of the land and its integrity as a charitable *waqf* (*religious endowment, unalienable property*), the significance of the holiness of Jerusalem, the exhortation to religious purification and creating a society based on Muslim values in Palestine. Al-Kaylānī rebukes the Palestinians and criticises a society based on secular values. Military defeat in 1967 is portrayed as punishment for departing from traditional Muslim values: "We ourselves spun the web of the defeat by our megalomania and indolence" (Al-Kaylānī 2008: 6). This view is in line with the ideology of the Muslim Brothers operating in the Gaza Strip and in the West Bank. Since the 1970s they have implemented the program of Islamisation of the Palestinian society that led to the spread of Islamic arguments and creating a positive atmosphere for political programs that apply Muslim terminology[6] (Philipp 2005: 502–505).

According to the ideology of Muslim Brothers, the first task of this organisation was to educate Palestinian society in the spirit of Islam and, consequently, change it into Muslim society. Only when this condition was met, was it to be possible to achieve another goal – the liberation of Palestine. The strategy adopted by the Palestinian Muslim Brothers initially relieved them of taking definite political or armed actions. At the same time, it allowed them to condemn the ineffectiveness of nationalist and Marxist ideology in the struggle for the liberation of Palestine (Philipp 2005: 504).

In his works, Al-Kaylānī argues with the PLO's secular and nationalist conception of the struggle for the liberation of Palestine. For example, in the novel, *Umar appears in Jerusalem* the figure of the Caliph Umar encouraged many atheists to convert as a result of his attitude and views (Al-Kaylānī

---

[6] It is worth emphasising that the growing fundamentalist tendencies were parallel to the growing importance of Likud using religious arguments to annex occupied areas.

2008.). In the novel, *The Land of the Prophets* Palestinian *fedayeen* are illustrated as pious Muslims (Al-Kaylānī 1969).

Thanks to the references to the Quran, Al-Kaylānī's message is very direct in form and clear: he believes it to be necessary to restore the principles and values that were in force in the time of early Islam in order to revive the greatness of the *ummah*. On the one hand, if the Palestinians want to defeat Israel, it is first necessary to fight against all the misconceptions accumulated during the 13 centuries. On the other, the struggle against Israel is a kind of *jihad* and should be lead by all Muslims in the World. This type of a postulate falls within the framework of fundamentalist ideologies, attempting to renew and strengthen Islam by returning to the roots. Such tactics are applied by radical organizations that operate in Palestine, e.g., Hamas.

Jihad and Martyrdom

As it has been already mentioned above, the concepts of Al-Kaylānī regarding the role of literature were formed under the influence of the ideology of Sayyid Quṭb, who, in the 1950s, started to criticise the regime in Egypt by using the context of the struggle (*ǧihād*) with paganism (*ǧāhiliyya)*. He was imprisoned as a result and then sentenced to death in 1966 to become one of the greatest contemporary martyrs of radical Islam. In his writings, Quṭb devoted much attention to the issue of martyrdom (*istišhād*), which was closely linked with his concept of *jihad*[7]. According to him, the martyr (*šahīd*) is God's chosen one. The loss of life in the struggle in the path of God (*fī sabīli Llāh*) does not bring loss or misery but is a kind of distinction and glory. Martyrs respond to the call of God, giving true testimony (*aš-šahāda*) (Quṭb, 2003: 481–482). Taking on the struggles and being ready to sacrifice constitutes an important part of strengthening character for the members of the Muslim community. Fighting is not about victory itself, but about the process of maturing of the *ummah* to take over the leadership of mankind. God, Quṭb argues, could send angels to fight against the Quraysh and facilitate the victory, but he did not do it, in order to provide the first Muslims with a valuable lesson during the battle of Uḥud in 625 (Quṭb, 2003: 484).

It is no wonder that the motifs of martyrdom in all Al-Kaylānī novels play such an important role. By studying them, we can observe how the presentation of heroic death varies according to the historical context, to what extent it is ideologically constituted and how deeply it is rooted in the Muslim and

---

[7] For information on *jihad* and martyrdom concepts in contemporary radical Islam see: David Cook, 2007: 35–48. In Arabic, see: Aṭ-Ṭībī 1994.

universal topoi. In his works, the author creates a chronicle of the persecution and martyrdom of Muslims, who have been facing the enemy and dying for their faith since the rise of Islam. Although the enemy takes various forms, depending on the time and location of the novel, he always represents the same hostile forces: Judaism (Zionism) and Christianity with its Imperialism.

The way of presenting the Jews in Al-Kaylānī's prose fits into the vision of the Zionist aspiration to dominate the world, embodied in *The Protocols of the Elders of Zion.* This book, written in the early 20th century in Russia, has become a generally credible historical source for many Muslims as a result of innumerable scientific and religious references. It has contributed to establishing "a paranoid outlook towards the world" to use the expression of David Cook. According to Cook, the writings of radical authors about *jihad* and martyrdom are difficult to understand without comprehension of this outlook. In 1968, a year after the defeat of the Arab army in the Six-Day war, a special edition of *The Protocols* was translated into Arabic by Gamal Naser's brother. This is the starting point of the propaganda of the idea of a Christian-Jewish conspiracy, aimed at capturing the world and destroying the Muslims who stand in the way to achieve this goal (Cook 2007: 137).

It is also important to stress that Al-Kaylānī created his series of historical novels by arguing with Ǧurǧī Zaydān (1861–1914) – the best-known author and pioneer of historical fiction in the Arabic language. According to Al-Kaylānī, Zaydān's Christian-nationalist vision of the past, presented in his 22 novels, was full of "deviations". Creating new historical concepts and presenting them as a historical tradition described as the *invention of tradition* is an important element of fundamentalist ideology. Modern Muslim fundamentalism also refers to history, although the traditions brought to life by fundamentalists do not reflect the past, but its contemporary imagery (Tibi 2004: 25). According to the authors of *Propaganda and Mass Persuasion: A Historical Encyclopedia, 1500 to the Present:* "opposition to imperialism and Israel have been the two central themes of modern propaganda in the Arab world" (Cull et al., 2003: 15).

Conclusion

In an attempt to evaluate or interpret Al-Kaylānī's writings, one should also take into account the religious and cultural context in which they were created. This important aspect is emphasised by Kenan Çayir: "Islamic novels are not fictional creations of meaning, but rather create particular views of reality. They cannot be thought to exist outside of a given political and cultural context since the author (and readers) operates within a linguistic and cultural tradition" (Çayir 2007: 28).

It is indisputable that Al-Kaylānī's works reflect the ideological engagement of the author, but they cannot be easily classified as propaganda writing. On the one hand, Al-Kaylānī was very conscious of his aims and used literature as a tool of *ad-da'wa*, i.e., spreading the true values. On the other hand, his works reflect the ideological changes which took place between the 1940s and the 1980s, not only in the Arab but also in the Muslim World. Initially, the writer, who grew up in an Egyptian province, was immersed in the ideas of Egyptian nationalism. Afterwards, he got closer to the ideas represented by Al-Bannā and Sayyid Quṭb. On many levels, his novels aim to implement the mission in the meaning given to this term by the ideologists of the Muslim Brothers. Thus, such issues as uniting the community of the Muslim world in the sense of danger, the necessity of *jihad* and martyrdom – in both collective and individual dimensions – move to the forefront in his works. However, his views presented in some novels not always stay in line with the ideology of Muslim Brothers. Although theorists of Islamic literature acknowledge Al-Kaylānī's merits for the development of *al-adab al-islāmī*, they accuse him first and foremost of flirting with the socialist and pan-Arabic ideas of Gamal Naser and referring to the ideas of a 19th century Egyptian activist, Qāsim Amīn (1863–1908), known for his advocacy of women's emancipation in Egypt. (Barīghish 1994 and Al-'Arīnī 2005). Perhaps these critical opinions prove that Al-Kaylānī's works elude unequivocal classifications. However, there is no doubt that the author deliberately used literature to express his ideological commitment and aimed to promote particular views among his readers.

Bibliography

Al-'Arīnī, 'Abdallāh (2005). *Al-Ittiğāh al-Islāmī fī A'māl Nağīb al-Kaylānī al-Qaṣaṣiyya.* Riyāḍ: Dār Kunūz Išbīliyā li-n-Našr wa-t-Tawzī'.

Barīğiš, Muḥammad Ḥasan (1994). *Dirāsāt fī l-Qiṣṣa al-Islāmiyya al-Mu'āṣira.* Bayrūt: Mu'assasat al-Risāla.

Berger, Rafał (2011). *Islam w Polsce.* Warszawa: Stowarzyszenie Jedności Muzułmańskiej. Instytut Muzułmański.

Çayir, Kenan (2007). *Islamic Literature in Contemporary Turkey. From Epic to Novel.* New York: Palgrave Macmillan.

Cook, David (2007). *Martyrdom in Islam.* Cambridge: Cambridge University Press.

Cull Nicholas J., Culbert David, and Welch David. (2003). *Propaganda and Mass Persuasion: A Historical Encyclopedia, 1500 to the Present.* Santa Barbara–Denver–Oxford: ABC-CLIO.

Danecki, Janusz (2002). *Podstawowe wiadomości o islamie II.* Warszawa. Wydawnictwo Akademickie Dialog.

Ḏikrā, Abū Bakr (n.d). *Ad-Da 'wa ilā al-Islām.* Al-Qāhira: Maktabat Dār al-'Arūba.

Dusūqī 'Alī, Muḥammad, 'Abd Al-Hādī (2011). *Manhağ ad-Da 'wa al-Islāmiyya.* Al-Qāhira: Dār al-Kalima li-n-Našr wa-t-Tawzī'.

Dziekan, Marek M. (2009). "Die islamische Literathurteorie und –kritik von 'Imād ad-Dīn Ḫalīl. Ein Vergleichendes Studium". *Rocznik Orientalistyczny* 62 (2): 15–25.

Ellul, Jacques (1967). *Histoire de la propagande.* Paris: Presses Universitaires de France.

Grabowski, Wojciech (2013). *Fundamentalizm muzułmański na Bliskim Wschodzie.* Gdańsk: Wydawnictwo Uniwersytetu Gdańskiego.

Hitti, Philip, Khuri (1970). *History of the Arabs.* 10th Edition, London: Macmillan.

Hołda, Renata (2008). *Dobry władca" Studium antropologiczne o Franciszku Józefie I.* Katowice: Wydawnictwo Uniwersytetu Śląskiego.

Al-Kaylānī, Nağīb (1961). *Al-Yaum al-Maw'ūd.* Al-Qāhira: Wizārat al-Tarbiyya wa-l-Ta'līm.

(1969). *Arḍ an-Anbiyā'.* Al-Kuwayt: Dār al-Bayyān.

—— (1974). *'Aḏrā' Jākartā.* Bayrūt: Dār an-Nafā'is.

—— (1974a). *Layālī Turkistān.* Bayrūt: Dār an-Nafā'is.

—— (1974b). *Ramaḍān Ḥabībī.* Al-Qāhira: Dār al-Muḫtār al-Islāmī.

—— (1975). *Lamḥāt Ḥayātī. Al-Ğuzz al-Awwal.* Bayrūt: Mu'assasat ar-Risāla.

—— (1977). *Qātil Ḥamza.* Bayrūt: Mu'assat ar-Risāla.

—— (1978). *Al-Nidā' al-Ḫālid.* Bayrūt: Mu'assat ar-Risāla.

—— (1979). *Nūr Allāh.* Bayrūt: Mu'assat ar-Risāla.

—— (1979a). *'Amāliqa al-Šamāl.* Bayrūt: Dār an-Nafā'is.

—— (1980). *Mawākib al-Aḥrār.* Bayrūt: Mu'assasat al-Risāla.

—— (1982) *Al-Ẓill al-Aswad.* Bayrūt: Dār an-Nafā'is.

—— (2006). *Lamḥāt Ḥayātī.* Vol. 1. Cairo: Kitāb al-Muḫtār.

—— (2008). *'Umar Yaẓharu fī al-Quds.* Al-Qāhira: Dār al-Muḫtār al-'Islāmī.

Kubarek, Magdalena (2014). "Współczesna literatura muzułmańska w krajach arabskich". *Litteraria Copernicana: Arabia. Stałe i zmienne w literaturze arabskiej*" 13: 39–53.

—— (2014a). "Muzułmańska perspektywa w twórczości Nağība al-Kaylanīego". In: *Orient w literaturze - Literatura w Oriencie. Spotkania.* Ed. Adam Bednarczyk, Magdalena Kubarek, Maciej Szatkowski Maciej. Toruń: Wydawnictwo Naukowe UMK.

—— (2016). "Should the Culture Be Engaged? Modern Islamic Literature and Its Religious and Political Engagement". *International Journal of Culture and History* 2 (1). On-line publication available at: http://www.ijch.net/index.php [accessed: April 2, 2017].

—— (2016a). "Paraenetic Character of Islamic Prose". *Comparative Literature in Education and Research* 3 (1). On-line publication available at: https://www.degruyter.com/view/ j/clear.2016.3.issue-1/ [accessed: April 2, 2017].

Mirek, Franciszek (1948). *Zarys socjologii.* Lublin: Towarzystwo Naukowe KUL.

Mrozek-Dumanowska, Anna (2001). *Islam i jego odnowa.* Warszawa: Wydawnictwo Naukowe Askon.

Nieć, Mateusz (2011). *Komunikowanie polityczne w społeczeństwach przedmasowych.* Warszawa: Wolters Kluwer.

Philipp, Thomas (2005). "Islam in ausgewählten Staaten. Israel und die Besetzten Gebiete". In: *Islam in der Gegenwart.* Ed. Werner Ende, Uno Steinbach. 5. aktualisierte und erw. Aufl. München: C.H. Beck Verlag:

Quṭb, Sayyid (2003). *Fī Ẓilāl al-Qur'ān.* Bayrūt: Dar aš-Šurūq.

Sivan, Emmanuel (1990). *Radical Islam: Medieval Theology and Modern Politics.* New Haven: Yale University Press.

Tibi, Bassam (2004). „Islam i polityka. Islam polityczny oraz fundamentalizm muzułmański". *Bliski Wschód. Społeczeństwo – polityka – tradycje* 1 (1): 19-40.

Aṭ-Ṭībī, 'Ukāša 'Abd al-Munān (1994).j *Aš-Šahāda wa-l-Istišhād fī Ẓilāl al-Qur'ān li-š-Šayḫ Sayyid Quṭb.* Al-Qāhira: Maktabat at-Turāṯ al-Islāmī.

Toth, James (2013). *Sayyid Qutb: The Life and Legacy of a Radical Islamic Intellectual.* Oxford University Press: Oxford.

Wehr, Hans (1993). *A dictionary of modern written Arabic: (Arabic-English),* 4th. Edition, Spoken Language Systems: Urbana, IL. Retrieved from: http://ejtaal.net/.

Zdanowski, Jerzy 1986. *Bracia Muzułmanie i inni.* Szczecin: Wydawnictwo Glob.

—— (2009). *Współczesna muzułmańska myśl społeczno-polityczna. Nurt Braci Muzułmanów.* Warszawa: Wydawnictwo Naukowe Askon.

Zwoliński, Andrzej 2003. *Słowo w relacjach społecznych.* Kraków: Wydawnictwo WAM.

Chapter 9

The Boundaries of Historical Accuracy: Contemporary Re-reading of Salman Rushdie's *Midnight's Children*

Olivier Harenda, *Nicolaus Copernicus University/Poland*

Introduction

Midnight's Children (1981), created by the then unknown Salman Rushdie[1], is undeniably a work of fiction of great literary significance. It went on to win the Booker Prize of 1981 and was later awarded the Booker of Bookers title in 1993 and 2008. Nowadays, it is considered an exemplary instance of the blend between historical fiction, magical realism, and postcolonial literature (British Fiction Today 2006; Eaglestone 2006: 93). This article examines the historical quality of Salman Rushdie's novel and the possible ways in which it can be interpreted today, 35 years after its original publication.

In order to conduct this analysis, the article firstly focuses on the novel's plot so as to correctly establish its most prevalent themes. Next, the novel's connection with the twentieth-century history of India (particularly the events of the Partition of India – 1947 and the State of Emergency – 1975) is outlined. This is done in order to indicate Rushdie's literary intent of blending real historical events with magical realism. Finally, the article proceeds to a detailed analysis of Midnight's Children from a modern perspective. That is to say, Rushdie's evaluation of "Indian history" and assumptions about the future of independent India conveyed in the novel are juxtaposed with actual events from Indian politics that followed after the book's publication.

The analysis of the novel consists of three parts: 1) How Rushdie described the Partition of India in the novel; 2) The eponymous Midnight's Children hailed as the Lost Generation of India; 3) Examination of Rushdie's accusa-

---

[1] The writer only had a debut fantasy novel to his credit at the time [cf. *Grimus* (1975)].

tions against India through the historical figure of Prime Minister Indira Gandhi. The analysis aims to show that a contemporary re-reading of Midnight's Children differs significantly from its initial reception due to major transformations on the political stage of India, which have taken place during the past 35 years. In consequence, certain historical inaccuracies may arise in the course of a modern interpretation of the novel.

1. *Midnight's Children* (1981)

The novel is a first-person perspective account of an Indian who was born at the stroke of midnight, on the 15th of August, 1947, which makes him permanently connected with the history of the newly created country. However, in spite of the book's fame in the First World countries, it became the subject of controversy among the Hindus and the Muslims. The plan for a BBC adaptation shortly after its release was banned by the Indian government, and similarly by Sri Lanka a couple of years later. It was not until 2012 that director Deepa Mehta made the adaptation with a limited cinematic release (Harikumar *Midnight's Children Screening Ignites Political Controversy*).

The novel's protagonist, Saleem Sinai, at the age of almost 31 is certain that he is approaching death. In view of this, he decides to write down the story of his life, moderated and occasionally interrupted by his loyal companion Padma, for his small son, Aadam Sinai. Saleem starts with an obvious statement that he came into this world at "the precise instant of India's arrival at independence" (Rushdie 2006: 3), but quickly shifts back over 30 years earlier and recounts how his grandfather, Ahmed Aziz, met and eventually married his wife. They had two sons and three daughters, one of which was Mumtaz Aziz. Due to an unfortunate coincidence, Mumtaz lost her first husband and married a prosperous businessman, Ahmed Sinai. When the couple arrived in Bombay, they settled on an estate belonging to an Englishman, Mr. William Methwold, a man occasionally entertained by a singing tramp, We Willie Winkie and his wife, Vanita. When Saleem is born, he has his grandfather's large, cucumber-like nose, which later proves essential in the boy's magical abilities. At the age of ten, Saleem discovers that he can hear and see other children born during the first hour of that fateful night. It turns out that each child has a different skill, depending on the exact time he or she came into the world, and Saleem's power is to summon them all, thus, he calls their meetings Midnight's Children Conference. However, it is unexpectedly discovered that Saleem is not his parents' biological child; in fact, he is the fruit of Mr. Methwold and Vanita's affair. When Vanita died in childbirth, in the act of rebellion, Saleem's nanny switched him with the Sinais' actual son called

Shiva. Forced to travel in-between his Indian and Pakistani relatives, and having his nose operated on, the teenage Saleem loses the connection with his magical peers. Later, all of his family members die in the bombings of the first Indo-Pakistani war of 1965. Saleem himself loses his memory, but he regains it as a soldier in Bangladesh in 1971. A fellow midnight child, Parvati-the-witch, harbours him back to India and the two form a relationship. Yet, in 1975, a State of Emergency is declared throughout India and Saleem has to face Shiva and the mysterious figure known as the Widow.

In terms of the novel's style, it has to be noted that it highly resembles the form of oral speech. Saleem knows he is going to die, hence, he does not waste time on grammatical structures, trying to encompass as much of his, and India's, history as possible (Ahmad 2014: 3–4). In consequence, some sentences consume the space of over a page. Yet, Saleem often diverges from the narrative, only to be called to order by Padma, evoking, as a result, the mode of the stream of consciousness, which can also be interpreted as a magic realist strategy. This can be seen through the elements of magic (children's extraordinary abilities), historical anchoring (the Partition), blurring of the protagonist's identity (his connection with the children and India), and hallucinations (dream about the Widow, Saleem's scattering into pieces at the end of the novel) (Faris 1995: 167, 171–172, 174). Also, the protagonist is revealed to be a subjective and unreliable narrator as he mixes up the dates of historical events with his life, but he explains that this is simply how he remembers them.

2. The Image of the Partition and India's History in *Midnight's Children*

In contrast to novels about the Partition of India, Salman Rushdie does not explore the motifs of fighting for one's rights, trauma, and violence, but he centres his focus on the figure of an individual who metaphorically stands for India. This reciprocity is outwardly reflected in Saleem's physical appearance. The protagonist's face is a literal personification of India's geography, with the birthmarks on his cheeks symbolising Pakistan West and Pakistan East and the combination of his nose and chin representing the Deccan peninsula (Horn 2014: 3).

Furthermore, Saleem constantly indicates his linkage with great important moments in history, even those before his birth (British Fiction Today 2006; Eaglestone 2006: 98). Therefore, we can notice a number of the following correlations: Ahmed Aziz is able to see the face of his future wife on the day when the First World War ended; in 1942, the leader of the Free Islam Convocation which opposed the establishment of Pakistan is killed and his supporter, Nadir Khan, goes into hiding in Aziz's house, falling in love with Mumtaz; after two years of their marriage it is revealed that Mumtaz is still a virgin and Aziz's wife, Naseem, breaks her three-year-long silence on the day the atomic bomb was dropped on Japan; Saleem and Shiva are born on the day of independence and the nanny Mary Pereira switches them so as to give the poor boy a rich life and the rich one – a poor one; in 1956, protests ensue across Bombay to divide the city between linguistic groups; the same year, India begins a Five-Year Plan, and Saleem cheats on his school exams; in 1961, Saleem participates in a coup d'état as his uncle, General Zulfikar, takes control of Pakistan; in 1962, when the Sino-Indian war ensues, Saleem's father suffers a heart attack; in 1965, the bombing of Karachi kills Saleem's whole family; in 1971 he is a soldier in Bangladesh; in 1975 he is captured by Shiva and sent to a sterilisation camp.

Needless to say, Rushdie provides more than enough evidence that Saleem's life represents that of India (Faris 1995: 177). However, in view of such great events over which Saleem has no control (Faris 1995: 168), he continuously views himself as a hero. The memorable moment of the Partition is described quite moderately. Saleem refuses to describe the violence, he "avert[s] [his] eyes from the brutality in Bengal and the long pacifying walk of Mahatma Gandhi" and adds: "Selfish? Narrow-minded? Well, perhaps; but excusably so, in my opinion. After all, one is not born every day" (Rushdie 2006: 125)[2]. In turn, the protagonist opts for describing the life at Methwold's estate. Mr. Methwold is keen on selling the property to Indian families who currently reside there, but on condition that the legal transfer of ownership will take place on the 15th of August, the date of the official handover of power by the British. Interestingly, as the families, including Saleem's parents, await the date, they acquire Methwold's habits by drinking cocktails, attending lunches, and speaking in the manner of English upper class. Meanwhile, as the countdown ensues, the community of Bombay cheerfully celebrates the advent of independence, whereas Mr. Methwold salutes the setting sun, accidentally removing his hairpiece in the process.

On the basis of such representation, a dichotomy of attitudes towards the Partition can be observed. First, there are the figures of the estate's residents

---

[2] Rushdie said that one of the motivations for writing the novel was his desire to recreate his childhood home from India. However, since he already lived in England, this attempt proved futile, because Rushdie himself was displaced in time and space. Consequently, he concluded that a reclaiming of the past is impossible, thus migrant writers have to write about "imaginary homelands," the ones in their minds (McLeod 2000: 210–211).

who are not prejudiced against Methwold, yet they willingly conform to his customs, as if driven by the political premise that the whole affair with the British will soon be over when they leave. Mr. Methwold, in contrast, evokes a feeling of nostalgia for British India. His salute to the setting sun signifies a symbolic twilight of the Empire on which the sun never sets, the end of Britain's territorial domination in the world. Is it a good thing that the British rule in India came to an end? Rushdie makes his answer to this question ambiguous as he develops the metaphor of Midnight's Children throughout the novel. Nevertheless, the removal of the hairpiece, much to the residents' amusement, may be viewed as referring to the double identity of the colonisers. They perceived themselves as the carriers of light, yet they inaptly tried to mask their atrocities and exploitations of the natives through creating the facade of romantic imagery about their rule.

3. *Midnight's Children* as India's Lost Generation

As it is explicitly described in the novel, Midnight's Children are those who were born in the first hour of independence. Initially, there were 1001 of them, an intertextual reference to *One Thousand and One Nights* (Faris 1995: 164). However, only 581 of them managed to survive when 10-year-old Saleem became aware of their existence. The powers the children have varied significantly. They are biological monsters who have such abilities as stepping into mirrors, making things invisible, multiplying fish, transforming into animals, changing sex, inflicting physical wounds with words, etc. Saleem, however, believes that they were endowed with such miraculous talents for a reason and that is why he proposes the formula of Midnight's Children Conference, by which all children could express their opinions. Nevertheless, Saleem is immediately attacked by Shiva who thinks that the group should be managed like a gang with a strong leader, instead of talking about purpose, because the unequal world proves there is no such thing. As time passes, the differences between Saleem and Shiva amplify. Eventually, the conference becomes meaningless, because the children undergo various changes. They become concerned with their personal problems and are influenced by class and religious prejudices. Saleem attempts to prevent the group's disintegration when saying:

> "Brothers, sisters! [...] Do not let this happen! Do not permit the endless duality of masses-and-classes, capital-and-labour, them-and-us to come between us! We [...] must be a third principle [...]; for only by being other, by being new, can we fulfil the promise of our birth!" (Rushdie 2006: 292)

Yet, Saleem's plea is opposed by the one of Shiva's:

> "No, little rich boy; there is no third principle; there is only money-and-poverty, and have-and-lack, and right-and-left; there is only me-against-the-world! The world is not ideas [...]; the world [...] is things. [...]. All that importance-of-the-individual. All that possibility-of-human-ity. Today, what people are is just another kind of thing." (Rushdie 2006: 292–293)

In consequence, a clear line of binary oppositions is established. Saleem is convinced that the children were born in order to change India, to ascertain the passage of the country into a brighter future, and he uses extremely leftist, if not communistic, rhetoric to substantiate this. Shiva, on the other hand, represents a strikingly capitalist approach. To him, the world is not about ideology and the fight against authority, but strictly about materialism and consumerism. Surprisingly, further on in the novel, Rushdie resorts to glorifying Saleem's sacrifice by turning him into a martyr, whereas Shiva is transformed into an unmerciful destroyer that needs to be condemned.

This clash of values leads us to the central message of Rushdie's story. That is to say, the first generation of independent Indians was betrayed by its own government. In a documentary entitled *A Tall Story – How Salman Rushdie Pickled All India,* the author explained his stance in the following words:

> "There is certainly a very strong political idea in the book [...] that independence despite the blood, the gore, [...] was, nevertheless, some kind of a time of optimism. People felt the sense of possibility [...], despite all the flaws of the event it was a time of hope, and the argument of the book is that during the course of the next 30 years that hope was betrayed, and... whatever the optimism that the independence represented, the next 30 years represented the annihilation of that optimism." (*A Tall Story* documentary, 00:34:34–00:36:28)

Through the allegory of the midnight conference that ridicules the Indian National Congress (Faris 1995: 179), Rushdie poses a claim that instead of forming a multicultural society on which India would thrive, the children were silenced and removed from the public spotlight by the politicians who wanted to maintain the dogma of nationalism. This ideology stood for the self-perpetuating circle of violence, which was exemplified, as Rushdie lays out in the novel, by the numerous military conflicts which occurred after the Partition of India.

4. The Destruction of *Midnight's Children* as the Critique of Indira Gandhi's Rule

In *Midnight's Children*, Salman Rushdie holds primarily one person accountable for eradicating the image of a peacefully co-existing, multicultural India – Indira Gandhi, to whom Saleem ambiguously refers to as the Widow. Halfway through the novel, the protagonist experiences a foreshadowing nightmare in which the so-called *Widow* destroys the children by literally ripping them apart:

> "The Widow is green but her hair is black as black. The Widow sits on a high high chair the chair is green the seat is black the Widow's hair has a centre-parting it is green on the left and on the right black. High as the sky the chair is green the seat is black the Widow's arm is long as death its skin is green the fingernails are long and sharp and black. Between the walls the children green the walls are green the Widow's arm comes snaking down the snake is green the children scream the fingernails are black they scratch the Widow's arm is hunting see the children run and scream the Widow's hand curls round them green and black. Now one by one the children mmff are stifled quiet the Widow's hand is lifting one by one the children green their blood is black unloosed by cutting fingernails it splashes black on walls [...] And children torn in two in Widow hands." (Rushdie 2006: 238)

In an interview, the writer claimed that he really had had this nightmare and pointed to the symbolism behind Indira Gandhi's hair, which had one large white streak on the right side of her head and black on the other, and this black and white contrast may epitomise the duplicity of her government that was open but also engaged in "black" economy (*A Tall Story* documentary, 00:38:23–00:39:00). In addition, Rushdie added that he had nothing against Jawaharlal Nehru who was a democrat and a statesman, but the leader was already planning to create a political dynasty when turning young Indira into his personal assistant (Kalmar 1989: 117). Indeed, nowadays it cannot be denied that the Nehru-Gandhi formed a political quasi-dynasty, yet history has shown that it was more due to a concurrence of unforeseeable events than deliberate intention.

It is not until the concluding section of the novel that the Widow is revealed to be Indira Gandhi. She is presented as a kind of a witch-like villainess who perceives the Midnight's Children as a threat to her power and seeks to destroy them (Faris 1995: 179–180). When in one of the final chapters Saleem meets his uncle, a civil servant called Mustapha Aziz, the man is visited by a stranger (in all probability Sanjay Gandhi) who leaves behind a folder titled Project M.C.C. With this incident, Rushdie implies that Mrs. Gandhi declared the Emergency essentially against the now grown-up children. Shiva, now a war hero, forces Saleem to disclose their whereabouts. Saleem and his peers undergo horrible forms of vasectomy in the Widows' hostels (Rushdie 2006: 499). The cruel fate of the victims is sealed when the ghetto in which Saleem lived is demolished due to a civic beautification programme (Rushdie 2006: 496). Subsequently, Parvati-the-witch dies, leaving her son Aadam, born out of a past affair with Shiva, to be taken care of by Saleem.

As a result, Saleem Sinai and Indira Gandhi are formed into adversaries who have distinct visions of India and personal premonitions about their connection with the country: "Did Saleem's dream of saving the nation leak [...] into the thoughts of the Prime Minister herself? Was my lifelong belief in the equation between the State and myself transmuted, in 'the Madam's' mind', into that in-those-days-famous phrase: India is Indira and Indira is India?" (Rushdie 2006: 483). Nevertheless, Rushdie shied away from admitting Mrs. Gandhi's important part in the book when stating that she was placed there only as "a joke," because the story needed a "terror figure" (*A Tall Story* documentary, 00:39:08–00:39:18).

Therefore, in view of the author's statement above and the general history of Indira Gandhi's time as a Prime Minister, a certain degree of inconsistency can be noticed on behalf of Salman Rushdie. The idea behind the book is to criticise the postcolonial politics of India and its elimination of a multicultural way of communal co-existence. Instead of focusing on the causality of the military conflicts and the Emergency after the Partition, the writer purposely chose to oversimplify the complex issues by attributing responsibility for them to one historical figure. It has to be mentioned here that the author has already been criticised for such practices of distorting post-colonial history in terms of satirising the legacy of Indian independence struggle (British Fiction Today 2006; Eaglestone 2006: 92).

Moreover, through the character of Ahmed Aziz and his adolescence in Kashmir, Rushdie seems to suggest that India thrived on diversity in pre-independence times (Horn 2014: 4). Thus, the writer hints that this diversity and multiculturalism may have saved India from the military and political upheavals of the 20th century; nevertheless, the author fails to acknowledge that the passage of India from colonialism to postcolonialism was inevitable. If it had not occurred in 1947, it would have happened later, perhaps with bloodshed avoided, yet still with partitioning of the nation. It is exactly that moment of division that is responsible for the internal and national events which the author is so dismissive of. The Sino-Indian War of 1962 ensued as a result of China's claim for territories along the 3000-kilometre-long border with India, the Indo-Pakistani War of 1965 broke out due to the dispute over territorial affiliation of Kashmir, whereas the source of the Indo-Pakistani War of 1971 was the rebellion of Pakistan East and the Pakistan West's invasion of India. In other words, the root cause of all these conflicts were territorial controversies that arose after the Partition of 1947.

The State of Emergency between 1975 and 1977 has much more complicated origins. This internal turmoil was triggered off by the subversive actions of Janata Party members that struck the country's economy. Indira Gandhi did not enforce the Emergency extemporaneously[3], but with the consultation and acceptance of the President of India (Kalmar 1989: 217). Indeed, such a state of affairs gave the Prime Minister autocratic rule by decree, yet also expanded the competences of law enforcement, causing the crime rate to drop drastically (Kalmar 1989: 218). Nevertheless, it has to be mentioned that the greatest stain of that period was the compulsory sterilisation programme, yet it significantly differed from its description in Rushdie's book. The blame for the programme's failure cannot be attributed solely to Mrs. Gandhi, because with its enforcement it achieved a nationwide snowball effect with numerous local government politicians urging, and even bribing their workers and relatives to undergo the procedure in order to improve the statistics (Singh *The Wonder That Was Indira*; Kalmar 1989: 221–223). Additionally, widespread corruption in the Congress party and the reckless actions of Sanjay Gandhi in terms of the civic beautification programme led to a public disdain of the government and eventually Mrs. Gandhi paid the price, losing the 1977 general election. "I have accepted all of the responsibility, because I happened to be the head of the government," she stated in a Thames Television interview (00:18:05–00:18:09).

However, Mrs. Gandhi did return to power when the coalition of the Janata Party, idealistically referred to in *Midnight's Children* as "the People's Front" (Rushdie 2006: 474), fell apart after only two years of being in power, failing to fulfil Rushdie's utopian vision of the country. Also, the refuelling of faith and trust of the public in Indira Gandhi's 1980 administration completely contra-

[3] The novel makes a false accusation that Mrs. Gandhi proclaimed the Emergency in response to the court ruling which found her guilty of electoral campaign malpractice. However, it is historically proven that after her appeal to the Supreme Court of India, the adjudication was suspended and she could perform her prime ministerial duties as normally (Kalmar 1989: 206–207).

dicts her image in the novel as a bloodthirsty Widow. Therefore, in view of such historical knowledge, a conclusion can be reached that what initially appears to be constructive criticism of post-Partition India in *Midnight's Children* is, in fact, a fictional misrepresentation whose exclusive aim is to demonise Indira Gandhi[4].

Furthermore, the flaws in Rushdie's reasoning stretch on to the end of the novel. With Aadam Sinai, the representative of a new, stronger, and smarter generation of Midnight's Children, the novel inflicts a belief that newborn Indians shall finish the objective of their parents regarding changing India into a multicultural place and will remember the atrocities of the Partition as well as the Emergency. Yet ironically, the new generation, for which the writer had such high hopes, chose a completely opposite direction. Nowadays, the popularity of Indira Gandhi is as high as ever with her being voted as *Woman of the Millennium* in a BBC poll[5] and the greatest Indian Prime Minister in *India Today's* survey[6]. In addition, the Facebook profile page dedicated to her has almost 900,000 followers, an unprecedented number for a historical figure[7]. Additionally, in terms of the present Indian political stage, Hindu nationalism is still as dominant as it is visible with a landslide victory of the right-wing Bharatiya Janata Party in the 2014 parliamentary elections.

Conclusions

All things considered, the contemporary re-reading of *Midnight's Children* significantly differs from the novel's initial reception in the First World. Referring to the statement by Salman Rushdie that the book was praised in the West due to its fantasy components, whereas in India, it was read like a history book[8], we can see that the author's statement, as well as his convictions about the future of India, are no longer valid from the present-day perspec-

---

[4] This argument can be justified even further by the fact of Mrs. Gandhi's winning a lawsuit against Salman Rushdie about having been directly defamed in chapter 28 of the novel (Rushdie 2006 [1981]: xiv).

[5] *Indira Gandhi 'greatest woman'*. 1999. http://news.bbc.co.uk/2/hi/543743.stm.

[6] *I am Courage – Indira Gandhi, The Iron Lady of Lady.* 2016. http://www.indiragandhi.in/.

[7] *Indira Priyadarshini Gandhi.* 2010. https://www.facebook.com/IndiraPriyadarshini Gandhi.

[8] "When 'Midnight's Children' came out, people in the West tended to respond to the fantasy elements in the novel, to praise it in those terms. In India, people read it like a history book" (Rushdie, https://www. brainyquote.com/quotes/quotes/s/salmanrush 580293.html).

tive. Indeed, the novel was regarded as a history book, but this happened in the First World countries, not in India[9]. A substantial quantity of historical errors and contextual inaccuracies incorporated by the author only propelled the stereotypical image of India throughout the 1980s and beyond. Needless to say, the present reinterpretation[10] of Indira Gandhi's rule and a strong prevalence of nationalist ideology in modern Indian politics renders the classic reading of *Midnight's Children* outdated.

Bibliography

A Tall Story- How Salman Rushdie Pickled All India (1981). Dir. Diana Mansfield. BBC Four Productions.

Ahmad, Naqui (2014). *Midnight's Children And The Art Of Narration.* On-Line Publication Available At: http://www.academia.edu/8998773/midnights_children_and_the_art_of_narration [Accessed: April 12, 2016].

British Fiction Today (2006). Ed. Phillip Tew And Rod Mengham. London: Continuum International Publishing Group.

Eaglestone, Robert (2006). "Salman Rushdie: Paradox And Truth," In: *British Fiction Today.* Ed. Philip Tew And Rod Mengham. London: Continuum International Publishing Group.

Faris, Wendy B. (1995). "Scheherazade's Children: Magical Realism And Postmodern Fiction," In: *Magical Realism: Theory, History, Community.* Ed. Lois Parkinson Zamora and Wendy B. Faris. Durham: Duke University Press.

Gandhi, Leela (2008) [1998]. *Teoria Postkolonialna. Wprowadzenie Krytyczne.* Trans. Jacek Serwański. Poznań: Wydawnictwo Poznańskie.

Harikumar, A. (2012). *Midnight's Children Screening Ignites Political Controversy.* On-Line Publication Available At: http://www.dailymail.co.uk/indiahome/indianews/article-2246648/midnights-children-screening-ignites-political-controversy.html [Accessed: April 9, 2016].

Horn, Madelaine (2014). "Women Have Always Been The Ones To Change My Life: Gendered Discourse In Salman Rushdie's *Midnight's Children*". *Undergraduate Journal Of Humanistic Studies,* 1 (Spring 2015): 1–9.

I Am Courage – Indira Gandhi, The Iron Lady Of India (2017). On-Line Publication Available At: http://www.indiragandhi.in/ [Accessed: April 12, 2017].

[9] Critical response of "Times of India" to the image of the country conveyed in *Midnight's Children* may serve as an additional substantiation (Gandhi 2008 [1998]: 148).

[10] Especially if we take into consideration a set of grand events in India (like lectures and exhibitions) whose aim is to celebrate the centenary of Indira Gandhi (1917–2017). For more information, please refer to *I am Courage – Indira Gandhi, The Iron Lady of Lady* at http://www.indiragandhi.in/.

Indira Gandhi 'Greatest Woman' (1999). On-Line Publication Available At: http://news.bbc.co. uk/2/hi/543743.Stm [Accessed: April 12, 2017].

Indira Gandhi Interview – TV Eye (1978). Hosted By Jonathan Dimbleby. Thames Television.

Indira Priyadarshini Gandhi (2010). On-Line Publication Available At: https://www.facebook.com/indirapriyadarshinigandhi [Accessed: April 12, 2017].

Kalmar, Gyorgy (1989) *Indira Gandhi.* Trans. Tomasz Kulisiewicz. Warszawa: Książka I Wiedza.

Magical Realism: Theory, History, Community (1995). Ed. Lois Parkinson Zamora And Wendy B. Faris. Durham: Duke University Press.

McLeod, John (2000) *Beginning Postcolonialism.* Manchester And New York: Manchester University Press.

Midnight's Children (2012). Dir. Deepa Mehta. Canada. Hamilton Mehta Productions.

Rushdie, Salman (2003). *Midnight's Children.* London: Vintage Classics.

Rushdie, Salman. https://www.brainyquote.com/quotes/quotes/s/salmanrush580293.html [Accessed: April 13, 2017].

Singh, Kushwant (2008). *The Wonder That Was Indira.* On-line publication available at: http://www.outlookindia.com/magazine/story/the-wonder-that-was-indira/211281 [accessed: April 23, 2016].

Chapter 10

Trifonov's Turkmenia: Optimism, Despair and the Intelligentsia

Benjamin Sutcliffe, *Miami University/USA*

The image of Turkmenia runs throughout the prose of Iurii Trifonov (1925–1981), despite this Soviet author being most famous for works focusing on the Moscow intelligentsia during the Brezhnev era. From the beginning Turkmenia is an ambiguous locale—at first, it is linked with youth and the promise of 1950s socialism. In the story *Hourglass* (*Pesochnye chasy*, 1959), the autobiographical protagonist stands near ancient ruins, pondering the rise and fall of empires through the ages. He then smugly notes that his time to die is still distant, claiming longevity and strength as birthrights.

Slaking the Thirst (*Utolenie zhazhdy*, 1963) incorporates the themes of "Hourglass" and expands on this assertion. The novel, the first Trifonov published after his debut novel *Students* (*Studenty*, 1950), has two plots set in 1957 and deeply embedded in the cultural anxieties of the Thaw. One, recalling narratives from the 1930s-1940s, deals with the struggles of those digging the Karakum Canal, a grandiose project to bring water from the Amu Darya River to irrigate Turkmenia. The second, parallel storyline depicts embittered Petr Koryshev, a struggling journalist in Turkmenia, whose father was repressed in 1937. Both plots intersect when Koryshev defends the canal's boss, the talented but unorthodox Ermasov, against political opponents associated with Stalinism (Trifonov 1959: 211-12)[1].

Turkmenia is the peripheral region Trifonov describes most extensively during the Thaw and, for that matter, in his entire oeuvre. At first glance *Slaking the Thirst* places this republic into the narrative of teleological optimism that the Khrushchev years continue from Stalinism. While flying over the Karakum sands and arguing with the more conservative Khorev, engineer Aleksei Ka-

[1] Discussion of *Slaking the Thirst* is modified from Sutcliffe (2016).

rabash curses the desert as a scoundrel that no one needs but whom he could beat into submission with 15 bulldozers. Such comments continue the previous epoch's drive to subdue and remake the environment, as well as heralding how the new scientific-technical revolution will change the USSR. Karabash's claim, however, also evokes a troubling past: before the Karakum project, there was Stalin's failed Main Turkmenia Canal. The region had long been a showcase for the USSR's attempts to control the natural world while demonstrating to recalcitrant locals the progressive might of Soviet power (Trifonov 1985, vol. 1: 648, 749)[2].

The desert must be conquered, as a scientist makes clear when warning Koryshev that otherwise, the Karakum could expand, the Caspian Sea could shrink, and even the distant Sahara could grow and thus excessively warm Europe's weather. This is a sadly prescient claim given climate change and the shrinking of the Aral (but not Caspian) Sea, with the second catastrophe mainly a result of the very same Karakum Canal. However, the message in *Slaking the Thirst* is quite different: the most enlightened part of humanity—Soviet workers and engineers—must act to correct nature's errors. One critic, applauding the (fictional) completion of the canal in the novel, paints a rosy picture that is darkly ironic in light of history. Celebrating those involved in the construction project, he asserts that they will see "the days when the canal becomes one of the cheapest trade routes between Europe and Asia and ships from the Baltic moor in the newly born ports of Afghanistan." For a number of obvious reasons, this utopian vision of the future never materialised (Trifonov 1985: 741)[3].

Trifonov's narrative depicts an era overshadowed by both the past and the future. Koryshev is consumed by Stalinism, which destroyed his father, while the Karakum Canal binds characters to the brighter era the state promises. The totalitarian past also taints the present as well as what has come before. The protagonist asks the well-read editor Diomidov why he fears a Stalinist colleague, Luzgin. For Koryshev, Luzgin should be a powerless "man of the past," yet he continues to impede those around him. Similarly, *Slaking the Thirst* appeared in 1963, soon after Aleksandr Solzhenitsyn's *One Day in the Life of Ivan Denisovich* and Evgenii Evtushenko's *The Heirs of Stalin*. These works depict the horrors of a past that Khrushchev-era society must confront, with Polly Jones noting that anti-Stalinists were confident that history was on

---

[2] Northrop (2004) discusses Soviet attitudes towards Central Asia.

[3] For one of the many studies on the shrinking of the Aral Sea, consult Micklin (1988). On the new ports of Afghanistan, see Tikhonov 1964: 212.

their side. The future is also a powerful force, ill-defined but alluring in its promises of justice and a better world (Trifonov 1985, vol. 1: 648, 749)[4].

In *Slaking the Thirst*, Koryshev has a number of affinities with Trifonov. Aside from the main character in the author's posthumously published novella *The Disappearance* (Ischeznovenie, 1987), he is the most autobiographical of Trifonov's protagonists. Koryshev recalls how in 1938 he stood outside the Matrosskaia Tishina prison in Moscow, trying to glean news of his father. Later, visiting the mountains in Turkmenia, the protagonist notes how the passage of years has little meaning since "real life" ended for him at eleven when his father was arrested. The protagonist then divulges that since this point his existence has been "unreal" as he and other victims of Stalin try to rectify what cannot be corrected. Both Koryshev's age and the year of his father's arrest match those of the author and his parent. This parallel and the image of the past strongly hint that the horror of the totalitarian era cannot be overcome, a basic truth that qualifies any search for justice for the victims of Stalin. *Slaking the Thirst* is an ambivalent narrative vacillating between a bright future and the unquiet ghosts of history, with its Central Asian setting an extension of these extremes (Trifonov 1985a, vol. 1: 477, 516)[5].

Trifonov's novella *Taking Stock* (*Predvaritel'nye itogi*, 1970) portrays Turkmenia as an alien frontier where isolation and silence reflect the lack of sincerity plaguing Trifonov's Moscow intelligentsia. As Igor' Reyf observes, Trifonov was a writer profoundly shaped by the Thaw-era problems such as coming to terms with the past and the collision of older and younger genera-

---

[4] Ivanova argues that these characters are mired in a moment of time that is nothing more than contemporaneity (Ivanova 1984, 66). Beginning in the late 1960s, novellas such as *The Exchange* will show how Trifonov retreats from the present—protagonists sink into despair after the moral missteps of the past. On history, see Jones 2013: 253–54.

[5] In another Thaw story by Trifonov, "Once on a Humid Night" (*Odnazhdi dushnoi noch'iu*, 1960) a Spaniard discusses his country's civil war, which, in turn, evokes the 1930s when the storyteller was a child in the Soviet Union (Trifonov 1978a, v. 1: 138). Trifonov's *House on the Embankment* depicts a similar scene when the narrator uses miniature flags to track the Republicans' defeat (Trifonov 1985a, vol. 2, 449–50). The troubling nature of the past has another level: even years later, Trifonov will not explain the reasons for his personal and creative crises before publishing *Slaking the Thirst*. These include problems resulting from authorities discovering his father's identity, the young author's difficulty in adjusting to his sudden fame and, in all likelihood, guilt over the novel *Students*, which glorified the system that destroyed his family (Trifonov 1985b: 240).

tions. However, *Taking Stock* and most of his well-known works were not published until after the invasion of Czechoslovakia (Reyf 2013: 12).

Turkmenia's image in *Taking Stock* is less a function of reality than of the conjoined moral and historical anxieties worrying the protagonist. The concept of this Central Asian republic as periphery is itself far from simple when discussing the USSR and its legacy. In his classic work, Hedrick Smith noticed inverse colonialism, where the standard of living was often better at the margins of the Soviet empire than in its heartland, with the notable exception of Moscow and Leningrad. Edith Clowes is more specific, asserting that an oppressive north (dominated by the capital often depicted by Trifonov) struggles to control an unruly southern and eastern periphery (Smith 1983; Clowes 2011: xi, 2, 126-27)[6].

Gennady Sergeevich flees wife Rita and adult son Kirill and eventually ends up in Tokhir, a scenic but isolated dacha for writers. He is translating a would-be epic poem by the hack Turkmen author Mansur, but his thoughts focus on family crises in the USSR's capital. Typical for the Moscow *povesti* that *Taking Stock* is part of, the plot is divided between the protagonist's present (here, in Turkmenia) and unsettling events from the past. The novella begins with the confluence of heat, illness, and despair. In Ashkhabad Gennady Sergeevich is afraid; the novella opens with physical, climatic, and spiritual complaints:

> "At the beginning of May the city was struck by a tropical heat wave and life became unbearable. From eleven in the morning until sunset the hotel room was as hot as an oven and I would begin to feel dizzy and short of breath. One night was particularly bad, and tormented by sleeplessness, pains in my chest, and the fear of death, I lost heart. The next morning I put in a call to Moscow." (Trifonov 1978b, 101)

Central Asia is a heat that signals the protagonist's distance from his wife and son in Moscow and spurs him to call them—soon he will move to cooler Tokhir. Already we see that locale is subordinate to a personal crisis. The reader quickly realises that Gennady Sergeevich's "fear of death" comes more from internal than external factors, factors prompting him to "lose heart"

---

[6] Theorising the periphery, an outlying region with overtones of isolation from the metropole, is closely related to the simmering debate over Orientalism in the Russian context. For a representative discussion of this extensive argument, see *Orientalism and Empire in Russia* (2006). Likewise, the trope of the visitor from a more central area describing an exotic locale is a familiar feature of colonialist writing. Layton (1994) provides an influential introduction to this literature.

(*smalodushnichat'*). Thomas Lahusen notes that this condition, which begins with the physical and quickly implicates morality, prompts Gennady Sergeevich to examine his life and make the preliminary conclusions that give the work its title (Lahusen 1986: 571)[7].

Even before abruptly departing Moscow, Gennady Sergeevich connects Central Asia with loss. His son by his first wife is now a geologist in the region, as the reader learns from a passing reference to the family that the protagonist abandoned to be with Rita. At the opening of the novella familial history is repeating itself (Gennady Sergeevich has left his second wife and second son) as he lives alone on the Soviet periphery. The "oven" of Ashkhabad drives the protagonist to Tokhir, which he hopes will protect him from the heat while allowing him to "take stock" of his failing relationship with Rita and Kirill (Trifonov 1978a, vol. 2: 76).

Unsurprisingly, Gennady Sergeevich finds Tokhir still more remote than the capital of the Turkmen SSR. Self-imposed isolation (whether personal or geographical) is a trope of Trifonov's prose, and distance from others hints at serious problems. In this sense critics examine *Taking Stock* as the second Moscow novella; it follows *The Exchange* (*Obmen*, 1969), which also features a middle-aged protagonist who realises that his life has changed for the worse. Introspective pessimism, the hallmark of Trifonov's best works, shapes Gennady Sergeevich's perception of this Soviet republic as an indication of internal disquiet. Trifonov himself had been more attentive to his surroundings: when writing the notes for the work that later became *Taking Stock*, he sat at a cafe in Turkmenia and inquired about the local names for birds. However, in Tokhir Gennady Sergeevich limits himself to worrying whether the humble establishment he frequents is serving him camel meat. The author knows (and cares) much more about Central Asia than his literary creation does — the gap between their levels of engagement shows that the *povest'* carefully envisions the totalizing narcissism of its protagonist.[8]

Taking Stock lacks one element that runs throughout Trifonov's works. As Natal'ia Ivanovna perceptively notes, the Moscow novellas *The Exchange* and *House on the Embankment* (*Dom na naberezhnoi*, 1976) contain a river, which symbolises loss of the past and the inexorable progression of time. Tokhir, however, has no such feature—instead, Gennady Sergeevich's inner mono-

[7] This trope is a hallmark of nineteenth-century realism and shapes ailing protagonists such as Lev Tolstoi's Ivan Il'ich and Fedor Dostoevskii's Underground Man.

[8] On Trifonov gathering local names, see Satretdinova 1984: 71; Trifonov 1978a, vol. 2: 78.

logue takes on this function as it inundates the reader, merging past and present in a current that the protagonist cannot stop. Water does appear at the end of the main plot. While embracing (and presumably having sex with) the young nurse Valya, Gennady Sergeevich slips into a memory of himself and Rita on a boating trip early in their marriage. At first, the scene is nostalgic and comforting, but its conclusion resembles the pressures crushing the protagonist from the novella's beginning: "The water was still warm, but the air seemed to disappear, and there was nothing to breathe. The water was choking us. It was that same staircase on which I always felt myself suffocating. For some reason, I had to keep climbing higher and higher—just one more step, just a little more effort—but there was simply no air" (Ivanova 1984: 109; Trifonov 1978b: 200).

Lying with Valya merges into being on the river with Rita, an initially soothing vision that soon becomes the literal and metaphorical suffocation threatening Gennady Sergeevich and his spouse. Even his one moment of pleasure in the narrative devolves into a memory of his wife and the troubles that have brought him to Tokhir. Ivanova asserts that this last scene, which precedes the epilogue with Gennady Sergeevich and Rita vacationing on the Baltic shore, permits the reader no illusions: the protagonist is doomed. Whether in his dream-state or in Central Asia, Gennady Sergeevich cannot escape the problems that he himself has created. These color his experience on the periphery but also suggest that Trifonov's "Turkmen text" of works about the region extends and develops the concerns that begin in Moscow (Ivanova 1984: 140)[9]. In Tokhir, Gennady Sergeevich hears the murmuring of an aryk, but mistakes it for a waterfall. He notes that the radio reports hot weather in Ashkhabad, but in Tokhir it is pleasant.

> The air is cool, there is always a breeze, and you can even hear the rustle of leaves. When you walk along the village's only street, which is long, gently sloping, and shaded by ancient poplars and plane trees, you can hear the loud, incessant roar of water running through an irrigation ditch. At first, whenever I heard this roar, I would involuntarily look around, trying to locate the waterfall which I imagined must be somewhere nearby.

---

[9] Ivanova identifies a more optimistic reference to Gennady Sergeevich as retreating to the desert like one of the prophets envisioned by nineteenth-century literature (Trifonov 1978b: 124). Durkin interprets this allusion as a sign that Gennady Sergeevich has realised his errors and can correct them. See Durkin 1984: 36.

> There are no Persian remains in Tokhir except for two wretched huts made of clay and dung. One of them is falling apart, and the other one has been converted into a shed." (Trifonov 1978b: 106-107)

Gennady Sergeevich is at first impressed by Tokhir's milder temperatures, quiet beauty, and "gently sloping" street, "shaded by ancient poplars and plane trees." The protagonist then twists this positive description into disappointment, mistaking the prosaic *aryk* for a waterfall. Then he recalls Tokhir's Persian past, which has been reduced to "two wretched huts made of clay and dung." For him, Turkmenia as periphery is a sorry reformulation of what has come before.

Taking Stock is not overly concerned with depictions of the region. Gennady Sergeevich's thoughts in Tokhir recall a referent usually closer to the Soviet capital: the dacha. Beginning with *Students* Trifonov has portrayed the dacha to discuss Moscow problems in an environment free of the city's distractions. Often, however, this change in venue intensifies these difficulties, as the protagonist Dmitriev in *The Exchange* discovers after a clash between his mother and mother-in-law at the summer house. Trifonov displaces the dacha and its discontents onto distant Turkmenia. Tellingly for Gennady Sergeevich, the other combatants (Rita, Kirill, snobby *intelligent* Gartvig) are absent, leaving the protagonist alone to wage war on himself. The inhabitants of Tokhir are irrelevant, even when they seem to be the focus of Gennady Sergeevich's attention. Thinking about the wife of Atabaly, the caretaker of the dacha where the protagonist is staying, Gennady Sergeevich muses that Yazgul's face is old and worn from her many children.

> "Her arms, however, which are usually bared to the elbow, look young and strong. And probably her body too, with its big stomach and heavy-hanging breasts just barely outlined under the folds of her kuynak, is still young and full of life. [...] Once, thinking about Yazgul, I had trouble falling asleep. It even frightened me a bit—though what did I have to be frightened about at this point? Actually, what I felt was a momentary flash of bitterness. A man becomes aware of his age only belatedly. It's the same way with a wife's infidelity: you don't suspect a thing, and everyone else already knows all about it." (Trifonov 1978b: 108-109)

Yazgul, whom Gennady Sergeevich believes to be in her mid-forties, is older than Rita. She, however, excites him in a way that his second wife does not. Following the logic of egocentrism that structures the image of Turkmenia, the protagonist's inner monologue, and the novella's plot as a whole, the desire for Yazgul leads him to realise that he himself is aging, an awareness he compares with discovering infidelity. While Rita and Gartvig may have had an affair, at the moment, it is Gennady Sergeevich who has disrupted his marriage as he sulks in Tokhir. Yazgul, one of the few Turkmen with whom he interacts, is a function of Gennady Sergeevich's pre-existing problems (Trifonov 1978a, vol. 2: 76).

Atabaly is similarly characterised. He supports eleven children, some of them (such as Valya) adopted; Gennady Sergeevich, by contrast, has a parlous relationship with his second son and none at all with his first. The protagonist romanticises the struggles of raising so many children in a remote region of the Soviet periphery, seeing Atabaly's situation to be difficult but invigorating, as husband and wife successfully raise their sons and daughters. This praise then shifts its focus to Gennady Sergeevich's own disappointing family—the protagonist naively wonders if even a modest four children would give meaning to his life (Trifonov 1978a, vol. 2: 117).

The bonds of kinship are a mystery to him. Valya, hiding from the drunken poet whose opus Gennady Sergeevich is translating, explains why she chose not to leave with her birth mother when the woman came to Tokhir. As Gennady Sergeevich conveys to the reader, "Undoubtedly [Valya's real mother] was a good woman. But it just happened that Valya had grown up without her. Your family is those who take care of you [Rodnye liudi—kto dobro delaet]." Here the words originally come from Valya, but the sentiment refers back to Gennady Sergeevich's relatives as proof of the opposite. The protagonist has abandoned his first family in favour of his second, which is now also under strain, a strain that intensifies after they refuse to let their mentally ill maid Nyura return to them from the psychiatric hospital. In *Taking Stock* the protagonist's discussion of kin and kindness is out of place, given that the Moscow novellas are an elaboration of familial dysfunction. Yet Gennady Sergeevich's statement is one of few hints Trifonov provides about what keeps loved ones together (Trifonov 1978b: 197; Trifonov 1978a, vol. 2: 99–98, 104)[10].

The final sentences of *Taking Stock* show isolation more than cohesion. A few months after Gennady Sergeevich returns from Turkmenia, Kirill goes to Novgorod, allowing his mother and father to vacation by themselves near Riga. The protagonist drily summarises: "August turned out to be beautiful—sunny and clear, and not too hot. I took long walks every day and, as always, the Baltic climate had a healing effect: I was able to breathe deeply and even-

[10] On Gennady Sergeevich's family abandoning Nyura, see Durkin 1984: 37.

ly, my blood pressure went down to normal, and at the end of our stay I got hold of a racket and even played a little tennis" (Trifonov 1978b: 200).

Husband and wife are together on this vacation, yet the emphasis remains on Gennady Sergeevich, who takes long walks (presumably by himself) and notes how his health improves but does not discuss Rita. His tone is hopeful, but it reminds readers of the preceding narrative, which begins with family troubles, loneliness, and a sensation of impending doom. The epilogue contains the ambiguity Trifonov ascribes to the human condition. Andrew Durkin believes that the final sentences illustrate Gennady Sergeevich's "success in achieving insight" and overcoming his problems, while Ivanova compares them to the devastatingly understated ending of *The Exchange*. From Ivanova's more convincing standpoint, Trifonov leaves the reader with few reasons for optimism: Gennady Sergeevich realises that his return to health and harmony is temporary and due, in part, to his son's absence. The conclusion of *Taking Stock* is far more circumscribed than the broad Baltic vistas it depicts (Durkin 1984: 39; Ivanova 1984: 133).

For Trifonov's protagonist lack of sincerity (*iskrennost'*) is a transgression driving Gennady Sergeevich to the literal and metaphorical edge of Soviet society. Kirill, who has inherited his father's dishonesty and his mother's love of material objects, is correct about one thing: his father produces "junk" (*mura*). Gennady Sergeevich is polishing the line-by-line translation of Mansur's poem about a Turkmen girl with a golden voice. The subject matter hints at ideal communication, beauty, and love—all elements whose absence harms Gennady Sergeevich. The protagonist himself does not speak Turkmen and, more to the point, knows that the poem is worthless; he is completing the translation for the money and for escaping his son and wife. This project is symptomatic of Gennady Sergeevich's underlying lack of sincerity, just as his trouble breathing at the novella's beginning is the latest of the health problems stemming from inner turmoil (Trifonov 1978a, vol. 2: 69, 77).

In helping to produce a poem which he knows lacks talent, Gennady Sergeevich profanes the sacral role of literature promoted by the intelligentsia while also contributing to the condescension Russians often displayed for the writing of the USSR's ethnic minorities. For Marina Selemeneva, such actions constitute the crass materialism that *intelligenty* abhor. Although he has a higher education and is well-read, Trifonov's protagonist knows that he does not belong to this group. When his wife complains that he is not *intelligent* because he does not love music, he responds to the reader that he has never thought of himself as one, but not because of disinterest in classical composers. Gennady Sergeevich hints that the actual reason is his cynicism. Cynicism implies a disjuncture between belief and action, and this gap is incompatible with the sincerity central to the intelligentsia. Trifonov himself was no stranger to this issue—he deeply regretted beginning his literary career with the odiously false Stalinist novel *Students*, which was partially an attempt to elide his father's execution. *House on the Embankment* is Trifonov's atonement for the mendacity of *Students*, but already in the earlier Moscow novellas, his characters are troubled by dishonest lives. Gennady Sergeevich bemoans this state: "I've never done what I wanted to, but only what was expected of me, what was needed to get by. And most likely I could have done what I wanted to. If only back then, right after the institute, in the late forties... Well, and so forth and so on." The protagonist has lived an insincere existence dictated by imagined exigency. The post-university experiences of Gennady Sergeevich resemble those of Trifonov, who published *Students* immediately after graduation, in the heat of Stalin's anti-cosmopolitan campaign. Following the success of the novel, he traveled to Central Asia and eventually wrote *Slaking the Thirst* (Selemeneva 2009: 16)[11].

Insincerity underlies Gennady Sergeevich's putative honesty as he presents his failures as husband, father, and friend. His confession is less atonement than gambit for sympathy. Naum Leiderman and Mark Lipovetsky correctly discern that *Taking Stock* represents an intensification of the corrupting process Dmitriev undergoes in *The Exchange*. Gennady Sergeevich's lack of *iskrennost'* is evident at the level of language as well as the events it depicts. When the protagonist criticises Gartvig for abandoning girlfriend and wife to travel throughout the USSR, the reader cannot help but compare this to Gennady Sergeevich's own situation. This is a deliberate and anomalously unsubtle move on Trifonov's part. Readers must reach the same realisation the protagonist gradually makes after coming to Tokhir: ignoring *iskrennost'* causes poor judgment, an inability to grasp consequences, and precludes understanding of one's true nature. Turkmenia as geographical periphery thus reveals how lack of sincerity is a concern at the center of Trifonov's late works. The absence of *iskrennost'* is reflected through the body; corporeality is Russian literature's favorite venue for displaying the torments of the soul. Josephine Woll observes that Gennady Sergeevich suffers from twenty years of the compromises Dmitriev fears, and this ailment takes on a psychosomatic

---

[11] Selemeneva is one of the best critics writing on Trifonov today (Trifonov 1978a, vol. 2: 69, 82). For a good, representative discussion of *House on the Embankment* as atonement for *Students*, see Dwyer (2005), (Trifonov 1978b: 110) Concerning Trifonov's later feelings about *Students*, consult Leiderman and Lipovetskii 2001: 7. On Trifonov and Central Asia, see Woll 1991: 20-21 and Ivanova 2000: 693.

form. It is significant that Gennady Sergeevich begins his narrative with a complaint about health; similarly, his heart problems begin when the family abandons Nyura. The body does not dissemble, and Gennady Sergeevich notes that he looks a decade older than his forty-seven years. Trifonov's best-known works are the narratives of middle age, with flabby stomachs and balding heads constituting the bodily indication of abrogated sincerity in Tokhir and Moscow (Leiderman and Lipovetskii 2001: 17; Trifonov 1978a, vol. 2: 90)[12].

Speaking underscores Gennady Sergeevich's insincerity, while silence signals disaster. Near the end of the novella, Mansur has arrived and brought Gennady Sergeevich only a portion of the money he promised the translator. Trifonov's protagonist senses that his previous freedom of movement (from Moscow to Ashkhabad to Tokhir) was illusory. Now he realises he is an animal caught in a trap, limited to a small radius the length of his own tail. His situation is no better than it was in Moscow. Indeed, now it has worsened: in the capital, he had news from his (second) wife and son, but in Tokhir its lack is disturbing. After arguing with Mansur, Gennady Sergeevich thinks: "Now, as I lay alone in complete silence, I realized that my unseemly shouting hadn't been about money at all. Apparently, I had been counting on news from home. I had been counting on hearing from [Rita and Kirill], and not they from me. But even if it was all over between us, still, this silence was unnatural" (Trifonov 1978a, vol. 2: 119; Trifonov 1978b: 191).

The oppressive quiet has little to do with Tokhir, which is slowly getting ready for the summer vacation season. It does not even come from Gennady Sergeevich's self-imposed sojourn to Central Asia: the terrible silence is within him and makes his current location on the periphery ultimately irrelevant. He will (and does) return to his wife and son, yet the ambiguous epilogue makes it clear that their summer of tentative reconciliation is only a ceasefire during what, in the post-Soviet parlance, would be termed a "frozen conflict." Ivanova points out that Trifonov believed that Gennady Sergeevich would die at the novella's conclusion, but then the author reconsidered. Gennady Sergeevich must not perish—that would be too easy an escape. He, like the writer's other amoral and immoral protagonists, must continue to suffer. In doing so, Gennady Sergeevich displays the consequences of insincerity that dominate Trifonov's works (Ivanova 1984: 132).

---

[12] Ivanova notes that Gennady Sergeevich has betrayed others so completely that he has betrayed himself (Ivanova 1984: 130). Woll 1991: 26; Trifonov 1978a, vol. 2: 69.

Gennady Sergeevich's dwelling on his shortcomings only reveals underlying levels of falsehood. He admits that he loves the pompous phrase "Also, sprache Zarathustra" but knows nothing about Nietzsche or, for that matter, Zoroastrianism and Persia (these are the provenance of annoyingly erudite Gartvig). Furthermore, the protagonist admits that his German is only good enough to order bread. These words constitute a superficial self-criticism yet cannot make up for the deeper lie: Gennady Sergeevich has lived in a way that has betrayed everyone, including himself. At the novella's conclusion, he lapses into silence—even it is another form of prevarication, fooling Gennady Sergeevich (and some critics) into believing that his time in Tokhir and "taking stock" have improved him. This is made clear when he is in bed with Valya and, embracing her, his thoughts turn to the day he and Rita were on the boat. Gennady Sergeevich recalls his wife while having sex with another woman, confirming that nothing will change in his profoundly insincere life, whether in Turkmenia or Moscow (Trifonov 1978a, vol. 2: 124–25)[13].

Gennady Sergeevich is an aged, cynical version of Koryshev, a young man who, for his part, already sees the radiant future overshadowed by the past. The Thaw-era enthusiasm of *Slaking the Thirst* and praise surrounding the Karakum Canal become the unsettling silence of self-imposed exile in *Taking Stock*. Both works illustrate how the setting is secondary and lacks the nuanced autonomy of the author's depictions of Moscow in narratives such as *The Exchange*. Indeed, the city's expansion serves as one of Trifonov's metaphors for history, which he sees as impersonal, destructive, and indifferent to the fate of the individual. Turkmenia as periphery has no such symbolic role. The flow of history that Koryshev sees in the Karakum Canal becomes the petty stream of water that Gennady Sergeevich mistakes for something more impressive. *Taking Stock* relegates Tokhir and, for that matter, Gennady Sergeevich to the backwater of existence. Turkmenia plays a large role in Trifonov's prose, yet it merely reiterates the worries and hopes of those who visit this periphery from the capital. The Central Asian region is a many-faceted mirror ultimately secondary to what it reflects: the Moscow intelligentsia who dominate Trifonov's prose.

Bibliography

Clowes, Edith (2011). *Russia on the Edge: Imagined Geographies and Post-Soviet Identity.* Ithaca: Cornell University Press.

[13] Durkin reads the scene with Valya and the epilogue in a more optimistic light (Durkin 1984: 38–39).

Durkin, Andrew (1984). "Trifonov's 'Taking Stock': The Role of Čexovian Subtext." *Slavic and East European Journal* 1: 32–41.

Dwyer, Anne (2005). "Runaway Texts: The Many Life Stories of Iurii Trifonov and Christa Wolf." *Russian Review* 64: 605–27.

Ivanova, Natal'ia (1984). *Proza Iuriia Trifonova,* Moscow: Sovetskii pisatel'.

—— (2000). "Trifonov, Iurii Valentinovich." In *Russkie pisateli 20 veka. Biograficheskii slovar'.* Comp. and ed. P A. Nikolaev. Moscow: Bol'shaia Rossiiskaia entsiklopediia and Randevu-AM.

Jones, Polly (2013). "The Personal and the Political: Opposition to the Thaw and the Politics of Literary Identity in the 1950s and 1960s." In *The Thaw: Soviet Society and Culture during the 1950s and 1960s.* Eds. Denis Kozlov and Eleonory Gilburd. Toronto: University of Toronto Press.

Lahusen, Thomas (1986). "Du 'dialogisme' et de la 'polyphonie' dans deux ouvrages russes des années soixantes: *Une semaine comme une autre* de Nat'ja Baranskaja et *Bilan préalable* de Jurij Trifonov." *Revue d'études slaves* 4: 563–85.

Layton, Susan (1994). *Russian Literature and Empire: Conquest of the Caucasus from Pushkin to Tolstoy.* Cambridge: Cambridge University Press.

Leiderman, N. L., and M. N. Lipovetskii (2001). *Ot "sovetskogo pisatelia" k pisateliu sovetskoi epokhi. Put' Iuriia Trifonova.* Ekaterinburg: Izdatel'stvo AMB.

Micklin, Philip (1988). "Desiccation of the Aral Sea: A Water Management Disaster in the Soviet Union." *Science* 241: 1170–76.

Northrop, Douglas (2004). *Veiled Empire: Gender and Power in Soviet Central Asia.* Ithaca: Cornell University Press.

Orientalism and Empire in Russia (2006). Eds. Michael David-Fox, Peter Holquist, and Alexander Martin. Bloomington: Slavica.

Reyf, Igor (2013). "Pisatel na vse vremena." *Voprosy literatury* 1: 9–29.

Satretdinova, Raisa S. (1984). *Turkmenia v tvorchestve Iu. V. Trifonova.* Ashkhabad: Ylym.

Selemeneva, Marina (2009). "Khudozhestvennyi mir Iu. V. Trifonova v kontekste gorodskoi prozy vtoroi poloviny XX veka." Synopsis of doctoral dissertation. Moscow State Humanities University.

Smith, Hedrick (1983). *The Russians.* New York: Times Books.

Sutcliffe, Benjamin (2016). "The Thin Present of Trifonov's Thaw: Time in *Slaking the Thirst.*" *Australian Slavonic and East European Studies* 1–2: 1–21.

Tikhonov, Ia. (1964). "Delo, kotoromu ty sluzhish'." *Oktiabr'* 1: 212–15.

Trifonov, Iurii. (1978a). *Iurii Trifonov. Izbrannye proizvedeniia v dvukh tomakh,* Moscow: Khudozhestvennaia literatura.

—— (1985a). *Iurii Trifonov: sobranie sochinenii.* 4 vols., S. A. Baruzdin et al. Eds. Moscow: Khudozhestvennaia literatura.

—— (1985b). *Kak nashe slovo otzovetsia….* Editor A. Shitov, notes by O. Trifonova and A. Shitov. Moscow: Sovetskaia Rossiia.

—— (1978b). *The Long Goodbye: Three Novellas.* Trans. Helen Burlingame. Ann Arbor: Ardis.

—— (1959). *Pod solntsem. Rasskazy.* Moscow: Sovetskii pisatel'.

Woll, Josephine (1991). *Invented Truth: Soviet Reality and the Literary Imagination of Iurii Trifonov.* Durham: Duke University Press.

Chapter 11

Bringing the Orient to the Empire – An Analysis of Frances Hodgson Burnett's *A Little Princess* and *The Secret Garden*

Karolina Marzec, *University of Lodz/Poland*

Children's literature is a vast and interesting genre. Unfortunately, it is typically associated with light reading, even though its educational value can still be appreciated by some adult readers. For years, academic scholars were not interested in analysing novels for children. The books were to promote desirable values within society, however, they were not considered profitable for an adult recipient. Nevertheless, the situation has changed and as Paula S. Fass states, "the history of children and childhood is a new and energetic field of inquiry that provides critical insights into the human past and contemporary social experience" (Fass 2004: xi). Bearing this in mind, scholars have started analysing children's literature with more respect and eagerness, as the genre can serve as a testimony to the social changes equally profoundly as any other. After all, it is worth remembering that novels for children are written by adult writers; thus, the values which may not be identified by the target reader may be indeed noticed and understood by the adult recipient.

With such a point of view in mind, one has to start perceiving books for children with more respect and concern. This paper thus will focus on the postcolonial perspective in Frances Hodgson Burnett's *A Little Princess* and *The Secret Garden.* The books were published respectively in 1905 and 1911. It is clear that the works cannot be classified as postcolonial ones, however, they can present a changing mindset within the British society and the changes Burnett was able to observe. In the aforementioned novels, Burnett presents a strident critique of British society. She comments on the position of a child, the social and political situation of women in general, as well as in the literary industry, but most importantly, she criticises imperialistic values. There are scholars who claim that writing for children is a way of colonising the young reader. Although, as it was already emphasised, the works of Frances Hodgson Burnett cannot be classified as ones showing a postcolonial point of view, they can be analysed along with this perspective, as Roderick McGillis states that "children remain the most colonialised persons on the globe" (McGillis and Khorana 1997: 7). Having that in mind, it becomes vital to look at children's literature as written for the benefit of an adult and not a child. Perry Nodelman, who is famous for analysing Edward Said's works in connection with children's literature, states:

> "As Orientalism is primarily for the benefit of Europeans, child psychology and children's literature are primarily for the benefit of adults. We may claim to study childhood in order to benefit children, but we actually do it so we will know how to deal with children; and... we write books for children to provide them with values and images of themselves we approve of or feel comfortable with." (Nodelman 1992: 30)

The scholar presents the educational value of the genre and a notion that, through literature, authors send messages by means of which they want to inspire the reader. This statement is of paramount importance, as Burnett's writing consists of a strident critique of the status quo in the British society and of proposals of changes which can and should be implemented by her readers. Nevertheless, the position of a child reader is presented as inferior to the adult writer, who imposes certain values through their work. McGillis elaborates that

> "Children, then, may not be in the position of postcolonial subjects, speaking for themselves and taking responsibility for their own actions. The literature which they read may also participate in a colonizing enterprise if we assume that it sets out to draw its readers into the world as adults see it and construct it. On the other hand, the postcolonial critic is not a quixote who sets out to de-colonize children; rather she or he tries to clarify how children's literature and the criticism of that literature manifest the powerful force of Eurocentric biases and in doing so tries to dismantle that powerful force." (McGillis and Khorana 1997: 8)

Applying such a strong parallel, an adult as the coloniser, a child as the colonised, one starts to perceive children's literature with a different mindset. The tropes of postcolonialism start to be more prominent when one reads about a child who is not allowed to speak for themselves or the imperialistic power abuse that is manifested in the way a protagonist treats a servant, even though the books – from the historical point of view – cannot be classified as postcolonial ones.

These examples can be found in both novels, but they can also be finally analysed from the contemporary perspective. Roderick McGillis expresses his certainty that "obviously, Burnett's evocation of India in both *The Secret Garden* and *A Little Princess* has a colonialist aspect that has remained unnoticed until recently" (McGillis 2000: xxvii) and that the latter novel "is a decidedly 'colonial' book, but one we need to examine from a postcolonial perspective" (McGillis and Khorana 1997: 11). The scholar strongly promotes looking at the well-known novels with a new approach: "One aspect of postcolonialism, then, identifies a revisionary reading of canonical texts that articulates how these texts construct worlds" (McGillis and Khorana 1997: 12). Gymnich and Lichterfeld also point out that "a number of literary critics have addressed the references to colonialism in Burnett's novels and have sought to evaluate them. In addition to Mary's childhood experiences in India, the references to Indian characters and the diamond mines in Burnett's *A Little Princess* of course also lend themselves to a discussion from a postcolonial perspective" (Gymnich and Lichterfeld 2012: 11). This is, thus, one of the examples of how Burnett's works present notions that look ahead of her times and can be analysed correspondingly with modern concepts.

A Little Princess depicts a story of a young girl, Sara Crewe, who comes to England from India, where she has been schooled by her father – a loving and caring person. Because their relationship is so warm and full of love, the girl will associate India with a place where she used to be happy, loved and cared for. The country will serve as a memory of kindness, happiness, tranquillity, and magic she experienced in her early childhood. Sara is brought to England to start her education in a school for young girls. Unfortunately, during his stay in India, Sara's father dies, and the young orphan, deprived of all her money, loses her position in the school and becomes a servant. The Orient thus serves Burnett as a starting point of the plot, as well as it enables the author to manipulate the story to her needs further on. Roderick McGillis sums it up by saying: "That Burnett's hope is to enter the debate over women's roles within an imperial context is clear from her casual use of India as the starting point for characters such as Mary Lennox and Sara Crewe" (McGillis

1996: 9). It becomes obvious that the author deliberately and consciously uses India to direct and stimulate the plots she created.

A mysterious appearance of a new neighbour, whose servant – Ram Dass – is a lascar is another plot twist connected with the Orient. Although the mysterious gentleman who moves next door should be or used to be, perceived as Sara's saviour, it is indeed the servant who notices the girl's situation and does what he can in order to help the poor orphan. Thanks to Ram Dass, the reader is again exposed to the Orient, which permeates the plot. The servant, however, is presented in a shallow and condescending manner. He lacks depth as a literary character and is a typical colonial servant, who should be perceived as a background figure. McGillis points out that:

> "He is an exotic stranger. He represents one aspect of the "other" against which Sara and her people identify themselves. Throughout the book Ram Dass appears to us as a willing servant, submissive and respectful. We never have the opportunity of knowing him from the inside. He remains a stereotypical figure rather than a character fully realized. In short, he servers Burnett's purpose as a figure of the exotic, the mysterious, the fey. The fact remains, however, that he is a character with a distinct historical and cultural life that is denied him in this novel." (McGillis 1996: 21)

The contemporary reader, however, should not be astonished by such a representation. One has to remember that it was typical for British society to treat the colonised people this way, not taking into consideration what they represent or think. It is also worth mentioning that while *A Little Princess* was published in 1905, the story itself was created much earlier. A serial publication of the story began in December 1887. Later on, it was adapted to be a play, and it was staged for the first time in 1902. As a book, *A Little Princess* shows values which were not only generally accepted, but also deeply rooted in the colonial mindset. The Orient presented in the novel is shown from the perspective of the colonisers, who insolently manifest their superiority over the conquered countries. Ram Dass himself represents the passivity and acceptance of the colonised nation. He knows how to serve his master, how to approach the British people in general. The book points out his gentility and politeness. The readers are able to recognise him as a colourful figure, a character who is associated by Sara with positive values, but they do not know what he thinks as a human being. He never speaks as an independent person. He was thus created as a shallow and trite character, which corresponded with the British idea of a colonised servant. Sara herself serves as an excellent example of such an attitude when she longs for Ram Dass' attention.

> "When he had gone Sara stood in the middle of her attic and thought of many things his face and his manner had brought back to her. The sight of his native costume and the profound reverence of his manner stirred all her past memories. It seemed a strange thing to remember that she the drudge whom the cook had said insulting things to an hour ago – had only a few years ago been surrounded by people who all treated her like Ram Dass had treated her; who salaamed when she went by, whose foreheads almost touched the ground when she spoke to them, who were her servants and her slaves. It was like a sort of dream. It was all over, and it could never come back. It certainly seemed that there was no way in which any change could take place." (Burnett 1996: 143–144)

The subservience of lascars is deeply rooted in the child's mind, even perceived as something positive, something she has lost and longed for. From the contemporary perspective, it is ironic that Ram Dass is to accept his position with no sign of objection whatsoever, even eagerly, while Sara opposes being treated as a servant. McGillis specifies that in fact, the position of the girl in relation to Miss Minchin is very similar to the position of Ram Dass in relation to Sara. The scholar notices the narrator pointing out that:

> "Sara does not respond to her "masters" with deference the way Ram Dass responds to her. In fact, the book has it both ways: Ram Dass and the other Indian servants are correct in their subservience to Sara, and Sara in her turn is correct in her resistance to the tyranny of Miss Minchin and her minions. In other words, Burnett never suggests that that Ram Dass or his Indian compatriots should resist their roles as acquiescent servants and slaves." (McGillis 1996: 20–21)

Burnett fails to notice the contradiction which was omnipresent in the British society, the contradiction which allowed people to ignore the fact that people are equal, as well as forget about respect towards other cultures and nations. This contradiction was responsible for the notion of the primacy of the Empire.

However, the Orient is not brought to England only by means of servants or local furniture. The Orient is brought to England in Sara's mind. When writing this novel, Burnett had not fully developed the concept of hybridity yet, however, a contemporary audience can notice that this notion was already slowly emerging in the author's work. Sara talks about India with affection and nostalgia, subconsciously identifying the place with her father's love but also with light-heartedness and magical atmosphere. Deprived of any relics from the past, she looks with yearning at the furniture the mysterious gentlemen from next door is bringing to his house. What is more, she speaks to the lascar in the language which is his mother tongue. It is an unfathomable practice, not common at the end of the nineteenth century because children of diplomats and soldiers who served in colonies were not allowed to fraternise with the local people. Learning the language of the colonised nations was considered scandalous among the British children.

> "She turned to the lascar, feeling glad that she remembered still some of the Hindustani she had learned when she lived with her father. She could make the man understand. She spoke to him in the language he knew.
>
> 'Will he let me catch him?' she asked.
>
> She thought she had never seen more surprise and delight than the dark face expressed when she spoke in the familiar tongue. The truth was that the poor fellow felt as if his gods had intervened, and the kind little voice came from heaven itself. At once Sara saw that he had been accustomed to European children. He poured forth a flood of respectful thanks. He was the servant of Missee Sahib." (Burnett 1996: 141–142)

The surprise does not only include the fact that a girl randomly met in London speaks his mother tongue. Ram Dass is surprised to see a British child who opposes the worldview and the pedagogical stereotypes of the coloniser. Sara exceeds the imperialistic ideas and presents a scandalous approach. A child who was brought up in the colonies acquires values and features of the conquered nation and manifests them in the very heart of the Empire. It constitutes an immensely intriguing direction of influence. The already mentioned hybridity – that is acquiring the features and values of two different cultures, which both make it impossible to identify specifically with one of them – usually exists in literature as presented within the colonised societies, not among the colonisers. Nevertheless, in *A Little Princess,* Burnett allows herself only to express what one may call a foreshadowing of a critique of British society and its imperialistic values, for the real breakthrough can be noticed in *The Secret Garden.*

The book, published in 1911, also draws a lot from the Orient. India again serves as a starting point for the plot. Mary Lennox is born, and she grows up in the colonies, this is the place where her personality develops. Because her parents die, and the uncle who lives in England is her only guardian, the girl is sent to live with him. This is the first opportunity for Mary to get to know her homeland. Again, a child grows up in India and comes to England with a set of some already ingrained characteristics. Twenty four years passed from the moment when *A Little Princess* was first published in a magazine (1887). The world Burnett observes is evolving and so does the author's approach to the presented values. Some scholars – like Jean Webb – state that "Frances Hodgson Burnett is [...] arguing an anti-imperialist position" (Webb 2002: 91). It can be easily noticed in the way the author describes Mary's parents:

> "Her father had held a position under the English Government and had always been busy and ill himself, and her mother had been a great beauty who cared only to go to parties and amuse herself with gay people. She had not wanted a little girl at all, and when Mary was born she handed her over to the care of an Ayah, who was made to understand that if she wished to please the Memsahib she must keep the child out of sight as much as possible." (Burnett 2010: 1)

The lengthy passage shows how badly the child is treated by her parents. The child feels she is unwanted, has never felt the love she needs, only to finally not even realise it is the love and warmth of a mother's touch and care that she truly and essentially craves. Mary thus becomes a sour and tyrannical girl, who, when not given her way, throws tantrums and hysterics. She becomes an "innocent victim of imperialism" (Webb 2002: 91) because of the way her parents neglect her. She is so accustomed to the servants obeying her orders that she does not realise that is not how she should treat other people. She overuses the power she is given on the grounds of her birth. There is, nonetheless, no one who would tell her that such behaviour is wrong and immoral. Webb sums it up by saying that:

> "the reasons for such neglect are directly related to British imperialism in India. Her father, as an administrator of imperialist power, was too involved with the work of British government, or too ill, to have time for his daughter. Her mother was also part of the invasive imperialist machinery of government social life. She was so entranced with the trappings of the rule, the Government dinner parties and balls, that she 'had not wanted a little girl at all'." (Webb 2002: 92)

The assumption concerning her mother, nevertheless, might seem a bit too farfetched. Roderick McGillis states that "true, Mary's parents represent British imperial power, but they are not models the reader admires. They are more interested in power and prestige than in family" (McGillis 1996: 13), which also points out their detachment from the norms of the society:

> "Victorians placed the need for a strong family at the center of their lives. The family disruptions caused by long separations between parents and their children commonly seen in Anglo-Indian families were not in tune with the Victorian emphasis on creating a stable home and family that would provide what historian Anthony Wohl called moral, ethical, religious, and social standards of good citizenship." (Chaudhuri 2004: 121)

Mary's parents are thus purposefully created as a pair who deviates from the social standards and norms. Burnett, when creating those characters, gives the reader all the reasons to be outraged at them. If the neglect of the child is not enough, the author presents the parents as people violating the tradition, mindset and the eagerly cultivated values of the British society, putting for a moment the imperialistic traits aside. There is not a single word in the story about Mary's mother being obliged by her husband's position to indulge herself in such a riotous life. It is a critique in itself. The figure of the father, nevertheless, is described in little detail, excluding him from the picture and only presenting the man as a government figure too absorbed with the issues of the Empire to care much about the baby, who presumably, was not wanted by him as well. Here lies the hidden accusation of the father being more concerned with the Empire than with his own daughter.

The child thus grows surrounded by the servants and does not understand the power she has over them. Burnett creates numerous situations in the novel where Mary scolds the servants, beats them and insults in the worst possible ways, only to hurt them and get what she wants. She has no limits in her cruelty and tyranny. It will be an element of a complex inner metamorphosis of the child, nevertheless, it is also a hidden critique of the imperialistic attitude which praises the primacy over other people or nations on the basis of nationality or social group. The Orientals were treated as something less than human. Edward Said's theory of "othering", which is explained further in his groundbreaking work *Orientalism,* applies here. Although his analysis is mainly devoted to the conflict between the Arabic countries and the West, his publication, along with the works of Homi K. Bhabha and Gayatri Chakravorty Spivak, has become the foundation stone for any postcolonial criticism, and thus also gave way to recognising the colonial tropes. In the chapter devoted to postcolonial criticism, Rafey Habib summarises: "constructions of Europe's self-image, resting on the Enlightenment project of rationality, progress, civilisation, and moral agency, were premised on the positing of various forms of alterity, or 'otherness', founded on polarised images such as superstitiousness, backwardness, barbarism, moral incapacity, and intellectual impoverishment" (Habib 2005: 740–741). The polarity is here understood as the superiority with which other nations were treated by the British. This idea was so popular in British society that it can also be found in the works devoted to younger generations. When talking about Orientals, Mary reaches her peak of outrage, contempt, and hysterics. She insults them, and even after coming to England she says the most disrespectful things about them. She shouts at Martha that "they are not people – they're servants who must salaam to you" (Burnett 2010: 23) and she is the most outraged when she is compared to a native. There is no risk, when it comes to the analysis of Mary's behaviour, that she might directly threaten the Empire, nonetheless, a more complicated issue arises when one fairly admits that Mary is not a child who is biased and antagonistic toward people from India, and praises the values of England and the Empire. She scolds everyone whom she perceives as someone in a lower social position, even in England; thus, this is not a behaviour directed towards a specific ethnic group. However, in its complexity, the issue shows that the child does not know how to behave in any of the ethnic groups because she is torn between the two cultures.

The Orient thus is again deeply rooted in the child's mind and is brought to England; however, the theory of hybridity is more noticeable in this novel. Habib summarises that "the notion of 'hybridity' is central to Bhabha's work in challenging notions of identity, culture, and nation as coherent and unified entities that exhibit a linear historical development. Hybridity expresses a state of 'in betweenness,' as in a person who stands between two cultures" (Habib 2005: 750). Not only does Mary not belong to anyone in the emotional sense of closeness between people, but she also does not belong to any of the cultures she is familiar with. Mary is a hybrid because she "is neither English, nor Indian, but is caught between two cultures, belonging to neither" (Webb 2002: 93). She does not realise it until she leaves India and finds herself in a land that is supposed to be her true home; however, she feels there even lonelier than ever. Trying to cope with the situation, and constantly torn between and confused by the two cultures, the girl compares England with India. The people she meets are compared with the servants she used to know in the colony. When puzzled, she often repeats "it is different in India" (Burnett 2010: 22), trying to prove people that she is not unintelligent, but accustomed to a totally different lifestyle and culture. The girl also often quotes her Ayah, who used to say "it was the custom" (Burnett 2010: 24), which in a way justifies her actions. When asked why she cannot put her own shoes on, Mary repeats the same phrase, knowing that in India it meant that nothing and no one would undermine such a statement: "The native servants were always saying it. If one told them to do a thing their ancestors had not done for a thousand years they gazed at one mildly and said, 'It is not the custom' and one knew that was the end of the matter. It had not been the custom that Mistress Mary should do anything but stand and allow herself to be dressed like a doll" (Burnett 2010: 24). The girl thus repeats what is known to her, unaware that she is following the traditions and customs of the native people whom she despises so much.

Just like Sara in *A Little Princess*, Mary speaks the language that was used by the colonised people. The Orient thus is again brought in the child's mind and memory. She calls her mother "the Memsahib… oftener than anything else" (Burnett 2010: 3) – using the Indian word for "British married women in India" (Chaudhuri 2004: 120) and repeating the expression after the servants. When Colin has trouble with falling asleep, she says "I will do what my Ayah used to do in India. I will pat your hand and stroke it and sing something quite low" (Burnett 2010: 112). Moments later the reader finds out that she "began to stroke and pat his hand and sing a very low little chanting song in Hindustani" (Burnett 2010: 112). Thus, the fear that was so common among the British people living in the colonies becomes a reality, as the child – exposed to the local language – starts to use it. The colonisers were afraid their children would "imitate 'native' habits, mannerisms, and language" (Chaudhuri 2004: 120). The scholar elaborates on the subject and summarises that "mothers were not often successful in shielding their children from learning the local language" (Chaudhuri 2004: 120) and even provides some examples of people being displeased and discontent with their children imitating local customs and words. Mary, as a cultural hybrid, also does not realise that she repeats the behaviour and has become accustomed to the language typical of the natives. This means that the fear and concern of the British Empire fulfils itself by means of a little girl. The child who, at the beginning of the book, shows all the negative traits of the colonial conquest, suddenly appears to know by heart and to be fond of a folk lullaby, an element of culture which was supposed to be so deeply despised.

Mary's metamorphosis into a healthy, strong and happy child is a slow process; however, thanks to the English servants who represent the romantic values, as well as thanks to the positive influence of the forces of nature, the girl sheds the negative imperialistic qualities. She no longer stands in the position of a tyrant who exercises cruel and mindless power, but, rather, she learns to be independent and learns how to respect other people – all this without rejecting the Oriental culture.

Both novels, *A Little Princess* and *The Secret Garden*, when analysed from the postcolonial perspective, present the same motif of bringing the Orient to the Empire in minds and hearts of children who grew up in India, and who have problems with assimilating in England, which is supposed to be their homeland. In both books India serves as a starting point and, although McGillis comments that "such plot devices are of less importance than the casualness with which Burnett uses the Empire, her complete lack of awareness that she appropriates another culture and people for her own purposes" (McGillis 1996: 56) in *A Little Princess*, the author's ideas evolve through years as she presents an anti-imperialistic stand in the latter novel. In both books the protagonists show traits of hybridity, they are torn between two different cultures and cannot explicitly identify with only one of them. This is thus an interesting and peculiar direction of influences, where a British child adapts and accustoms the influences from the colonised regions. It is a unique harbinger of a revolutionary transformation, but also fulfilment and expression of the worst fears of the Empire – the Orient surpasses all expectations and influences the lives and views of the next generation of the colonisers, propelling the changes in the general worldview.

Bibliography

Burnett, Frances Hodgson (1996). *A Little Princess.* London: Penguin Books.

—— (2010). *The Secret Garden.* London: Harper Press.

Chaudhuri, Nupur (2004). "British Colonialism in India." In: *Encyclopedia of Children and Childhood: In History and Society.* Ed. Paula S. Fass, Macmillan Reference USA.

Fass, Paula S. (2004). Preface. In: *Encyclopedia of Children and Childhood: In History and Society.* Ed. Paula S. Fass, Macmillan Reference USA.

Gymnich, Marion and Imke Lichterfeld (2012). "*The Secret Garden* Revisited." In: *A Hundred Years of* The Secret Garden: *Frances Hodgson Burnett's Children's Classic Revisited.* Ed. Uwe Baumann, Marion Gymnich and Barbara Schmidt-Haberkamp. Bonn University Press.

Habib, Rafey (2005). *A History of Literary Criticism and Theory: From Plato to the Present.* Oxford: Blackwell Publishing.

McGillis, Roderick (1996). *A Little Princess: Gender and Empire.* New York: Twayne Publishers.

——, and Meena Khorana (1997). "Postcolonialism, Children, and their Literature". *ARIEL: A Review of International English Literature,* 28(1): 7–20.

—— (2000). *Voices of the Other: Children's Literature and the Postcolonial Context.* New York: Routledge.

Nodelman, Perry (1992). "The Other: Orientalism, Colonialism, and Children's Literature". *Children's Literature Association Quarterly* 17(1): 29–35.

Webb, Jean (2002). "Romanticism vs. Empire in *The Secret Garden*". In: Thacker, Deborah Cogan, and Jean Webb, *Introducing Children's Literature.* London: Routledge.

IV

Crossing Borders in Travel: Journey in Oriental Literature and Inspired by Orient

Chapter 12

The Great Wall of China in Polish and Serbian Travel Writing (From the 18th until the Middle of the 20th Century)

Tomasz Ewertowski, *Adam Mickiewicz University/Poland*

Introduction

A typical narration about the Great Wall of China, which can be found, for example, on the UNESCO World Heritage List website, maintains that the Wall is the only man-made structure visible from the Moon, "was continuously built from the 3rd century BC to the 17th century AD", its total length is more than 20,000 kilometres, and "Its purpose was to protect China from outside aggression, but also to preserve its culture from the customs of foreign barbarians" (*The Great Wall of China* 2017). Information given by the UNESCO should be trustworthy, however, the statements quoted above are a part of a widespread myth. Not only the claim of visibility from the Moon is rejected (Hvistendahl 2008; López-Gil 2008). Based on the works of Arthur Waldron (Waldron 1990) and Julie Lovell (Lovell 2006)[1], popular opinion can be confronted with views of historians. Imposing brick wall, parts of which are often visited by tourists, were built during the Ming dynasty (1368–1644). The history of the construction of fortifications in northern China started more than 2000 years ago, however, the famous wall of Qin Shi Huangdi is not the same as brick fortifications observed today. According to Waldron, problems appear already on the level of terminology. A Chinese expression *chang cheng* (长城),

[1] Both of these books tackle the problem of the myth of the Great Wall; however, it should be emphasised that Lovell's book, newer than Waldron's, is less original and more biased.

literally meaning "a long wall" and nowadays translated as the Great Wall, appeared in Chinese sources from the 1st century BC, however, it was used to designate any long wall. The In Ming period, when many of barriers currently described as "the Great Wall of China" were constructed, frontier fortresses were called *jiu bian zhen* (九边镇), "the nine border garrisons" (Waldron 1990)[2].

In stereotypical views, the Great Wall was a border between agricultural civilisation and "barbarian" nomads of the steppes and helped to preserve peace-loving Chinese from attacks. However, such a point of view is a simplification. Interactions between nomad and settled societies were complicated, and trade may have had as big significance as military conflicts. Some Chinese dynasties stemmed from nomads. Furthermore, some of the walls were built far away from farming territories and may be seen as *"less land-protecting than land grabbing"* (Lovell 2006: 21).

The myth of the Great Wall can acquire various senses. The structure is considered a symbol of China and a prestigious trademark, so we can find brands of cars or wine called "The Great Wall". Besides being a border between civilisation and barbarism, it also has many other meanings:

> "'The Great Wall,' another wall theorist has projected, 'is not only to be understood as a barrier, but also as a river uniting people of various ethnic background and providing them with a common haven and meeting place.' Luo Zhewen, vice-president of the Chinese Great Wall Society, has transformed the wall into the ultimate multipurpose historical mascot, declaring that it is simultaneously a product of feudal society and an inspiration for 'the Chinese people to forge ahead on the road of constructing socialism with Chinese characteristics'; that it created the first unified, centralized Chinese nation and helped build a multinational China" (Lovell 2006: 13–4).

The structure can also have a negative meaning. The construction of it is seen as a waste of resources and lives. The futility of fortifications is also emphasised, because many times the barriers did not save China from conquerors. The ancient wall of Qin Shi Huangdi served as a figure of tyranny and cruelty in Chinese literature. For instance, the legendary widow Mengjiang broke the wall up by her sobbing and revealed the bones of her husband and other workmen who died carrying out the will of the emperor. This legend

[2] A quotation is taken from an e-book provided by Amazon.com in the .azw format, therefore page numbers are not given.

was reinterpreted in an interesting way during the Cultural Revolution. The first emperor was described as a visionary who wanted to unite the country, and the widow was presented as pro-Confucian reactionary and "Great Poisonous Weed" (Waldron 1990).

Travelers on the Great Wall

The paper will analyse and interpret how the Polish and Serbian travelogues in the period from the 18th century until the middle of the 20th century interpreted the Wall and its myth[3]. Travel writing can be seen as a textual trace of a journey, created as an effect of a dialogue of the writer's personality and intellectual judgements with a new experience (Gvozden 2011). Contemporary studies analyse links between travel writing and production of knowledge, imperial rhetoric, representation of other cultures (Said 1977; Pratt 2011; Spurr 1993; Huigen 2009)[4]. The topic of the image of China was analysed in general terms (Dawson 1967; Mackerras 1989; Spence 1998) or from the point of view of a specific group in a particular period of time (Лукин 2007; Fogel 1996). Taking into account writers from Poland and Serbia makes it possible to introduce an interesting comparative perspective. Furthermore, Polish and Serbian authors are especially valuable for analysis of imperial dimension of travel writing and representation of China. In the period from the 18th until the middle of the 20th century Poland and Serbia did not participate in the political, military and economic exploitation of China, on the contrary, these countries themselves were objects of imperial actions. Nevertheless, Poles and Serbs often travelled to China while representing foreign institutions. Therefore, Polish and Serbian travelogues can show an interesting ambivalence between imperialism and Eurocentrism on the one hand, and sympathy towards abused nation and aversion to great powers on the other.

In the Eyes of a Diplomat

Probably the first Serbian traveller who visited China was Sava Vladislavić (1668–1738). He lived in Russia from 1708, where he was involved in military affairs and achieved successes in trade and diplomacy[5]. In 1725–1728

[3] For general information about Polish travelers in China, see Kajdański 2005; Kałuski 2001; Cyrzyk 1966. For Serbian authors, see Pušić 1998; Pušić 2006.

[4] It should be noted that the aforementioned works sometimes represent very different approaches, e.g. Huigen is very critical towards Pratt.

[5] For biographical information about Sava Vladislavić, see Dučić 2004; Sindik 2012; Kosanović 2009.

Vladislavić was a Russian envoy to China. This mission ended with signing the Treaty of Kyakhta and is recognised as a very significant event (Мясников 1990; Mancall 1971: 255). According to two secret points added to Vladislavić's instructions, he was concerned with gathering intelligence (Бантыш-Каменский 1882: 434–55). His findings are included in *Секретная информация о силе и состоянии Китайского государства* (The Secret Information on Strength and Situation of the Chinese State), a secret report, which was called one of the most important pieces of writing on China (Мясников 2006: 442).

Vladislavić's text was an intelligence report, so he mentioned the Great Wall most frequently in the context of possible military actions of Russian army, as well as in the context of Chinese history and the meaning of the Wall for Chinese politics, e.g., Chinese never sent an army bigger than 50,000 beyond the Great Wall (Vladislavić 2011: 178–9). While writing on the history of China, Vladislavić repeated, probably after his Jesuit sources, the widespread assertion that the Wall was built in the Qin dynasty period to save the country from Tatars. Sava's remarks emphasised the hugeness of the structure, its length and the number of people involved in its construction (allegedly 60 million). The Serbian diplomat's intelligence report was written in a dry manner, so adducing so many numbers can be seen a sign of great interest in a structure. As we will see, many travelers quoted numbers to express their admiration for the Great Wall. It seems to be one of the examples of a common image of China as a land of excess (Kerr and Kuehn 2010: 1). The description of the structure was also a sign of respect, especially given that in other parts of his report Vladislavić was very Eurocentric, full of confidence in the power of European armies and biased toward the "barbarian" Chinese[6]. Aleksandr Lukin does not mention Sava in his analysis of the image of China in Russia, although the researcher's general conclusion on Russian views on the Middle Kingdom in 18th century can also be applied to the Serbian diplomat: Russian Empire was perceived as a part of the progressive European civilisation, contrasted with backward Asia (Лукин 2007: 46).

---

[6] For a detailed analysis of Vladislavić's writings on China, see Ewertowski 2014.

Glorification of Chinese Achievements

Vladislavić's being a Serb serving at the Russian court is an instance of accommodation to imperial gaze. Another Serbian author, Milan Jovanović (1834–1896) shows how democratic and liberal worldview can influence a positive image of China[7]. In the late 1870s and early 1880s Jovanović travelled around the Mediterranean and in Asia while working as a ship's doctor for the steamship company Lloyd from Triest, hence, his travels in Asia were conditioned by the steamship revolution and European commercial expansion. The Serbian author represented liberal and humanistic ideas, therefore becoming very critical towards European imperialism[8]. His writings expressed a strong sense of European identity, although he was willing to appreciate the achievements of Asian civilisations, which led him to the idealisation of China and the Chinese. For Jovanović, the Great Wall was an example of the greatness of the Middle Kingdom:

> "In his work, a Chinese does not ask how much time he will need: he works, and what he does not finish today, he will continue tomorrow, and like that for many years, and if he dies while working, someone else will continue. This continuity can be seen in any kind of work, and mainly in economy and literature, so these works have broad fundaments. A book after a book like a canal after canal and its continuity there is a plan, which is executed by whole generations. The Great Wall of China and Chinese literature have the same proportions" (Jovanović 1895: 179)[9].

In Jovanović's words, we can find an echo of stereotypes characteristic for Jesuits' writings on China, which emphasised rationality and efficiency, as

---

[7] For Jovanović's life and work, see Tartalja 1984; Maksimović 2008. On Jovanović's travel writing see also Kostadinović 2012.

[8] On Jovanović's attitude towards colonialism and the image of China, see Ewertowski 2016.

[9] All translations into English are our own, unless otherwise indicated. For the convenience of readers, all Serbian Cyrillic texts have been transcribed into the Latin script. The original says: "U radu svom Hinez ne pita koliko će ga ovaj stati vremena: on radi, pa što ne svrši danas, nastaviće sutra, pa tako kroza čitave godine, i ako ga u tome zateče smrt – nastaviće neko drugi. Taj kontinuitet opaža se u svakoj vrsti rada a poglavito u ekonomnoj i književnoj, te su s toga u njih ovi radovi na širokoj osnovici. Knjiga se ređa na knjigu, kao kanal na kanal, i u tome kontinuitetu ima plana koji izvršuju čitave generacije. Hineski zid i hineska književnost jednake su proporcije".

well as the image of China as a land of "ritcheness and plentiffullnesse", as originating in the Middle Ages (Dawson 1967: 9–34).

A similar perspective can be found in writings of a Polish author Przecław Smolik (1877–1947). As an Austrian subject, he was taken as a prisoner by Russians during the First World War, lived in a POW camp in Siberia, and after the October Revolution, he was one of many Polish refugees who came to China[10]. This author had a positive attitude towards the East Asian peoples, and he wrote books about Buryats and Mongols. Smolik observed fortifications in Mukden (nowadays Shenyang), the old capitol of the Manchu state. Nevertheless, an observation of local ramparts prompted the Polish author to write a discourse linked with the myth of the Great Wall. "What I saw, even today makes an imposing impression, a structure built by giants, next to which the remains of our Middle Age fortifications [...] look like children toys"[11] (Smolik 1921: 131). Similarly to the Jovanović account, the Wall was perceived as a symbol of great achievements of the Chinese civilisation, which dwarfed European buildings. It revealed that the Middle Kingdom inhabitants, masters of crafts and manual skills, were also able to construct huge barriers to defend themselves from "wild barbarians". Based on these assumptions, he formulated a generalization on the Chinese

> "[...] gentle and cheerful as a child, and as a child honest; diligent over any European measure, attached to his family and his land [...], breeds as sand in a sea and populates still new virgin and barren lands of Asia, in front of which a white man falls back, and where he [a Chinese] quietly brings his wonderful, eternal culture [...]. Indeed, this nation de-

---

[10] Besides Smolik, a few other authors wrote travelogues based on their escape from revolutionary Russia to China, e.g. Kamil Giżycki *Przez Urianchaj i Mongolię. Wspomnienia z lat 1920-21* and *Ze Wschodu na Zachód. Listy z podróży,* Ferdynand Antoni Ossendowski *Przez kraj ludzi, zwierząt i bogów,* Jerzy Bandrowski *Przez jasne wrota.* General information about Polish migrations in East Asia caused by the war and revolution can be found in Cabanowski 1993: 42–72; Kałuski 2001: 97–104. A migration movement caused by the First World War and Russian revolution included also Serbs and other Yugoslavian nationals. E.g. Aleksandar Đurić, *Ka pobedi,* Jovan Milanković, *Uspomene iz Sibira 1918–1919 i put okeanom u domovinu 1920,* Vlada Stanojević, *Moje ratne beleške i slike,* Ariton Mihailović, *Kroz plamen ruske revolucije.*

[11] „To, co zobaczyłem, czyni jeszcze dziś wrażenie imponujące, budowli, przez gigantów stawianej, przy której resztki naszych średniowiecznych fortyfikacyj (...) wyglądają jak chłopięce igraszki!".

serves appreciation and imitation, in spite of the unpleasant smell of garlic and broad bean oil"[12].

Smolik glorified the Chinese, also dealing with aspects of everyday life, which were often criticised (e.g., the unpleasant smell). The comparisons with Europe are also very important. In the previously quoted fragment, the Great Wall was dwarfing European fortifications, now the Chinese traits which allowed them to build the majestic structure are presented as enabling them to colonise lands inhabitable for Europeans. Being very favourable for the Chinese, the analysed account still remains in the framework of European imperial discourse. As David Spurr points out, at the end of the classical period classification moved to the assessment of "a character based on the internal principle" (Spurr 1993: 63). While observing a phenomenon, a deep root is being looked for. "Such a system of understanding—one that orders natural beings according to function and establishes a hierarchy based on internal character—has consequences for the classification of human races in the Western mind" (Spurr 1993: 63). Smolik is prompted by an observation of the Wall to classify its builders and prescribe some essential characteristics to them.

Finally, the Polish traveller presented a sharp criticism of European imperialism that is also analogical to Jovanović's views. He wrote that "a white barbarian" was trying in vain to teach the Chinese how to kill, as the East Asians are a great nation without such instincts (Smolik 1921: 132). A moral, social and state discipline made Chinese human, while "white tigers from the West" were not humanised by Christianity even after two thousand years (Smolik 1921: 133). By describing Europeans as "barbarians", Smolik seemed to adopt the Chinese point of view, although it should be noted that he also projected Western ideas on China. Colonising new lands, civilising mission and humanism are seen as merits of value. Furthermore, his views on the Chinese can be treated as a reinvention of the "noble savage". He appreciated the achievements of the Chinese civilisation, but while writing about people he used a patronising tone, calling "a Chinese" a child who did not know the value of his deeds. As Spurr states, Western writers' idealization of extra-European peo-

---

[12] „Chińczyk [...] łagodny i wesoły, jak dziecię i jak tylko dziecię dziś u nas uczciwy; pracowity ponad wszelką naszą europejską miarę, przywiązany gorąco do rodziny i do swej ziemi, [...] rozmnaża się niby piasek w morzu, i zaludnia wciąż nowe dziewicze i jałowe przestrzenie Azji, przed któremi cofa się biały człowiek ze strachem, i w które wnosi on cicho swą cudowną, odwieczną kulturę, [...]. Zaiste — naród to godny, by go uwielbiać i naśladować, pomimo niemiłego zapachu czosnku i oleju z bobów [...]".

ples in a "noble savage" style was often prompted by a crisis of their own culture, so Smolik's apotheosis of the Chinese can be linked with experiencing the horrors of the First World War. Criticism of the West and glorification of China were conducted within a Western worldview, which is not surprising, considering that his stay in East Asia was a relatively short episode in Smolik's life.

Emphasising Chinese Troubles

An inversion of Jovanović's and Symonolewicz's thoughts can be found in a description of the trip to the Great Wall written by the well-known Polish architect Stefan Bryła (1886–1943) from his book *Daleki Wschód* (The Far East). This author also used the Great Wall to formulate a general conclusion on the Chinese culture, although his assessment was totally different. Bryła visited a section of the Great Wall near Beijing. His account began with a description of the landscape, and it expressed esteem for the fascinating setting. Yet a closer examination of the structure led Bryła to a claim of its futility.

> "Its [the Wall's] cobbled surface is made out of big, mighty stones. They still hold, but moss and weeds have squeezed among them; and time started to bite them. It has made huge breaches already [...]. Guards do not stand at the gate. The wall is just a trace and a witness of an enormous, not very productive work, but will not fulfill its role. It did not fulfill it in the days of yore, two and a half centuries ago!"[13] (Bryła 1923: 178).

During the trip, while observing Chinese workers and comparing them with his experience in America, the architect-turned-writer claimed that the Chinese did not know how to work because their diligence was just a routine repetition of actions. Where Smolik and Jovanović praised diligence and perseverance, Bryła saw only the lack of innovation. Jovanović extolled the continuity in Chinese work, Bryła despised it, saying that small toys started by a grandfather and finished by a grandson resulted in disrespect for time and punctuality (Bryła 1923: 181). This is also reflected in thinking about the Great Wall. Smolik saw it as a great structure which protected China from barbarians and overshadowed European fortifications, whereas Bryła emphasised

---

[13] „Bruk jego z wielkich potężnych kamieni. Jeszcze trzymają się, ale już wcisnęły się pomiędzy nie mchy i chwasty; a czas je gryźć poczyna. Wyrwy poczynił już wielkie [...]. U bramy straż już nie stoi. Mur jest tylko śladem i świadkiem ogromnej, niezbyt produkcyjnej pracy, ale roli swej spełnić już me zdoła. Nie zdołał jeszcze ongi przed półtrzecia wiekiem!".

the fact that the Wall was in ruins and had been ineffective. The architect disquisition was crowned by using the Wall as a symbol of Chinese backwardness and isolation. Between the Middle Kingdom and the rest of the World, there was the Great Wall of China, stronger than a stone one, which had not been crossed yet. Chinese must demolish it themselves (Bryła 1923: 182). The usage of the Wall as a symbol of barriers preventing communication between the Middle Kingdom and the world can also be encountered in the works of another Polish traveller, who visited China in the first half from the 20th century, a well-known sinologist Witold Jabłoński (1901–1957)[14]; however, this author wrote about "the wall of our prejudices": "Thousands of our prejudices and biases separated us then from China with a wall more unreachable than the famous Great Wall of China"[15] (Jabłoński 1958: 201).

A Sublime Experience

The works of Jovanović, Smolik, and Bryła used the Great Wall as a pretext to make a general statement about the Chinese civilisation. This dimension is also present in an account by Milutin Velimirović (1893–1973), but the dominant feature is his emotions. Velimirović stayed in China in 1918 as a member of a Russian-Mongolian trade mission, and in this period he also visited Mongolia and Japan (Pušić 2006: 129–30). Descriptions of the Great Wall can be found in two Velimirović's travelogues – *Kroz Kinu* (Through China) and *Po Japanu i Mongoliji* (In Japan and Mongolia)[16]. A fragment of the first book is the most interesting:

> "The Great Wall of China is one of the wonders of the world, created by human hand. It leaves an extraordinary and heavy impression; a thought is strange itself, that the Wall spreads for three thousand kilometres, winding on mountain slopes and crossing streams and deserts, and was build 230 years BC.

---

[14] On Jabłoński biography and research, see Golik 2009.

[15] „Wtedy tysiące naszych uprzedzeń i przesądów oddzielało nas od Chin murem bardziej niedostępnym niż słynny Mur Chiński".

[16] For more about the image of China in Velimirović's works, see Ewertowski 2015.

> This Great Wall, which is over 11 meters high and on which a few carriages can pass each other, was to defend China against invasions [...]" (Velimirović 1930: 23)[17].

Even if Velimirović reproduced information about the length and history analogically to others, still his emotional tone made a difference. He admired the Wall, but simultaneously he was overwhelmed by its hugeness. This feeling can be described using the theory of the sublime. The sublime creates excitement and may appear to contravene the limits of one's power of judgment, so it is called an outrage on the imagination (Kant 2004: 132). The greatness of the Wall is such an outrage, and so it left a heavy and extraordinary impression on Velimirović. Later he also claimed that the majesty of the Wall was transformed into "incomprehensibility" (Velimirović 1930: 24).

Still, there was one more side of the edifice which gave Velimirović bad feelings. He mentioned that not infrequently workers rioted because of hunger. Unrests were brutally quashed, and hundreds of men were buried in the Wall.

Nevertheless, his final words on the Wall are full of appreciation. He even stated that their grandeur and boldness could be compared only with the canals on the surface of Mars, thus elevating the structure on an interplanetary level. Furthermore, contrary to Bryła's thought about a destruction of the barrier, Velimirović claimed that even if the ancient walls were not in good shape, the damage was caused by people, not the time. Thus, to Velimirović the Great Wall was a timeless monument, and he remarked that only Chinese patience and workforce could finish such a colossal work. As we see, in this way he classified the essence of the Chinese national character on the basis of the observation of the Great Wall, like other authors.

In terms of emotions, we can compare his account with the passionate words of a Polish aristocrat Paweł Sapieha (1860–1934), who travelled in Asia in 1888–1889[18]. Sapieha made a journey from China to Mongolia and observed various fortifications, all of which were treated as Chinese walls. A fragment devoted to "the furthest, the oldest, great wall of China" is the most

---

[17] „Veliki kineski zid – to je jedno od zemaljskih čuda, koje je stvoreno čovečjom rukom! On ostavlja neobičan i težak utisak; čudnovata je i sama pomisao da se taj zid prostire u dužinu od 3300 kilometara, vijugajući po planinskim kosama i prolazeći preko strmeni i pustinje, a da je sagrađen 230 god. pre Hrista!/ Taj Veliki zid, koji je visok preko 11 metara i na komes e, na bedemu mogu nekoliko kola mimoići, trebao je da zaštiti Kinu od najezda [...]".

[18] See Mazan 2010.

interesing: "An unheard, magnificent view. We are on a great altitude, I am sitting under a half-ruined, completely black fort, under my foot [there is] this ancient wall, today only a heap of blacked stones marks a place where the wall was"[19] (Sapieha 1899: 307). Then followed a description of a scenery "[...] further away there are mountains, rocks are piling over terraces higher and higher, up to clouds, from which far away, [...] magnificent, sapphire peaks are protruding – they are probably Himalayas!"[20] (Sapieha 1899: 307). According to Grażyna Królikiewicz, within romantic perception ruins belonged simultaneously to culture and nature, and contemplation of them showed a mechanism of memory and imagination (Królikiewicz 1993). We can see it in Sapieha's account. His imagination, impressed by a crumbling wall and the scenery, was able to see the Himalayas, despite the fact that they were a few thousand kilometres away. This incomparable experience is expressed once again at the end of the fragment devoted to the Wall:

> "I have never seen in my life anything equal to this view, anything so touching. After all, I had a third of Asia at my feet, in front of my eyes: these two colossi, China and Mongolia. Behind Mongolia one can also feel the third: the "holy" Russia [...] I admit that sitting there and watching and involuntarily looking if somewhere in this expense I will not see the lord of these worlds, Satan, I was trembling as a leaf – whether because of cold, or because of emotions, let others judge; but only they, who can look at such colossi and expanses with an eye different from an ordinary tourist"[21].

Analogically to Velimirović, the Wall and the view from it gave Sapieha a feeling of the sublime, which overwhelmed a subject, so it felt deeply moved and vulnerable, "trembling as a leaf". Postcolonial analyses of writings con-

---

[19] „Widok niesłychany, przepyszny. Jesteśmy na wysokości ogromnej; siedzę pod rozwalonym na poły, zupełnie zczerniałym karaułem; u stóp moich ów prastary mur, dziś już kupa kamieni zczerniałych, znaczy zaledwie miejsce gdzie stał mur".

[20] „[...].dalej znowu góry, skały piętrzą się terasami coraz wyżej aż pod chmury, z których [...] sterczą szafirowe teraz, przepyszne szczyty — to już chyba Himalaje!".

[21] „Nic równego jak ten widok, nic tak przejmującego w życiu nie widziałem. Wszak prawie trzecią część Azyi miałem u stóp, przed oczami: te dwa kolosy, Chiny i Mongolię. Za Mongolią czuć mimowoli trzeciego: Rosyę «świętą»! [...] Wyznaję, że siedząc tu i patrząc i mimowoli szukając, czy gdzie w tem przestworzu nie ujrzę unoszącego się pana tych światów, szatana, dygotałem jak listek — czy z zimna, czy ze wzruszenia, niech osądzą inni; ale ci tylko, co umieją na takie kolosy i przestworza innem jak zwykłem okiem turysty spoglądać".

cerning an observation of a landscape introduce a rhetoric gesture of "monarch of all I survey" (Spurr 1993: 17–9; Pratt 2011: 283–92). In this kind of stylistic manner, a writer proceeds with an aesthetic, or economic valorisation of the landscape and turns a foreign country into a painting, thus expressing the idea of domination. Some aspects of this rhetoric can be seen in Sapieha's account, although his writing lacks of a strong colonial subject. Sapieha was not a Victorian explorer with the ideology of the British Empire in his backpack, but rather a romantic-minded traveller concentrated on a subjective experience of the sublime. This kind of sensitivity is also expressed by a contrast between the elitist look of the traveller and an ordinary tourist gaze. This dichotomy is typical of the 19th century and 20th-century travel writing and is often used to emphasise a distinction between a subject and "others" in many fields, including a class (Gvozden 2011: 187–207). As it might be expected, Sapieha, an aristocrat, presented himself as a sensible traveller in opposition to an ordinary tourist. Another very interesting figure is the reference to Satan as "the lord of these worlds". Such a formula adds sublimity to the described landscape in a way which can be associated with conventions of dark romanticism. It can also be read as a reflection of a tradition which has its roots in the Middle Ages, in which distant Asian lands were presented as belonging to evil powers.

Imaginative History and Geography

Another author who modified geography while standing on the Wall was the Polish reporter Roman Fajans (1903–1976), one of the most highly regarded Polish reporters of the 1930s (Szczygieł 2015: 261). The journalist visited China in 1937–1938. In his book *W Chinach znowu wojna* (A war in China once again) he described a trip to a section of the Great Wall next to Beijing. He was very impressed by the landscape, but analogically to Bryła, he wrote that the fortifications were empty. He called them an effect of the Emperor's despotic whim (Fajans 1939: 312), a waste of resources and manpower. But had it not been for the Emperor's urge, "we would not have one of the most great and picturesque panoramas in the world" (Fajans 1939: 313)[22]. The view is breathtaking: "looking towards the four sides of the world, we gaze towards Mongo-

[22] „jednej z najpotężniejszych i najbardziej malowniczych panoram, jakie istnieją na świecie".

lian steppe and towards Che-li, towards Tibet and the fertile lowlands of South China" (Fajans 1939: 313)[23].

Fajans had a double point of view. On the one hand, in terms of rational analysis, he saw the Wall as a useless extravagance of the Emperor and a place of people's suffering. On the other hand, he was deeply impressed by the aesthetic qualities of the edifice and, in a similar way to Sapieha, he imagined new geography, linking distant lands. To some extent, this can be seen as an effect of a strong connection between the Wall and the idea of the border. Looking at the structure with this idea in one's mind inspired imaginative geography, in which fortifications became a boundary between faraway territories.

In Fajans's and Sapieha's works we encountered examples of imaginative geography, in Serbian traveller's Miodrag Rajčević's account, we read an imaginative history. Of course, as Hayden White shows, history is, in general, a narration, so inevitably it involves storytelling and imagination. The majority of analysed authors reproduced popular myths about the structure, and they could not be blamed for it because they simply used knowledge which was available to them. However, if we agree that imaginative geography and history are „helping mind to intensify its own sense of itself by dramatizing the distance and difference between what is close to it and what is far away" (Said 1977: 55), Rajčević still can be singled out because his travelogue contained the best example of such a process of intensifying one's identity, even if his method consists in linking, rather than dramatising a difference. This Serbian author was a globetrotter who travelled around the world in the first half of the 20th century for a few years. While writing about the Great Wall, Rajčević revived a famous myth that the Rome fall because China built the Wall, thus redirecting Huns to the West. Rajčević went even further, implicitly linking all historical invasions from Asia to Europe with the building of the Wall, claiming that because of the Chinese fortifications Serbs had been suffering under a Turkish rule since the Kosovo battle in 1389 (Rajčević 1930: 113–4). An imaginative history of the Wall acted as a trigger for the expression of Serbian identity.

---

[23] „Widok za to jest z góry niezrównany: patrząc w cztery strony świata, spoglądamy ku mongolskim stepom i ku Cze-li, ku przedpolom Tybetu i ku żyznym nizinom Chin południowych".

In the Eyes of a Reporter

The last author whose accounts will be examined here is another reporter, but also a poet and an editor, Aleksander Janta-Połczyński (1908–1974), who in the 1930s wrote two books about his travels in Asia: *Ziemia jest okrągła* (The Earth is round) and *Na kresach Azji* (On the frontiers of Asia)[24]. *Na kresach Azji* pays more attention to the Great Wall. Janta recognised that the Wall could make a big impression, but his attitude is to some extent different from the other analysed authors, as he is more critical towards stereotypes. As he wrote, while seeing the Wall the third time in his life, he laughed at some news about these fortifications from the European press, e.g., about the idea of building a highway on the top of the structure (Janta-Połczyński 1939: 173). While giving information about the visibility from Mars, he indicated its source, Hendrik van Loon's *Geography.* The writer also claimed that it was surprising that there had not been an expedition along a whole Wall, from Shanhaiguan into the depths of Mongolia, where the Wall allegedly ends. According to Janta, such an expedition could discover how long and how full of tangles fortifications are. His research interest and his scepticism made him quite different from the other analysed authors, nonetheless, we can still notice some inaccuracies, e.g., the expedition projected by Janta had been already conducted at the beginning of the 20th century (Geil 1909).

Conclusion

The accounts analysed above have a number of common features, especially reproducing historical myths or being impressed by the sheer size and length of the Wall along with the spectacular setting. However, the authors' views depended on their individual predilections, their personalities as well as the social and intellectual background. The best example is a comparison between Bryła's criticism and Smolik's and Jovanović's idealisation. Writers of romantic sensibility are more emotional and can be carried away by the sublime nature of the fortifications like Velimirović and Sapieha did. Imaginative history and geography of the Wall can enhance subject's identity, the most telling example being Rajčević. In the field of imperial rhetoric, authors whose identities are strongly linked with great powers seem to be much more critical towards Chinese and full of self-confidence, like Vladislavić. This variety of approaches is very significant. Robert Dawson entitled his book on European conceptions of China *The Chinese Chameleon*, and the Great Wall also constitutes such a chameleon.

---

[24] For more information about Janta-Połczyński, see Palowski 1990.

Bibliography

Bantysh-Kamienskij, Nikolaj [=Бантыш-Каменский, Николай] (1882). *Дипломатическое собрание дел между российским и китайским государствами с 1619 по 1792 гг.* Казань: Типография Императорского Университета.

Bryła, Stefan (1923). *Daleki Wschód.* Lwów: Księgarnia Naukowa.

Cabanowski, Marek (1993). *Tajemnice Mandżurii. Polacy w Harbinie.* Warszawa: Muzeum Niepodległości.

Cyrzyk, Leszek (1966). "Literatura podróżnicza o Chinach w Polsce XIX w.". *Przegląd Orientalistyczny* 3(59): 205–16.

Dawson, Raymond (1967). *The Chinese Chameleon. An Analysis of European Conceptions of Chinese Civilisation.* New York: Oxford University Press.

Dučić, Jovan (2004). *Grof Sava Vladislavić: Jedan Srbin Diplomat na dvoru Petra Velikog i Katarine I.* Valjevo: Glas Crkve.

Ewertowski, Tomasz (2014). "Slika Kine u'Tajnoj informaciji o snazi i stanju Kineskog Carstva' Save Vladislavića". *Dositejev Vrt* 2: 71–93.

—— (2015). "Cultural Exchange between China and the West from the Perspectve of Two Eastern European Travelers – Travelogues of Milutin Velimirovic and Konstanty Symonolewicz". In: 第三届 '利玛窦写中文化交流' 国际学术研过会论文集. Guangzhou: Sun Yat-Sen University Press.

—— (2016). "The Image of the Chinese in the Southeast Asian Contact Zone. National Comparisons in the Travelogues of Milan Jovanović and Władysław Michał Zaleski". *Imagologiya i komparativistika* 2(6): 40–57.

Fajans, Roman (1939). *W Chinach znowu wojna.*Warszawa: Rój.

Fogel, Joshua (1996). *The Literature of Travel in The Japanese Rediscovery of China. 1862–1945.* Stanford: Stanford University Press.

Geil, William Edgar (1909). *The Great Wall of China.* New York: Sturgis & Walton Company.

Golik, Katarzyna (2009). "Witold Jabłoński – niesłusznie zapomniany polski sinolog". *Azja-Pacyfik* 12: 218–229.

Gvozden, Vladimir (2011). *Srpska putopisna kultura 1914–1940. Studija o hronotopičnosti susreta.* Beograd: Službeni Glasnik.

Huigen, Siegfried (2009). *Knowledge and Colonialism: Eighteenth-century Travellers in South Africa.* Leiden; Boston.

Hvistendahl, Mary (2008). *Is China's Great Wall Visible from Space?* Scientific American. On line publication available at: Https://Www.Scientificamerican.Com/Article/Is? Chinas?Great?Wall?Visible?From?Space [Accessed: April 8, 2017].

Jabłoński, Witold (1958). "Przed ćwierćwieczem po niezmierzonych obszarach Chin (1932)". In: *Ze wspomnień podróżników.* Ed. Bolesław Olszewski. Warszawa: Wiedza Powszechna.

Janta-Połczyński, Aleksander (1939). *Na kresach Azji.* Warszawa: Rój.

Jovanović, Milan (1895). *Tamo amo po Istoku. Sveska druga.* Beograd: Srpska književna zadruga.

Kajdański, Edward (2005). *Długi cień Wielkiego Muru: Jak Polacy odkrywali Chiny.* Warszawa: Oficyna Naukowa.

Kałuski, Marian (2001). *Polacy w Chinach.* Warszawa: Instytut Wydawniczy Pax.

Kant, Immanuel (2004). *Krytyka władzy sądzenia.* Trans. Jerzy Gałecki. Warszawa: PWN.

Kapija od žada. Putopisi Srba o Kini: 1725–1935 (1998). Beograd: Biblioteka Grada; Želnid.

Kerr, Douglas, and Julia Kuehn (2010). "Introduction". In: *A Century of Travels in China. Critical Essays on Travel Writing from the 1840s to the 1940s.* Ed. Douglas Kerr and Julia Kuehn. Hong Kong: Hong Kong University Press.

Kosanović, Bogdan (2009). *Sava Vladislavić-Raguzinski u svom i našem vremenu.* Beograd: Svet Knjige.

Kostadinović, Aleksandar (2012). "Putnička projekcija intime (Putopisna priča Milana Jovanovića Morskog)". In: *Filologija i univerzitet. Tematski zbornik radova.* Ed. Bojana Dimitrijević. Niš: Filozofski Fakultet.

Królikiewicz, Grażyna (1993). *Terytorium ruin. Ruina jako obraz i temat romantyczny.* Kraków: Universitas.

Lovell, Julia (2006). *The Great Wall. China Against The World 1000 Bc–Ad 2000.* New York: Grove Press.

López-Gil, Norberto (2008). "Is it Really Possible to See the Great Wall of China from Space with a Naked Eye?". *Journal of Optometry* 1: 3–4.

Lukin, Aleksandr Vladimirovich [=Лукин, Александр Владимирович] (2007). *Медведь наблюдает за драконом. Образ Китая в России в XVII-XXI веках.* Москва: Восток-Запад: АСТ.

Mackerras, Colin (1989). *Western Images of China.* Oxford, New York: Oxford University Press.

Maksimović, Goran (2008). "Putopisna proza Milana Jovanovića Morskog". Zbornik *Matice Srpske za književnost i jezik* LVI: 623–38. Online Publication Available At: Http://Scindeks.Nb.Rs/Article.Aspx?Artid=0543-12200803623m [Accessed: September 4, 2012].

Mancall, Mark (1971). *Russia and China: Their Diplomatic Relations to 1728.* Cambridge, Massachusetts: Harvard University Press.

Mazan, Bogdan (2010). "„Opisać… niepodobna". Z notat podróżnych arystokraty galicyjskiego o Chinach końca XIX wieku (Paweł Sapieha „Podróż na wschód Azji 1888–1889")". In: *Europejczyk w podróży 1850–1939.* Ed. Ewa Ihnatowicz and Stefan Ciara. Warszawa: Neriton.

Myasnikov, Vladimir Stepanovich [=Мясников, Владимир Степанович] (1990). "Посольство С. Л. Владиславича-Рагузинского в Пекин", *Русско-китайские отношения в XVIII веку. Том Ii. 1725–1727,* In Владимир Степанович Мясников (Ed.). Москва: Наука.

Palowski, Franciszek (1990). *Aleksander Janta-Połczyński. Ballada o wiecznym szukaniu.* Warszawa–Kraków: PWN.

Podnebesko carstvo. Srbi o Kini 1725–1940 (Putopisi i članci) (2006). Beograd: Čigoja Štampa.

Pratt, Mary Louise (2011). *Imperialne spojrzenie: Pisarstwo podróżnicze a transkulturacja.* Trans. Ewa Elżbieta Nowakowska. Kraków: Wydawnictwo Uniwersytetu Jagiellońskiego.

Rajčević, Milorad (1930). *Na Dalekom Istoku. Beograd*: Štamparija 'Đura Jakšić'.

Russko-kitajskije otnosheniya u XVIII vyeku. Tom III. 1727–1729 [=*Русско-китайские отношения у XVIII веку. Том III. 1727–1729*] (2006). Москва: Российская Академия Наук, Институт Дальнего Востока. Министерство Иностранных Дел РФ, Историко-документальный департамент. Федеральное Агентство Архивов РФ.

Said, Edward (1977). *Orientalism.* London: Penguin.

Sapieha, Paweł (1899). *Podróż na wschód Azyi.* Lwów: Księgarnia Gubrynowicza i Schmidta.

Sindik, Dušan (2012). "Zanimljivosti iz života grofa Save Vladislavića". *Glas* 420. Beograd: SANU, Odeljenje Istorijskih Nauka: 197–208.

Smolik, Przecław (1921). *Przez lądy i oceany. Sześć lat na Dalekim Wschodzie.* Warszawa–Kraków: Księgarnia J. Czarneckiego.

Spence, Jonathan (1998). *The Chan's Great Continent. China in Western Minds.* London: W.W. Norton.

Spurr, David (1993). *The Rhetoric of Empire. Colonial Discourse in Journalism, Travel Writing, and Imperial Administration.* Durham: Duke University Press.

Tartalja, Ivo (1984). "Jedan zaboravljen majstor srpske proze iz perioda ranog realizma". *Naučni sastanak slavista u Vukove Dane, Zbornik radova* 13/2: 129–36.

The Great Wall of China (2017). On-line publication available at: Http://Whc.Unesco.Org/En/ List/438 [Accessed: April 8, 2017].

Velimirović, Milutin (1930). *Kroz Kinu: Putopis.* Beograd: S. B. Cvijanović.

Vladislavić, Sava (2011). *Tajna informacija o snazi i stanju kineske države.* Секретная информацiя о силѣ и состоянiи китайскаго государства. Ed. Vladimir Davidović. Beograd: Radio-Televizija Srbije.

Waldron, Arthur (1990). *The Great Wall of China. From History to Myth.* Cambridge: Cambridge University Press.

Chapter 13

Ar-Riḥla in the Service of *An-Nahḍa*. Rifā ʻa aṭ-Ṭahṭāwī's Concept of Crossing Geographical and Cultural Boundaries

Magdalena Lewicka, *Nicolaus Copernicus University/Poland*

Arabic travel literature (*adab ar-riḥlāt*) developed from the 9th century alongside other genres of geographical literature such as encyclopaedias and dictionaries, works of descriptive and analytical geography (Kraczkowski 1963: 19–21; Ḍayf 1987: 11–67; Bielawski 1995: 183–190, 241–243; Al-Mawāfī 1995: 21–30, 35–47; Bosworth 1999: 778–780; Walter 2008: 99–110). Its development was facilitated by the high mobility of medieval Arabs and other inhabitants of the caliphate moving across the enormous, at that time, the territory of *dār al-islām* and beyond. Travels were undertaken for personal and business reasons as a result of various factors of a political, religious and social character. There were a few basic goals of these travels, including commercial contacts, diplomatic missions, postal service, the obligatory pilgrimage to Mecca, a desire to acquire knowledge from scholars residing in metropolises such as Mecca, Baghdad, Damascus, Jerusalem, Cairo and Tunis, exploring unknown territories for various reasons or, finally, a desire to experience adventure and face challenges connected with travelling to faraway lands (Ḍayf 1987: 8–10; Al-Samaany 2002: 19–21).

The first proper description of a journey in Arabic literature, translated in its entirety into Polish, (Ibn Fadlan 1985), was written by Ibn Faḍlān. He presented his journey to the north, to the country of the Volga Bulgars in the years 821–822. Little is known about the author except for the fact that he was accompanying the envoys of the Abbasid Caliph Al-Muqtadir, and his account is a valuable source of ethnographic information on the pagan Turkish peoples whose territories he crossed, as well as the Volga Bulgars (Walter 2008: 106, for a detailed description of the account, see Bahayy 2006).

From the 12th century, the term *riḥla* was used to denote descriptions of travels by Andalusian and Maghrebi scholars to the East which they found particularly appealing as a more developed region in terms of learning and culture. The best known work of this kind, recorded by Ibn Ǧuzayy, the secretary of the court of the Marinid Sultan of Fez (Ibn Battuta 2008), describes the nearly thirty-year journey of Abū 'Abd Allāh Muḥammad Ibn Baṭṭūṭa, the most famous mediaeval Arab author-traveller whose travels took him to the most distant places at that time. During his seven expeditions, between his journey from Tangier to Mecca across northern Africa, Egypt and Syria in 1325 and his last journey in the years 1352–1353, he explored the lands of Europe, Asia and Africa, gathering knowledge about the everyday life of people in the whole Arab and Muslim world of the day and beyond it[1].

Account of a Journey by Ibn Ǧubayr (1145–1217), describing his journey to Mecca in the years 1183–1185, is regarded as a model work of this kind. The author explains that the pilgrimage from Granada to Mecca via Alexandria is his penance for surrendering to the temptation to drink wine. Hence, one-third of the account is devoted to pilgrimage rituals and life in the holy cities Mecca and Medina[2]. He spent over a year there and, after an eventful stay in Syria and Iraq, came back to Spain. The exemplary character of Ibn Ǧubayr's work was reflected in the repeated inclusion of fragments of his text in other travel accounts, such as *Riḥla* by Ibn Baṭṭūṭa, already mentioned above (Walter 2008: 109; Chapter *Riḥla* [in:] Dunn 2012).

With regard to content, classic travel accounts share characteristics such as providing information on the condition of the roads, possibility, and safety of travel; information on the current political situation in the lands visited; information on the level of development of the areas and cities visited, including the functioning of trade and agriculture; information on the life of the people inhabiting the regions visited, particularly scholars and clergy; presenting extraordinary, unusual events (Moudden 1990: 69–76; Al-Mawāfī 1995: 48–57; Al-Samaany 2002: 201–237; Garden 2015: 1–17).

---

[1] Among studies devoted to Ibn Baṭṭūṭa's travel accounts, it is worth noting Dunn 2012. For brief mentions, see also: Kraczkowski 1963: 425–431; Kowalska 1973: 118–132; Ḍayf 1987: 95–122; Bielawski 1995: 289; Qindīl 2002: 488–528; Al-Samaany 2002: 40–41; Euben 2008: 47–89; Walter 2008: 108–109.

[2] For more information on Ibn Ǧubayr's travel account, it is worth noting Netton 1991. For mentions of this account, see also Ḍayf 1987: 70–94; Bielawski 1995: 243; Qindīl 2002: 384–405; Walter 2008: 108.

In terms of form, the characteristics of classic travel accounts include the presentation of events by a narrator who was also the protagonist of *riḥla* from the perspective of personal observation and experience as the basic research and narrative technique; borrowing of information from other authors of travel accounts; finally, the tendency to cross genre boundaries manifested in the inclusion of autobiographical, biographical, journalist, encyclopaedic or poetic fragments in the travel account (Kraczkowski 1963: 24; Al-Samaany 2002: 250; ʿAbd ar-Raḥīm 2006: 40–42; Šuʿayb 2006: 48–49).

With regard to structure, classic travel accounts typically consist of a preface with a characteristic invocation to God and Prophet Muḥammad and definition of the goal of the travel; conclusion of the work with the formula of thanksgiving to God for his assistance in its completion and indication of the completion date; finally, the author's organisation of the material in the main part of the work, i.e. division of chapters according to temporal, spatial or thematic units (Al-Mawāfī 1995: 63–67, 68–74; Al-Samaany 2002: 247–249).

All these distinguishing characteristics can be found in Rifāʿa aṭ-Ṭahṭāwī's account of his stay in Paris, with the classical title *Kitāb taḫlīṣ al-ibrīz fī talḫīṣ Bārīz (Extraction of Pure Gold or a Short Description of Paris)*[3]. This account was first published on the eve of reforms in Arab countries, in the 19th century marked by the confrontation between the developed and increasingly influential West and the Arab and Muslim world, stagnating and surrendering to European supremacy. The inevitability of this confrontation and the profound awareness of the Muslim community's helplessness against the dominance of the West were at the basis of every subsequent Arab political concept and became the driving force behind the effort to regain the previous position of power that had played a special role in the Islamic world-view since the dawn of time[4]. Such a path was sought by Aṭ-Ṭahṭāwī,[5] a reformer who, similarly to

---

[3] The author gave two titles to this work: *Kitāb taḫlīṣ al-ibrīz fī talḫīṣ Bārīz* (Extraction of Pure Gold or a Short Description of Paris) and *Ad-Dīwān an-nafīs bi-īwān Bārīs* (Precious Carpet in a Paris Salon). It was first published in print by Al-Būlāq publishing house in 1834, then in 1849; the next edition was not published until 1974. In recent years, it was reissued several times; the author of this article cites the work based on the volume published by Dār al-Hilāl in 2001.

[4] The times of the Arab Renaissance as well as the social and intellectual background of the epoch are presented in, for example, Aš-Šayyāl 1951; Al-Ḥuṣrī 1960; Mūsà 1973; ʿAbd al-Malik 1978; Šarābī 1978; Al-Qāḍī, Ṣawwāh 1992; Lewis 1993; Lewis 1995; Mūsā 1995; ʿAmmāra 1997; Hourani 1998; Ḥūrānī 2001; Hourani 2002; ʿAmmāra 2003; Lewis 2003; Jamsheer 2008; Jamsheer 2009; Lewicka 2012a; Lewicka 2014a; Lewicka 2015.

other representatives of the nineteenth-century Arab Renaissance,[6] was deeply affected by the situation of his native Egypt and the entire world of Islam at that time. That is why he focused on analysing the reasons for the backwardness and the mechanisms leading to the renewed development of this civilisation and its restoration to its due place on the international stage. Convinced that Europe's development and wealth did not stem from the philosophical and religious system, but only from knowledge and rationalism, he called for taking advantage of them in order to steer the Arab and Muslim world out of its crisis on the one hand and, on the other, to find their source in Sharia law to reconcile them with Islam and traditional Muslim political theory.

His reformatory ideas became part of an interesting discussion which had been going on in the Arab and Muslim world since the beginning of the 19th century. The discussion was centred around very important matters concerning the political system, social and political reforms, comparison of the representative system and democracy with their antithesis – despotism as well as a search for the way out of stagnation and backwardness, which essentially included the reform of the educational system – an idea emphasised by all thinkers. His objective was to find the answer to the basic question facing the representatives of the Muslim world: the question about the reason for its decline and backwardness, the basis of European supremacy considering the role of the oppressive governments, anachronistic state structures, lack of modern school system and other issues and, most of all, the crystallisation of the ideas and notions concerning the relationship between tradition and modernity[7].

---

[5] On the life and work of the reformer, see Aš-Šayyāl 1958; Ḥiğāzī 1974; Altman 1976; ʻAmmāra 1984; An-Naṣr 1987; Abū Ḥamdān 1992; Jamsheer 2008; Jamsheer 2009; ʻAmmāra 2010; Lewicka 2012b; Lewicka 2014a.

[6] Ğamāl ad-Dīn al-Afğānī (1838–1897), Muḥammad ʻAbduh (1849–1905), Aḥmad Ḫān (1817–1898), Muḥammad Iqbāl (1877–1938), ʻAbd al-Raḥmān al-Kawākibī (1855–1902), Muḥammad Rašīd Riḍà (1865–1935), Ḫayr ad-Dīn at-Tūnusī (1822–1890). On the key representatives of Arab Renaissance, see Amīn 1965; Husry 1966; Abū Ḥamdān 1992–1994; Danecki 2007; Jamsheer 2008; Jamsheer 2009.

[7] What is significant in this context is that Aṭ-Ṭahṭāwī combined two personalities—that of a thinker and an actor of socio-political life thanks to holding several public functions in education and culture: he was a lecturer at Al-Azhar, an imam of the Egyptian Army and a cleric of the Egyptian student missions in Paris, a translator at specialist schools in Cairo, the director of Madrasat al-Alsun language school, the editor-in-chief of "Al-Waqā'iʻ al-Miṣriyya" ("Egyptian News"), a translator and coordinator of

He was one of the first Arab thinkers to observe the modern civilisation of the West with great discernment and awareness[8]. However, his views on the state and society were neither a simple reflection of the ideas he became familiar with abroad nor a repetition of the traditional, religious outlook, but, rather, an attempt at working out a compromise between European models and the law of *aš-šarī'a* and embedding it in the Muslim tradition. This method was based on the necessity to prove that, firstly, European knowledge and sciences had belonged to the Arab and Muslim world before being taken over by the West and, secondly, there was no contradiction between faith and modernity. Quite to the contrary, the development of the state and society was part of the religious duties of the government that should ensure the pursuit of the common good, development of public assets and public services, prevalence of justice, elimination of injustice and oppression, respect of civil liberties and support of economic activity and civic engagement. Thus, his admiration for European political thought concerning power and society as well as legal, political and social systems did not imply the abandonment or indifference to Muslim tradition. On the contrary, this admiration was based on the conviction that, since the dawn of time, the socio-political thought of Islam had been advocating ideas that formed the cornerstone of the European Enlightenment thought. Thus, his socio-political thought was based on the ideas of the Great French Revolution and the principle that the nation should benefit from political and personal freedom while the mechanisms regulating the relations between the government and society should be based on the respect for the laws. The rulers and the ruled *(al-ḥākim wa-al-maḥkūm)* constitute, in the opinion of Aṭ-Ṭahṭāwī, two cornerstones of the state, mutually complementary and having mutual interests, i.e., relationships of rights and duties of one group towards the other: "The government is like the soul and the people are like the body and the body does not exist without the soul (Aṭ-Ṭahṭāwī 2002: 101).

translations of European works into Arabic, an author of textbooks, a member of successive education committees and the initiator of several educational and cultural institutions.

[8] For five years (1826–1831) Aṭ-Ṭahṭāwī stayed in Paris as an imam accompanying the mission of Egyptian scholarship holders.

In *Kitāb taḫlīṣ al-ibrīz fī talḫīṣ Bārīz,*[9] a work that was the only detailed description of a European country in Arabic until 1834 and, until World War One, was on the required reading list for all Egyptian clerks and officials, Aṭ-Ṭahṭāwī presents the political, social, cultural and educational institutions that he encountered in Paris and regarded as a model worth replicating in his homeland, in accordance with the *ahadith* "Seek knowledge even as far as China" (Aṭ-Ṭahṭāwī 2002: 18) and "Wisdom is the weapon of the believer, he seeks it everywhere, even among non-believers" (Aṭ-Ṭahṭāwī 2002: 18), as well as the Arabic adage: "He who walks first takes priority" (Aṭ-Ṭahṭāwī 2002: 16).

The book, comprised of six extensive chapters, opens with the *Introduction* (*Al-Muqaddima*) (Aṭ-Ṭahṭāwī 2002: 13–33)[10] where the author, after explaining the reason for the trip to France and confirming the necessity of acquiring knowledge and becoming familiar with the sciences, arts, crafts and manufacturing, describes this country against the background of other European countries and presents the distinguishing features of its inhabitants, based on which France has been chosen as the destination for Egyptian students seeking good education and appropriate civilisation models. As indicated by the first verses of the main part of the volume, appearing right after the *Introduction, Kitāb taḫlīṣ al-ibrīz fī talḫīṣ Bārīz* presents the "journey from Egypt to Paris and extraordinary things that we had the opportunity to see during this journey, the stay in this city filled with all kinds of sciences and arts and astounding justice and extremely virtuous conduct that deserve to become first-rate issues in the world of Islam, in countries where the Shari'a of the Prophet prevails, peace be with Him. And this is the goal contained in the

[9] Translated into English as *An imam in Paris: account of a stay in France by an Egyptian cleric (1826-1831),* trans. Daniel Newman, Saqi, London 2004; into German as *Aṭ-Ṭahṭāwī in Paris: ein Dokument des arabischen Modernismus aus dem frühen 19. Jahrhundert,* trans. Karl Stowasser, Univ. Diss., Münster 1968; into Polish as *Wydobycie czystego złota czyli krótki opis Paryża,* trans. Magdalena Lewicka [under preparation for printing].

[10] The *Introduction* consists of four chapters with the following titles: Chapter One – *On what appears to me as the reason for our journey to that country* [France – M.L.], *in the world of unbelievers, so remote from us and so expensive because of the exorbitant prices* (pp. 14–19), Chapter Two – *concerning the desired sciences and arts* (pp. 20–21), Chapter Three – *On the situation of foreign countries in comparison with other states, on the superiority of the French nation over other nations there, on its designation by our superiors as the destination of our journey among the foreign kingdoms* (pp. 22–31), Chapter Four – *About those who were at the head of our expedition* (pp. 32–33).

subsequent chapters divided into successive subchapters" (Aṭ-Ṭahṭāwī 2002: 33).

In the first chapter, entitled *On what happened from the moment of departure from Egypt to the moment of arrival in Marseilles* (pp. 34–46) and consisting of four subchapters,[11] Aṭ-Ṭahṭāwī writes about Alexandria. Chapter Two, entitled *On what happened from the moment of departure from Marseilles to the moment of arrival in Paris* (pp. 47–56) and divided into just two parts,[12] is devoted to Marseilles, while the third one, entitled *On the arrival in Paris and all that we had the opportunity to see and experience* (pp. 57–198) and consisting of thirteen subchapters,[13] contains a detailed description of France and Paris including the geographical location, natural resources and description of the region and country. This is followed by a presentation of social and welfare issues, including housing conditions and standard of living, kinds of clothing and leisure activities, traditions related to food, religious situation, healthcare and the special interest in medical sciences, charity organisations, progress and achievements in the field of arts and sciences, issues related to state administration including the rights enjoyed by the French, ways of exer-

---

[11] Chapter One – *On the departure from Egypt to the moment of arrival at the port in Alexandria* (p. 35), Chapter Two – *In brief, about the details concerning this city obtained from Arabic and French works and about the details that we believe to be right* (pp. 36–38), Chapter Three – *On the travel across the salty sea connected with the port in Alexandria* (pp. 39–41), Chapter Four – *On the mountains, countries and islands that we had the opportunity to see* (pp. 42–46).

[12] Chapter One – *On our stay in Marseilles* (pp. 48–54), Chapter Two – *On the departure from Marseilles to the moment of arrival in Paris and on the distance between these cities* (pp. 55–56).

[13] Chapter One – *On the map of Paris from the perspective of the city's geographical location, natural conditions, distinguishing features of the region and the country* (pp. 58–75), Chapter Two – *On the inhabitants of Paris* (pp. 76–97), Chapter Three – *On the administration of the French state* (pp. 98–115), Chapter Four – *On the housing customs of the inhabitants of Paris and the resulting issues* (pp. 116–123), Chapter Five – *On the nutrition of the inhabitants of Paris and their customs concerning food and drink* (pp. 124–129), Chapter Six – *On the clothing of the French people* (pp. 130–132), Chapter Seven – *On the parks of Paris* (pp. 133–141), Chapter Eight – *On the health policy in Paris* (pp. 142–144), Chapter Nine – *On medical sciences in Paris* (pp. 145–164), Chapter Ten – *On charity in Paris* (pp. 165–168), Chapter Eleven – *On the achievements and skills of the inhabitants of Paris* (pp. 169–174), Chapter Twelve – *On the religion of the inhabitants of Paris* (pp. 175–178), Chapter Thirteen – *On the progress of the inhabitants of Paris in the field of the arts, sciences and crafts, on their classification and the related issues* (pp. 179–198).

cising judicial, legislative and executive power, as well as the participation of society in the government. In Chapter Four (pp. 199–230), divided into six parts[14] and entitled *On the effort and actions with regard to the required arts that we had to take in order to achieve our goal and that benefited me, on the organisation of term assignments in reading, writing and other sciences, on the considerable costs on the part of the superiors, on my correspondence with educated foreigners about teaching, on the books I read in Paris,* the reformer devotes his attention to the situation of the Egyptian students taking up studies in Paris and the problems facing them during their stay abroad, and then presents his correspondence with representatives of French academia and the works that he became familiar with during his mission. In Chapter Five (pp. 231–258), entitled *On discord in France and the deposition of the king before our return to Egypt* and consisting of seven subchapters,[15] he presents the situation in France: the July Revolution of 1830, deposition of Charles X, and instalment of Louis Philippe I, as well as the socio-political changes resulting from those events. Chapter Six (pp. 259–286), entitled *On the outline of the sciences and arts mentioned in Chapter Two of the Introduction*, and divid-

---

[14] Chapter One – *On what we encountered at the beginning with regard to the system of reading and writing and other sciences* (pp. 202–204), Chapter Two – *About the regulations on leaving the boarding house* (pp. 205–207), Chapter Three – *On our desire to take up work and effort* (pp. 208–210), Chapter Four – *On my correspondence with French scholars* (pp. 211–217), Chapter Five – *On books that I read in Paris, on the method of examination, on what Mr Ǧūmār wrote to me, on what he observed in the results of the last examination* (pp. 218–224), Chapter Six – *On the examinations I took in Paris, particularly the last one that preceded my return to Egypt* (pp. 225–230).

[15] Chapter One – *On the first events that enable the understanding of the reasons why the French people forsook their allegiance to their ruler* (pp. 232–234), Chapter Two – *On the changes that occurred and on the discord that they resulted in* (pp. 235–240), Chapter Three – *How the ruler behaved at the time, on his satisfaction with the settlement as time went by as well as on his dethronement* (pp. 241–243), Chapter Four – *On what caused the difference of opinions and on how the discord led to the handover of royal power to Louis Philippe I* (pp. 244–249), Chapter Five – *On what happened to the ministers who signed the royal decrees that led to the downfall of the rule of the first king who committed what he committed , on the unforeseen effects and on the covetousness that did not prevail* (pp. 250–253), Chapter Six – *On the French people's mocking of Charles X following that discord and the resultant dissatisfaction among the French* (pp. 254–256), Chapter Seven – *On the response of foreign countries to the news of the dethronement of one king and handover of power to the other king, and on their satisfaction with it* (pp. 257–258).

ed into seven parts,[16] is devoted entirely to sciences and arts, including the European classification of these domains, including the genetic classification of languages, description of literature, rhetoric, logic, philosophy and arithmetic. The discussion of issues related to the French cultural, social and political life ends with the *Conclusions* (*Al-Ḫātima*) (Aṭ-Ṭahṭāwī 2002: 287–304), entitled *On our return from Paris to Egypt and various other issues*, where the author attempts to draw conclusions from his observations and deliberations with regard to a comparison between France, a Western country, and Egypt, a representative of the Muslim world, with a view to following the example of Europe, which will enable the development of the Muslim civilisation in accordance with the Arabic adage: "He who walks first takes priority" (Aṭ-Ṭahṭāwī 2002: 285).

The description of the state administration, political institutions and the scope of rights enjoyed by the citizens, presented in the subchapter *On the administration of the French state*, is of particular significance (Aṭ-Ṭahṭāwī 2002: 98–115). There, the Egyptian reformer explains concepts related to the French models of government (Aṭ-Ṭahṭāwī 2002: 98–101), translates the French constitution of 1830 (Aṭ-Ṭahṭāwī 2002: 101–109) and expresses his admiration for this document, indicating that by introducing constitutional principles the French people achieved "the heyday of their country, development in various fields of knowledge, accumulation of resources and peace of heart. They have chosen rational behaviour, consistent with the principles of justice *(al-'adl)* and rule of law (*al-inṣāf*); thus injustice disappears, and justice becomes the basis of the development of civilisation (*al-umrān*)" (Aṭ-Ṭahṭāwī 2002: 100). He emphasises that the king of France did not hold absolute power because it was limited by law; the Chamber of Peers (the Supreme Chamber), appointed by him, represented the interests of the monarch whereas the Chamber of Deputies (the Lower Chamber) represented the people and thus exercised control over legislation, government policy, as well as state revenues and spending (Aṭ-Ṭahṭāwī 2002: 100). He cites the provisions of the constitution that defend the rights of the French people, their freedom, and equality (equality before the law and in state post appointments, freedom

---

[16] Chapter One – *On the classification of sciences and arts according to the foreigners*(pp. 260–261), Chapter Two – *On the classification of languages as such and on the term "French language"*(pp. 262–269), Chapter Three – *On the art of writing* (pp. 270–271), Chapter Four – *On rhetoric, comprising oratory, semantics and the art of the beautiful word*(pp. 272–273), Chapter Five – *On logic* (pp. 274–277), Chapter Six – *On ten works ascribed to Aristotle* (pp. 278–280), Chapter Seven – *On the science of reckoning referred to as arithmetics in the language of the foreigners* (pp. 281–286).

of expression, religion and beliefs, the right to property protection, etc.) on the one hand, and, on the other, those strengthening the prerogatives of the ruler: his central position in the state or right of legislative initiative (Aṭ-Ṭahṭāwī 2002: 98–100).

He devotes a lot of attention (the chapter *On discord in France and the deposition of the king before our return to Egypt*, Aṭ-Ṭahṭāwī 2002: 231–258) to the political events in France in the period before his return to Egypt, i.e. the July Revolution (27–29 July 1830) that thwarted the attempt to restore absolutism by Charles X (1824–1830) through his deposition and the installation of Louis Philippe I (1830–1848) as the monarch. Noting that those events "belonged to the period that was fondly remembered by the French" (Aṭ-Ṭahṭāwī 2002: 257), he explains their origin: the crystallisation of two factions in the country, i.e. the royalist faction, whose supporters, originating mainly from clerical circles, advocated entrusting all matters to the ruler without questioning the scope of his powers, which was tantamount to absolute monarchy; and the liberal faction, supported by the majority of citizens, as well as a number of philosophers, scholars and sages who opted for the rule of law and limitation of the absolute power of the king, introduction of a constitutional monarchy or a republic. The "July monarchy", a period of changes in all the fundamental areas of the nation's life-formation of the parliamentary system and modern political parties, the development of modern capitalism, the changes in economy and culture (Romanticism), as well as the *Charte constitutionnelle* granted by Louis XVIII (translated into Arabic in this work) confirmed, in the eyes of Aṭ-Ṭahṭāwī, the rights and duties of French citizens (Aṭ-Ṭahṭāwī 2002: 112–115).

The reformatory thought of Aṭ-Ṭahṭāwī is a peculiar compromise between two sources of culture, i.e., the civilisation of Islam and the civilisation of the West. This compromise does not entail the slightest feeling of inferiority, either on the part of the author or the community he represents, and to which his concept applies, i.e., the community of the Arab and Muslim world, or a sense of subordination to the culture of the West. His goal is for all Muslims to thoroughly examine the historical reasons behind the backwardness and downfall of the Arab and Muslim world, and to study the means with which European countries achieved their current strength and power, so that they can choose what is appropriate for them in their circumstances and what is consistent with Muslim law.

Aṭ-Ṭahṭāwī's reforms focused on one significant problem, namely the need for the Arab and Muslim world, which is lagging behind, to imitate Western civilisation, which has achieved the peak of progress (*al-iqtibās 'an al-Ġarb*), as well as the directly related problem of giving legitimacy to this imitation and confirming it with Islamic law. As a pioneer of the revival in the Arab and Muslim world, he put forward an idea of civilisational development (*at-tamaddun*) in order to improve the outdated structures of political and social life, living conditions, educational development and, consequently, progress and prosperity. The attributes of this development were to be as follows: respect of Muslim law (*aš-šarī'a*), emulating the sciences and arts of the West (*al-'ulūm wa-al-ma'ārif*) and, thus, following its path, which was only possible by opening up the Muslim world to the achievements of European culture and civilisation. This conviction was the starting point for his deliberations on various aspects of the reform of government and society, and served as the basis for his own doctrine aimed at accomplishing a political, social and cultural transformation and, consequently, developing the abilities and potential of the Muslim community (*al-umma*) and restoring the Arab and Muslim world to its due place in the international stage.

Aṭ-Ṭahṭāwī's work contributed considerably to the preparation of the minds and dissemination of the idea of the modern Egyptian state and society and also referred to other Arab and Muslim countries. The renewal of their political, social, economic and educational institutions that he called for in his works and activity in order to overcome the backwardness inherited from the Ottomans and Mamluks could be effected only with the help of modern knowledge and science and, consequently, the opening up of the Orient to the achievements of Western culture and civilisation. This conviction was the starting point for his deliberations, and he decided to express them in the form of a *riḥla* in which he describes his travel to the West, not an interesting destination for Arab travellers in the preceding centuries. He thus employs the *riḥla* in the service of *an-nahḍa*. The Egyptian, very well acquainted with the conventions of classic Arabic travel accounts and applying them in his work, thus engages in an intertextual dialogue with the legacy of Arabic culture, as well as his contemporary readers, representing the community from which he comes and to which he addresses his reformatory ideas. By crossing geographic and cultural boundaries, in his writings as well as his life and activity, Aṭ-Ṭahṭāwī made his name as the "precursor of European modernism" and the "pioneer of renewal in the Arab and Muslim world", and *Kitāb taḫlīṣ* was recognised as one of the most outstanding Arabic works of the Renaissance.

Bibliography

'Abd al-Malik, Anwar (1978). *Al-Fikr al-'arabī fī ma'raka an-nahḍa*. Bayrūt: Dār al-Ādāb.

'Abd ar-Raḥīm, Mu'aḏḏin (2006). "Ar-Riḥla bi-waṣfihā ğinsan adabiyyan". *Alif: Journal of Comparative Poetics* 26: 26–46.

Abū Ḥamdān, Samīr (1992–1994). *Mawsū'at 'aṣr an-nahḍa*. Bayrūt: Aš-Šarika al-'Ālamiyya li-l-Kitāb.

—— (1992). *Rifā'a Rāfi' aṭ-Ṭahtāwī: Rā'id at-taḥdīṯ al-ūrūbī fī Miṣr*. Bayrūt: Aš-Šarika al-'Ālamiyya li-l-Kitāb.

Altman, Israel (1976). *The Political Thought od Rifa'ah Rafi at-Tahtawi, a Nineteenth Century Egiptian Reformer*. Los Angeles: University of California.

'Ammāra, Muḥammad (1997). *Aṣ-Ṣaḥwa al-islāmiyya wa-at-taḥaddà al-ḥaḍārī*. Bayrūt – Al-Qāhira: Dār aš-Šurūq.

—— (1984). *Rifā'a aṭ-Ṭahṭāwī : Rā'id at-tanwīr fī al-'aṣr al-ḥadīṯ*. Al-Qāhira: Dār aš-Šurūq.

—— (2003). *Mustaqbalunā bayna at-taḥdīd al-islāmī wa-al-ḥadāṯa al-ġarbiyya*. Al-Qāhira: Maktabat aš-Šurūq ad-Duwaliyya.

—— (2010). *Al-A'māl al-kāmila li-Rifā'a aṭ-Ṭahṭāwī*. Al-Qāhira: Dār aš-Šurūq.

Maktabat aš-Šurūq ad-Duwaliyya.

Amīn, Aḥmad (1965). *Zu'amā' al-iṣlāḥ fī al-'aṣr al-ḥadīṯ*. Al-Qāhira: Maktabat an-Nahḍa al-Miṣriyya.

Bahayy, 'Iṣām (2006). "Risālat Ibn Faḍlān. Qirā'a ṯaqāfiyya". *Alif: Journal of Comparative Poetics* 26: 105–137.

Bielawski, Józef (1995). *Klasyczna literatura arabska*, Warszawa: Wydawnictwo Akademickie Dialog.

Bosworth, Clifford Edmund (1999). "Travel Literature". In: *Encyclopedia of Arabic Literature*. Eds. Julie Scott Meisami, Paul Starkey. London – New York: Routledge.

Danecki, Janusz (2007). *Podstawowe wiadomości o islamie*. Warszawa: Wydawnictwo Akademickie Dialog.

Ḍayf, Šawqī (1987). *Ar-Riḥlāt*. Al-Qāhira: Dār al-Ma'ārif.

Dunn, Ross E. (2012). *The Adventures of Ibn Battuta: A Muslim Traveler of the Fourteenth Century*. Berkeley: University of California Press.

Euben, Roxanne L. (2008). *Journeys to the Other Shore – Muslim and Western Travelers in Search of Knowledge*. Princeton: Princeton University Press.

Garden, Kenneth (2015). "The Rihla and Self-reinvention of Abu Bakr Ibn al-'Arabi". *The Journal of American Oriental Society* 135(1): 1–17.

Ḥiğāzī, Maḥmūd (1974). *Uṣūl al-fikr al-'arabī al-ḥadīṯ 'inda Aṭ-Ṭahṭāwī: ma'a an-naṣṣ al-kāmil li-kitābihi Taḫlīṣ al-ibrīz*. Al-Qāhira: Al-Hay'a al-Miṣriyya al-'Āmma li-l-Kitāb.

Hourani, Albert (1998). *Arabic Thought in the Liberal Age 1798–1939*, London – New York – Toronto: Cambridge University Press.

—— (2002). *Historia Arabów*, Transl. Janusz Danecki, Gdańsk Wydawnictwo Marabut.

Ḥūrānī, Albert (2001). *Al-Fikr Al-'Arabī Fī 'Aṣr An-Nahḍa 1798–1939*, Transl. Karīm 'Azqūl. Bayrūt: Dār An-Nahār Li-N-Našr.

Al-Ḥuṣrī, Ḫaldūn Sāṭi' (1960). *Al-Bilād Al-'Arabiyya Wa-Ad-Dawla Al-'Uṯmāniyya.* Bayrūt: Dār Al-'Ilm Li-L-Malāyīn.

Husry, Khaldun Sati (1966). *Three Reformers: A Study In Modern Arab Political Thought.* Beirut: Khayats.

Ibn Battuta, Muhammad (2008). *Osobliwości Miast I Dziwy Podróży*, Transl. Tadeusz Majda, Halina Natorf. Warszawa: Książka I Wiedza.

Ibn Fadlan, Ahmad (1985). *Kitab*, Transl. Anna Kmietowicz, Franciszek Kmietowicz, Tadeusz Lewicki, Wrocław: Ossolineum.

Jamsheer, Hassan Ali (2008). *Reforma Władzy I Społeczeństwa W Arabsko-Muzułmańskiej Myśli Politycznej Wieków XIX I XX.* Łódź: Wydawnictwo Ibidem.

—— (2009). *Historia Powstania Islamu Jako Doktryny Społeczno-Politycznej.* Warszawa: Wydawnictwo Akademickie Dialog.

Kowalska, Maria (1973). *Średniowieczna Arabska Literatura Podróżnicza.* Kraków: Zeszyty Naukowe UJ.

Kraczkowski, Ignacy Julianowicz (1963). *Tārīḫ Al-Adab Al-Ǧuġrāfī Al-'Arabī*, Transl. Faḍl Ad-Dīn 'Uṯmān Hāšim. Al-Qāhira: Maṭba'at Laǧnat at-Ta'līf wa-at-Tarǧama wa-an-Našr.

Lewicka, Magdalena (2012a). "Relacje świata arabskiego i państw islamu z cywilizacją Zachodu w dobie odrodzenia arabskiego na podstawie 'Aqwam al-masālik fī ma'rifat aḥwāl al-mamālik' (Najprostsza droga do poznania sytuacji w Królestwach) Ḫayr ad-Dīna at-Tūnisīego". *Gdańskie Studia Międzynarodowe* 10, 1–2: 156–165.

—— (2012b)., "Rifa' at-Tahtawi – między islamem a Europą". *Muzułmanie Rzeczypospolitej* 2–3: 18–21.

—— (2014a). "Europa w arabskiej myśli społeczno-politycznej doby odrodzenia". *Litteraria Copernicana* 1(13): 82–97.

—— (2014b). "Between the East and the West. Aqwam al-masālik fī ma'rifat aḥwāl al-mamālik of Ḫayr ad-Dīn at-Tūnusī (1822–1890)". *Planeta literatur. Journal of Global Literary Studies* 1: 53–68.

—— (2015). "European patterns versus Muslim political tradition in the Arab reformist ideas in the 19th century". In: *Aspects of contemporary Asia: culture, education, ethics.* Ed. Joanna Marszałek-Kawa. Toruń: Wydawnictwo Adam Marszałek.

—— (2016). „Zwischen Tradition und Modernität. Europäische Vorbilder und islamische gesellschaftspolitische Tradition aufgrund des *Kitāb taḫlīṣ al-ibrīz fī talḫīṣ Bārīz von Rifā'a aṭ-Ṭahṭāwī*". *Acta Philologica* 49: 359–372.

Lewis, Bernard (1995). *Arabowie w historii*, Transl. Janusz Danecki. Warszawa: Państwowy Instytut Wydawniczy.

—— (1973). *Islam in History. Ideas, People and Events in the Middle East* London: Oxford University Press.

—— (2003). *Muzułmański Bliski* Wschód, Transl. J. Danecki, Gdańsk: Wydawnictwo Marabut.

Al-Mawāfī, Nāṣir 'Abd ar-Rāzzaq (1995). *Ar-Riḥla fī al-adab al-'arabī ḥattà nihāyat al-qarn ar-rābi' al-hiǧrī.* Al-Qāhira: Dār an-Našr li-l-Ǧāmi'āt al-Miṣriyya.

Moudden, Abderrahmane (1990). "The Ambivalence of Riḥla: Community Integration and Self-definition in Moroccan Travel Accounts 1300–1800". In: *Muslim Travelers: Pilgrimage, Migration, and the Religious Imagination.* Ed. Dale F. Eickemann. Berkeley: University of California Press.

Mūsà, Munīr (1973). *Al-Fikr al-'arabī fī al-'aṣr al-ḥadīṯ,* Bayrūt: Dār al-Ḥaqīqa.

—— (1995). *Al-Fikr as-siyāsī al-'arabī fī al-'aṣr al-ḥadīṯ.* Ṭarābulus: Maktabat as-Sā'iḥ.

An-Naǧǧār, Ḥusayn Fawzī (1987). *Rifā'a aṭ-Ṭahṭāwī: Rā'id fikr wa-imām nahḍa.* Al-Qāhira: Al-Hay'a al-Miṣriyya al-'Āmma li-l-Kitāb.

Netton, Ian Richard (1991). "Basic Structures and Signs of Alienation in the Rihla of Ibn Jubayr". *Journal of Arabic Literature* 22(1): 127–144.

Al-Qāḍī, Muḥammad, Ṣawwāh, 'Abd Allāh (1992). *Al-Fikr Al-Iṣlāḥī 'Inda Al-'Arab Fī 'Aṣr An-Nahḍa.* Tūnis: Dār Al-Ǧanūb Li-N-Našr.

Qindīl, Fu'ād (2002). *Adab Ar-Riḥla Fī At-Turāṯ Al-'Arabī.* Madīnat Naṣr: Maktabat Ad-Dār Al-'Arabiyya Li-L-Kitāb.

Al-Samaany, Nasser S. (2000). *Travel Literature Of Moroccan Pilgrims During The 11–12th/17–18th Centuries: Thematic And Artistic Study,* Phd Thesis. Leeds: Department Of Arabic And Middle Eastern Studies, The University Of Leeds, Http://Etheses.Whiterose.Ac.Uk/ 542/1/Uk_Bl_Ethos_420414.Pdf.

Šarābī, Ḥišām (1978). *Al-Muṯaqqafūn Al-'Arab Wa-Al-Ġarb.* Bayrūt: Dār An-Nahār.

Aš-Šayyāl, Ǧamīl Ad-Dīn (1958). *Rifā'A Rāfi' Aṭ-Ṭahṭāwī: 1801–1873.* Al-Qāhira: Dār Al-Ma'Ārif.

—— (1951). *Tārīḫ At-Tarǧama Wa-Al-ḥaraka Aṯ-ṯaqāfiyya Fī 'Aṣr Muḥammad 'Alī.* Al-Qāhira: Dār Al-Ma'Ārif.

Šu'ayb, Ḫalīfī (2006). "Ar-Riḥlāt Al-'Arabiyya: An-Naṣṣ Wa-ḫiṭāb Al-Huwiyya". *Alif: Journal Of Comparative Poetics* 26: 47–63.

Al-Ṭahṭāwī, Rifā'A Rāfi' (2004). *An Imam In Paris: Account Of A Stay In France By An Egyptian Cleric (1826–1831),* Transl. Daniel L. Newman. London: Saqi.

—— (2002). *Kitāb Taḫlīṣ Al-Ibrīz Fī Talḫīṣ Bārīz.* Bayrūt: Dār Al-Hilāl.

—— (1968). *Aṭ-Ṭahṭāwī in Paris: ein Dokument des arabischen Modernismus aus dem frühen 19. Jahrhundert,* Transl. Karl Stowasser. Münster: Universität Münster.

Walter, Wiebke (2008). *Historia literatury arabskiej,* Transl. Agnieszka Gadzała. Warszawa: Wydawnictwo Naukowe PWN.

"Wanderlust: Travel Literature of Egypt and the Middle East / Šahwat at-tirḥīl. Adab ar-riḥla fī Miṣr wa-aš-Šarq al-Awsaṭ" (2006). Ed. Ferial Jabouri Ghazoul. *Alif: Journal of Comparative Poetics* 26: 1–282 (English), 1–238 (Arabic). Cairo: American University in Cairo Press.

Chapter 14

Crossing the Borders of Decency. Gustave Flaubert, Maxime Du Camp and their Oriental Journey

Małgorzata Sokołowicz, *University of Warsaw, The Fryderyk Chopin University of Music/Poland*

"Le temps des oies blanches et des bordels", the time of white geese and brothels. This was the expression used by Alain Corbin, a French historian, to name the 19th century (Corbin 2003: 102). The hypocritical century represses the sex and is obsessed by it at the same time. The morality is different for women and men. The former are to be Romantic innocent angels, while the latter are allowed to visit brothels to satisfy their most perverted desires. Consequently, sexuality is experienced differently by women and men. Daughters brought up in good families live in the total ignorance of their own body. Museums of anatomy are closed to the female public, and special bath salt is added to water when they take a bath so as they should not contemplate their nudity (Corbin 2003: 102–110). Marital sex is perpetuated only for the reasons of procreation and excludes all pleasure for woman. Convinced that the main duty of their wives is to be mothers and that the coitus is needed only to make them conceive, men look for pleasure and fulfilment of their fantasies elsewhere (Corbin 2015: 361–364). Brothels of different types flourish, offering to their clients what they lack at home, namely nudity, mirrors and debauchery (Pludermacher 2015: 241–242). Needless to say that syphilis becomes the plague of the century, and the most prominent figures of the period suffer from it. Touched by the illness, Pasteur tries in vain to find a cure against it during the last years of his life (Richard, Richard-Le Guillou 2002: 75).

A lack of sexual satisfaction at home, regular visits to houses of ill repute and a growing fear of contracting syphilis result in permanent frustration and evasion into the worlds of fantasies (Corbin 2015: 372–374). The Middle East becomes a perfect destination for those voyages conducted in dreams. For a long time, it has been believed that the Orient is synonymous with eroticism and love passion. Sexually, women are treated in the same way as men and have the same access to pleasure (Colonna 2006: 78–81). Turkish baths, sensual scents, and, above all, inaccessible harems become not only a popular way of depicting the nude in the arts but also a predominant setting of erotic fantasies (cf. Gallet 2016: passim).

Over the course of time, travelling to the Oriental countries is becoming more and more popular. Many artists and writers go to see those distant lands and, willingly or not, contrast their exotic and erotic fantasies with reality. Usually, the image of sensual Oriental worlds persists in their travel writing and is reflected by the praise of Arab beauties (Lamartine) or declared fascination with harems (Delacroix, Nerval). However, there is a single French text that is entirely different. Gustave Flaubert's (1821–1880) travel writing states openly that the function of the Oriental world is to satisfy sensual needs of a European traveller.

According to Eric Lawrence Gans, young Flaubert expressed his first sexual desires in texts about Oriental worlds (Gans 1971: 125). Nevertheless, these texts did not differ a lot from others of the period, in which protagonists dreamt about veiled beauties with languishing eyes. In 1849, the future author of *Madame Bovary* sets off to the Middle East with his friend, writer, and photographer, Maxime Du Camp (1822–1894). As he is very close to his mother, an undecided person and home lover, Flaubert finds it difficult to leave France for such a long time. But, encouraged by his friend, he decides finally to accompany him to Egypt, Syria, Palestine, and Greece (Gothot-Mersch 2006: 10-12). Both men write down their travel impressions, Maxime Du Camp publishes them soon after coming back home (in 1852 he publishes *Égypte, Nubie, Palestine, Syrie* and in 1854 *Le Nil, ou lettres sur l'Égypte et la Nubie*), while Flaubert uses his notes only to create Oriental atmosphere of his future writings and does not plan to publish them separately. Consequently, Maxime Du Camp writes just another account of Oriental journey, whereas the notes and letters by Flaubert build a completely different image of their travelling, according to which the two young men profit to an extreme from the escapade, using their money and position to frequent prostitutes, launching themselves into homosexual experiments and audaciously crossing all borders of European decency.

Very bold, published posthumously and censored still in 1910 (Gothot-Mersch 2006: 27), the description of the activities of the two young men in the Oriental world becomes an unusual fulfillment of the 19th-century Oriental dream. In the present paper, we would like to focus on this realisation, explain its origins and consequences, taking as their basis the Egyptian part of the journey, which according to many was the most important for the travellers (Naaman 1965: passim). To do so, we have decided to divide the paper into three parts. The first one focuses on the description of the Oriental world, promoting its most perverted and corrupted features. In the second, some homoerotic aspects of the journey are discussed. The third part describes the relations of the two travellers with Egyptian prostitutes.

A Perverted World

According to Antoine Youssef Naaman, Flaubert was obsessed with Egypt. The obsession started in 1832 when, as a young boy, he saw in the port of Rouen the ship *Louxor* transporting the famous obelisk, currently exposed on the Place de la Concorde in Paris (Naaman 1965: 7). Not only do Oriental subjects appear in his juvenile writings, but he also has an important collection of books about the Middle East (Gothot-Mersch 2008: 17–18). It may be for that reason that the world he saw in Egypt was not so strange for him:

> "I sum up my feelings so far [he wrote from Cairo]: very little impressed by nature here – i.e. landscape, sky, desert (except the mirages); enormously excited by the cities and the people. […] It probably comes of my having given more imagination and thought, before coming here, to things like horizon, greenery, sun, trees, sun, etc., than to houses, streets, costumes and faces. The result is that nature has been a rediscovery and the rest a discovery" (Flaubert 1996: 42).

This discovery also concerns all that is obscene and perverted in this world, that transgresses the borders of European decency. Flaubert delights in "*bizarreries*, never attempting to reduce the incongruities before him" (Said 1979: 184). Like many others, he wants to escape from the monotony of European life, the prison of conventions (Czyba 1994: 73). That is why his first descriptions seem to go beyond all norms, focusing on obscene jokes or events having strong sexual connotations:

> "Clowns at a wedding, one made up as a woman. Obscene jokes between patient and doctor: «Who is it? No, I'll not let you in. Who is it?» «It's…», «No. Who? Who? » «A whore. » «Oh, do come in. » «What's the doctor doing? » «He's in his garden. » «Who with? » «His donkey» – «He's buggering it. »" (Flaubert 1996: 37–38).

His first impressions of Egypt resemble an inventory of perversions that he writes down scrupulously and sends to one of his best friends, Louis Bouilhet:

> "To amuse the crowd, Mohammed Ali's jester took a woman in a Cairo bazaar one day, set her on the counter of a shop, and coupled with her publicly while the shopkeeper calmly smoked his pipe.
> On the road from Cairo to Shubra some time ago a young fellow had himself publicly buggered by a large monkey – as in the story above, to create a good opinion of himself and make people laugh.
> A marabout died a while ago – an idiot – who had long passed as a saint marked by God; all the Moslem women came to see him and masturbated him – in the end he died of exhaustion – from morning to night it was a perpetual jacking-off. Oh, Bouilhet, why weren't you that marabout?" (Flaubert 1996: 44).

"His tastes", comments Said, "run to the perverse, [to] extreme animality, even of grotesque nastiness" (Said 1979: 184). Paradoxically, for Flaubert, those aberrant behaviours seem perfectly natural and prove the unhypocritical character of Egyptians. Surely, it results from a comparison with his own society where natural needs should be deeply hidden.

Therefore, he is delighted by a "short, ugly, stocky" boy he meets on the street and finds him "excellent" because of the proposal the child puts forward: "If you'll give me five paras, I'll bring you my mother to fuck. I wish you all kinds of prosperity, especially a long prick" (Flaubert 1996: 38). This event shows clearly how the two young Europeans are perceived in Cairo: they are considered to be sex tourists looking for exotic, and erotic, entertainment. Said talks about this "almost uniform association between the Orient and sex" (Said 1979: 188). According to Flaubert, it is mainly Maxime Du Camp who gets overexcited by the exotic reality: "Max, the old lecher, got excited over a negress who was drawing water at a fountain. He is just as excited by little negro boys. By who is he not excited? Or, rather, by what?..." (Flaubert 1996: 43). In Egypt, the travellers have no restraints. Their desires, fouled by the conventional European society, re-emerge and are boosted in the Oriental country.

It is not only the question of sexuality, but also nudity, illness, deformation, all that is taboo in European world – all of that becomes an important issue in Flaubert's notes. The two travellers visit, for instance, a hospital or a mental asylum. Especially, the description of the hospital is striking due to an unnatural fascination with the macabre:

> "Pretty cases of syphilis; in the ward of Abbas's Mamelukes, several have it in the arse. At the sign from the doctor, they all stood up on their beds, undid their trouser belts (it was like army drill), and opened

> their anuses with their fingers to show their chancres. Enormous infundibula; one had a growth of hair inside his anus. One old man's prick entirely devoid of skin; I recoil from the stench. A rachitic: hands, carved backwards, nails as long as claws; one could see the bone structure of his torso, as clearly as a skeleton; the rest of his body, too, was fanatically thin, and his head was ringed with whitish leprosy.
> Dissecting room: ...On the table an Arab cadaver, wide open; beautiful black hair..." (Flaubert 1996: 65).

While commenting on this extract, Said says that the Orient presents itself to Flaubert "sometimes horribly, but always attractively" (Said 1979: 186). It seems appealing by its truth, naturalness, lack of hypocrisy or dissimulation; an attitude which is a complete reverse to the one observed in Europe.

According to Said, Flaubert was also impressed by "decrepitude and senescence" of the Oriental world (Said 1979: 185), which is particularly well visible in the extract on the mental asylum the travellers visit. It shows an image of the Orient in decay, where the power and beauty had gone, but debauchery was left:

> "The black eunuch of the Grande Princess came up and kissed my hands. One old woman begged me to fuck her – she uncovered her long – flat beasts that hang down to her umbilicus and stroke them; she had an exquisitely sweet smile [...]. Another woman catching sight of me in the courtyard, began to do handsprings and showed me her arse; she does it whenever she sees a man. A woman dancing in her cell, beating her tin chamber pot like a 'darabukeh'" (Flaubert 1996: 67-68).

Everything looks like in a distorting mirror. The sensual and beautiful Oriental world is no longer pleasing but continues to have strong sexual connotations and attract the travellers.

This emphasis put on the perversity and obscenity of the Orient seems to result from the need to liberate oneself from the restraining conventions of European society, but also to break the awful boredom tormenting the writer: "What is it, oh Lord, this permanent lassitude that I drag about with me?", he asks himself (Flaubert 1996: 151). Describing things that are new, unknown and salacious helps to forget the spleen.

Homoerotic Experience

It may be because of this lassitude that both travellers are keen on completely new experiences. In one of his letters, Flaubert states that in Egypt everyone speaks openly about sodomy and this practice is "quite accepted". His comment is ironic:

> "Travelling as we are for educational purposes, and charged with a mission by the government, we have considered it our duty to indulge in this form of ejaculation. So far the occasion has not presented itself. We continue to seek it, however. It's at the baths that such things take place. You reserve the bath for yourself (five francs including masseurs, pipe, coffee, sheet and towel). And you skewer your lad in one of the rooms. Be informed, furthermore, that all the bath-boys are bardashes. The final masseurs, the ones who come to rub you when all the rest is done, are usually quite nice young boys. We had our eye on one in an establishment very near our hotel. I reserved the bath exclusively for myself. I went, and the rascal was away that day!" (Flaubert 1996: 84).

It does not mean that his staying in the baths was completely innocent. Once, a "little boy in red tarboosh [...] massaged [his] left thigh with a melancholic air" (Flaubert 1996: 63). Another "adventure" takes place the day he has not met "the rascal" in the bath:

> "That day [...] my kellaa was rubbing me gently, and when he came to the noble parts, he lifted up my *boules d'amour* to clean them, then continuing to rub my chest with his left hand he began to pull with his right on my prick, and as he drew it up and down he leaned over my shoulder and said "baksheesh, baksheesh". He was a man in his fifties, ignoble, disgusting – imagine the effect, and the word "baksheesh, baksheesh". I pushed him away a little, saying "làh, làh" ("no, no") – he thought I was angry and took a craven look – then I gave him a few pats on the shoulder, saying "làh, làh" again, but more gently – he smiled a smile that meant, "you're not fouling me – you like as much as anybody, but today you've decided against for some reason." As for me, I laughed aloud like a dirty old man, and the shadowy vault of the bath echoed with the sound" (Flaubert 1996: 85).

Egyptians seem to be perfectly aware of the specific needs of European travellers and accept homosexual practices, very negatively perceived in Europe (cf. Richard, Richard-Le Guillou 2002: 120). Once more, Flaubert goes far beyond European decency. However, his boldness is close to a caricature. The subject reappears in another letter to Louis Bouilhet written at the end of the Egyptian journey: "By the way, you ask me if I consummated that business at the baths. Yes – and on a pockmarked young rascal wearing a white turban. It's made me laugh, that's all. But I'll be at it again. To be done well, an experiment must be repeated" (Flaubert 1996: 204). Scholars do not agree whether Flaubert really had homosexual relations with Egyptians or whether that was just a joke (cf. Flaubert 1996: 204 note). The particular tone of the description may be in favour of the second option and Flaubert's perceptible will to shock.

What was particularly shocking for European travellers already in the 18th century were Oriental men who were dancing, dressed as women. "The Orientals often look for criminal pleasures beyond nature", Jean Potocki commented on that (Potocki 1980: 53). Obviously, Flaubert immediately takes to this kind of dance and asks Hassan el-Belbeissi, a famous Egyptian dancer of that period, to dance for him at least two times. The description of male dancers returns in his notes and letters, the longest being given in a letter to Louis Bouilhet:

> "As dancers, imagine two rascals, quite ugly, but charming in their corruption, in their obscene leerings and the femininity of their movements, dressed as women, their eyes painted with antinomy. For costume, they had wide trousers… From time to time, during the dance, the impresario, or pimp, who brought them plays around them kissing them on the belly, the arse, and the small of the back, and making obscene remarks in an effort to put additional spice into a thing that is already quite clear in itself. It is too beautiful to be exciting. I doubt whether we shall find women as good as the men; the ugliness of the latter adds greatly to the thing as art. I had a headache for the rest of the day, and I had to go and pee two or three times during the performance – a nervous reaction that I attribute particularly to the music. – I'll have this marvellous Hassan el-Belbeissi come again. He'll dance the Bee for me, in particular. Done by such a bardash as he, it can scarcely be a thing for babes" (Flaubert 1996: 83–84).

Flaubert does not describe the famous strip dance, so Hassan has probably not come to dance for him. Nonetheless, it is important to notice that Egyptians do their best to satisfy European tourists. They know that corruption and obscenity please them the most. Consequently, in the Middle East, the travellers get all they might have ever dreamt of in Europe. Of course, they pay for it (which is rarely mentioned in the notes or letters). It is well known that

Flaubert's journey was costly and had to be shortened due to excessive expenditures (Gothot-Mersch 2006: 19).

Egyptian Prostitutes

Except for the particular obscenity of male dance, there is another reason for which Flaubert describes those dancers. In June 1834, Mohammad-Ali prohibited female dances and prostitution in Cairo. Since that moment every woman caught dancing or prostituting was arrested and, after the third recidivism, sent to Esna, which became the main place of prostitution in Egypt (Naaman 1965: x). "We have not yet seen any dancing girls; they are all in exile in Upper Egypt. Good brothels no longer exist in Cairo, either", complains Flaubert (Flaubert 1996: 83). The question may be asked what "good brothels" mean. Indeed, venereal diseases are present not only in Europe. In a letter from Constantinople Flaubert writes to Louis Bouilhet:

> "I must tell you, my dear sir, that I picked up [...] VII (sic) chancres, which eventually combined to form two, then one. I travelled in that condition from Marmaris to Smyrna on horseback. Each night and morning I dressed my poor prick. Finally it healed. In two more days the scar will have closed. I am madly taking care of myself. I suspect a Maronite – or was it a little Turkish girl? – of having given me this present" (Flaubert 1996: 215).

The writer suffers from syphilis and seems to be proud of it (Steegmuller 1980: 239). It is difficult to say when he has contracted it, but the brothels he describes are surely not very luxurious, nor hygienic.

The first Oriental sexual experience of the two travellers takes place in Cairo in a shabby illegal brothel, at la Triestina. The women are poor, probably sick, the place is an absolute slum, there are even some kittens on the bed that need to be removed before the coitus. Even though dances and music are forbidden, the women dance as if having sex was impossible without this special introduction. Flaubert describes the event in a quasi-ethnographic way: "On the mating: firm flesh, bronze arse, shaven cunt, dry though fatty; the whole thing gave the effect of a plague victim or a leperhouse" (Flaubert 1996: 40). They try to talk afterwards, but they do not understand each other. Flaubert rewrites the event in a letter to Louis Bouilhet: "a strange coitus, looking at each other without being able to exchange a word, and the exchange of looks is all the deeper for the curiosity and the surprise. My brain was too stimulated for me to enjoy it much otherwise" (Flaubert 1996: 44). The writer seems to be much more excited by transgressing the taboo, possessing the Oriental woman he has dreamt of before coming to Egypt than by the sex itself.

Nevertheless, the most important Oriental erotic experience takes place in Upper Egypt. The woman-symbol of Flaubert's trip is Kuchuk Hanem (cf. Auriant 1943: passim), "Pretty little princess" or simply "Dancing woman", the star of Esna "of whom the travellers had undoubtedly heard in Cairo" (Flaubert 1996: 112-113 note). Remarkably picturesque, the vision of a woman in pink trousers, surrounded by light becomes a subject of a poem by Louis Bouilhet (cf. Flaubert 2008: 610): "She had just come from the bath, her firm breasts had a fresh smell, something like that of sweetened turpentine" (Flaubert 1996: 114). The woman must have impressed the travellers: "She asks us if we would like a little entertainment, but Max says that first, he would like to entertain himself alone with her, and they go downstairs. After he finishes, I go down and follow his example" (Flaubert 1996: 115). It is important to notice that Du Camp does not mention this event in his book. He describes the dance of Kuchuk, calls it even "quite coarse" and declares to say her goodbye immediately afterwards (Du Camp 1889, 116–119). It shows perfectly the distortion between what was said in the published travel writings and what had happened in reality. The travel writing of 19th century was obviously (self-) censored.

According to the notes by Flaubert, the real evening of debauchery starts. Women dance, play the instrument and really serve the men. They do know how to please Europeans (cf. Tritter 2012: 192):

> "*Coup* with Safia Zugairah ("Little Sophie") – I stained the divan. She is very corrupted and writhing, extremely voluptuous. But the best was the second copulation with Kuchuk. Effect of her necklace between my teeth. Her cunt felt like rolls of velvet as she made me come. I felt like a tiger" (Flaubert 1996: 117).

Believing he is in the centre of the universe, the traveller feels strong and powerful. The Oriental dream about women serving one man comes true. Kuchuk dances the famous Bee, the dance during which the dancer progressively strips. The musicians have their eyes covered. The view of the naked woman is not for them, but for the strangers, the privileged ones.

Flaubert stays at the house for the night. Then, the register changes. In spite of a number of *coups* described, one may easily notice the tenderness of the European who puts his pelisse over the blanket to make Kuchuk feel warmer and who watches her sleep. The conclusion is also singular: "How flattering it would be to one's pride if at the moment of leaving you were sure that you left a memory behind, that she would think of you more than of the others who have been there, that you would remain in her heart!" (Flaubert 1996: 119). It is still a Romantic who speaks. In front of the decay of the world, Flaubert goes to prostitutes to search for the last traces of beauty, Auriant says (Auriant 1943: 30–31). This is another way of transgressing the norms of European society.

That is not the end of the erotic adventures of the two travellers. Continuing their trip up to the Nile, the Frenchmen meet black female dancers: "This is no longer Egypt; it is negro, African, savage" (Flaubert 1996: 121). Flaubert himself makes a reference to the stereotype of the black woman seen as a fusion of animal sexuality and uncontrolled desires (Le Bihan 2006: 518). The writer profits from the opportunity presented to him: "I have lain with Nubian girls whose necklaces of gold piasters hung down to their thigs and her black stomachs were encircled by colour beads – they feel cold when your rub your own stomach against them. And their dancing! *Sacré nom de Dieu!!!*" (Flaubert 1996: 126). The dance reflects lack of modesty, total liberation, but also something primitive and primary (Le Bihan 2006: 521–522). Edward Said writes about "sexual promise (and treat), untiring sensuality, unlimited desire, deep generative energies" (Said 1979: 188). All of that happens during the Oriental journey of the two travellers: "At Kena I had a beautiful whore who liked me very much and told me in sign language that I had beautiful eyes. Her name is Hosna et-Taouilah, which means 'the beautiful tall one'; and there was another, fat and lubricious, on top of whom I enjoyed myself immensely..." (Flaubert 1996: 201). There is something extremely primary in this action, as liberated sexuality may evoke some primitive fecundity rite. According to Lucette Czyba, during his journey, Flaubert looked for the eternal Orient (Czyba 1996: 74), and it seems that this eternal Orient is the Orient of sexual freedom. Doing what one wants, being guided by desires, forgetting all norms become the essence of the escapade.

Louise Colet, Flaubert's lover, who read his travel notes, became fanatically jealous of Kuchuk. She immediately understood that the writer treated the dancer differently from other women he had met during his Oriental journey. To calm her down, Flaubert answered her in a letter:

> "The oriental woman is no more than a machine: she makes no distinction between one man and another man. Smoking, going to the baths, painting her eyelids and drinking coffee – such is the circle of occupations within which her existence is confined. As for physical pleasure it must be very slight, since the well know button, the seat of same, is sliced off at the early age" (Flaubert 1996: 220).

The extract shows the objectification of Oriental woman, depicts her as a sexual slave, whose role is to please the European man. Lowe criticises Flaubert: "As 'machine', the 'femme orientale' produces this sensual pleasure for a man to consume, because she is not 'human'" (Lowe 1986: 53). It can easily be used as an example of colonial discourse. In the 19th century, the Orient started to be perceived "as a female counterpart to masculine Europe" (Lowe 1986: 45), the female that masculine Europe wants to possess. Nevertheless, taking into consideration the importance of Kuchuk in future writings of Flaubert (cf. Auriant 1943), it can easily turn into abuse.

Conclusion

Flaubert dreamt of coming back to Egypt until the end of his life. In 1880, a few days before his death, he wrote to his niece that he wanted to see palm trees standing out against the blue sky one more time (Flaubert 1996: 222 note). The Oriental world became a paradise lost, though regularly revisited while writing and dreaming. It is undeniable that the sensual aspect of the journey contributed to this vision. The travellers crossed the borders of European decency there, but by doing that, they fulfilled all their dreams. Edward Said criticised Flaubert much; and his writings helped him to construct his theory: "He was foreign, comparatively wealthy, male, and these were historical facts of domination that allowed him not only to possess Kuchuk Hanem physically but to speak for her and tell his readers in what way she was 'typically oriental'" (Said 1979: 6).

Even though the behaviour of the two travellers may be morally dubious, it seems that what was "typically oriental" had been defined in Europe long before Flaubert. It is true that "in all his novels Flaubert associates the Orient with the escapism of sexual fantasy" (Said 1979: 190), but he is surely not the first to do so. The image of the Oriental world in the Occident had been being created for centuries, showing the power of man, sensuality approaching debauchery, violence, and subordination of women. In the art of the 19th century, Oriental scenes by Ingres or Gérôme connoted brothels (Pludermacher 2015: 232). "[T]he exotic and the erotic ideal [went] hand in hand" to quote the famous sentence by Mario Praz (1951: 197). Flaubert is just the first writer in France to speak about that so openly (even though his writings were not supposed to be published). He was surely not the first to travel in this way, but he was the first to describe his excesses, and he did not destroy his papers. The thoughts verbalised by Flaubert were surely hidden behind paintings depicting odalisques and apparently innocent descriptions of Oriental dances and baths. As a tempting alternative to the hypocritical Europe of the 19th century, this sensual dreamland could easily turn out to be perverted and obscene. Crossing the borders of European decency in the Orient was a revolt against the European society, a dramatic way of expressing oneself.

Bibliography

Auriant [Alexandre Hadjivassiliou] (1943). "Koutchouk-Hanem, L'Almée De Flaubert". In *Koutchouk-Hanem, L'Almée De Flaubert Suivi De Onze Essais Sur La Vie De Flaubert Et Sur Son Œuvre*, Paris: Mercure De France.

Behdad, Ali (1990). "Orientalist Desire, Desire Of The Orient", *French Forum* 1: 37–51.

Colonna, Vincent (2006). "Amours d'Orient Et d'Occident, Le Miroir Brisé". *La Pensée De Midi* 17 (1): 78–85.

Corbin, Alain (2003). "Le Temps Des Oies Blanches Et Des Bordels". In *La Plus Belle Histoire De L'amour*. Ed. Dominique Simmonet. Paris: Le Seuil.

—— (2015). *Les Filles De Noce. Misère Sexuelle Et Prostitution (Xix^e^ Siècle)*. Paris: Flammarion.

Czyba, Lucette (1994). "Le Voyage En Orient De Gustave Flaubert", *Acta Universitatis Lodziensis. Folia Literaria* 35: 64–76.

Du Camp, Maxime (1887). *Le Nil. Egypte Et Nubie*. Paris: Librairie Hachette Et Cie.

Flaubert, Gustave (1996). *Flaubert In Egypt. A Sensibility On Tour. A Narrative Drawn From Gustave Flaubert's Travel Notes & Letters Translated From The French & Edited By Francis Steegmuller*. London: Penguin Books.

Gallet, Valentine (2016). *Harem. L'Orient Amoureux*. Paris : Éditions Place Des Victoires.

Gans, Eric Lawrence (1971). *The Discovery Of Illusion. Flaubert's Early Works, 1835–1837*. London: University Of California Press.

Gothot-Mersch, Claudine (2008). "Préface". In: Gustave Flaubert, *Voyage En Orient*. Paris: Gallimard.

Le Bihan, Yann (2006). "L'ambivalence Du Regard Colonial Porté Sur Les Femmes d'Afrique Noire". *Cahiers d'Études Africaines* 46 (183): 513–537.

Lowe, Lisa (1986). "The Orient as Woman in Flaubert's *Salammbô* and *Voyage en Orient*". *Comparative Literature Studies* 1 (23): 44–58.

Naaman, Antoine Youssef (1965). *Les Lettres D'Egypte De Gustave Flaubert*. Paris : A. G. Nizet.

Pludermacher, Isolde (2015). "« Les Beau Dans L'Horrible ». Prostitution Et Modernité". In : *Splendeurs Et Misères. Images De La Prostitution. 1850–1910*. Paris : Musée D'orsay/Flammarion.

Potocki, Jean (1980). *Voyages En Turquie Et En Egypte, En Hollande, Au Maroc*, Introduction Et Notes De Daniel Beauvois, Paris : Fayard.

Praz, Mario (1951). *The Romantic Agony*. Trans. Angus Davidson. London: Oxford University Press.

Richard, Guy, Richard-Le Guillou, Annie (2002). *Histoire De L'Amour. Du Moyen Age À Nos Jours*. Toulouse: Editions Privat.

Said, Edward W. (1979). *Orientalism.* New York: Vintage Books.

Steegmuller, Francis (1980). "Flaubert And Syphilis". In Gustave Flaubert, *The Letters Of Gustave Flaubert 1830–1857. Selected, Edited, And Translated By Francis Steegmuller.* Cambridge: Harvard University Press.

Tritter, Jean-Louis (2012). *Mythes De l'Orient En Occident,* Paris: Ellipses.

V

Multidimensionality of Cultural, Social and Emotional Borders in Oriental Literature

Chapter 15

The World of Haruki Murakami – a Hidden World of Ourselves

Milica Obrenović, *Independent researcher/Serbia*

Introduction

In order to present the world of Haruki Murakami, which is implicitly the world of each of us, it is important to present his literary work and Murakami as the author. As Haruki Murakami's literary work developed, the characters in his novels are becoming increasingly developed and more complex. We can notice this through the examples of the novel *Hard-Boiled Wonderland and the End of the World*, which was originally published in 1985 and whose female characters were not that well represented, as it is the case with the characters of Naoko and Midori in the novel *Norwegian Wood*, published in 1987, or the strong and outstanding character Aomame in the novel *1Q84*, the first two books of which were published in 2009, while the third book was published in 2010. In the analysis of his work, we recognise psychological and sociological approach in creating characters, describing their lives and the world around them. In developing their personalities Haruki Murakami uses such important aspects as the motif of childhood, relationships within their families and relationships among peers in school. The lack of love, care, support and understanding in their early age reflects in their future life on the possibilities to build various types of relationships. In this paper, these statements are supported by examples from Murakami's novels *Sputnik Sweetheart, Norwegian Wood, South of the Border, West of the Sun, After Dark, 1Q84* and *Coloreless Tsukuru Tazaki and His Years of Pilgrimage*, as well as by the scientific facts of Erich Fromm, a German social psychologist, psychoanalyst, sociologist and humanistic philosopher, David Riesman, an American sociologist, and Daniel Goleman, an American psychologist.

The reason for introducing these scientific points of views lies in the fact that Murakami provides us with the richness of the inner world of his characters. The outer world, on the other hand, serves only as an asset for a more authentic presentation of the layers of that inner world. Furthermore, while reading his novels, we feel like reading about a world distant from us. If we try to understand what that world looks like, we realise that we are familiar with the described world.

Haruki Murakami creates quite genuine characters, with whom we can not only easily identify, but also empathise. We might make the conclusion that the reason for his genuine and sincere style of writing lies in the fact that he started to write rather suddenly. He felt an impulse that he should write, so he did it, and, luckily, still does that and, moreover, he does it very successfully and intrigues us as readers and members of the world he creates.

The position of an Individual in a Society

The motif of a search for lost or hidden identity and inner fights, as well as the position of the individual in society, are frequent and timeless motifs and themes in the world literature. That is something that occupies an individual in every society during one's lifetime and has done so over centuries.

Daniel Goleman, in his book *Emotional Intelligence*, emphasises, within the subheading *A Cost of Modernity: Rising Rates of Depression*, the characteristics of the new age which increases not only sadness among people, which starts at earlier and earlier age, but also listlessness, dejection and overwhelming hopelessness, also stating the following: "These millennial years are ushering in an Age of Melancholy, just as the twentieth century became an Age of Anxiety" (Goleman 1996: 240).

A quite frequent motif is also the relationship between men and women, and perhaps at first we might feel free to state that nothing new is mentioned and described in Murakami's novels, but at the same time, we must add that Murakami's specific writing style and his approach to creating characters and describing these themes and motifs have a recognisable basis. However, he, due to his creative writing techniques, develops different characters and gives us his own, unique way of seeing those themes and motifs that make him distinctive and eminent in world literature.

Haruki Murakami presents us a completely different inner world of his characters. His characters do not succumb to temptation or pressure of societal norms. On the contrary, by living in their own way, following the rules of their inner world, they defy it. If we analysed Japanese society through historical and traditional aspects, we might have a different starting point while reading his novels, i.e., we would expect men to have leading roles in comparison with women. However, Murakami sees and describes their positions quite differently from the expected one. The way he sets his characters in the novels and the relationships among the male and female characters might be something that distinguishes his point of view of Japanese society or society in general, not bound by social constraints, but framed with human emotions, wherever and whenever they live. In the world of emotions, we cannot set the rules and expect those rules to be followed, hierarchically, socially or historically. The world of emotions bares an individual and makes them vulnerable, weak and fragile. At the same time, that world offers us a richness and wide palette of colours of the inner world, depending on the mood and condition in which, in this case, Murakami's characters are.

Even though Murakami's characters are not living souls, at least one small part of them lives in each of us, in the conscious, unconscious or subconscious part of our souls. Therefore, there is no need to perceive the mystery of his female characters as the inability of their analysis from the point of view of literature, but from the point of view of psychoanalysis also, through the theory of personality which concerns an individual or a reader, who sometimes identify themselves with "seemingly unreal and imaginary" characters.

The Alienation of the Individual

As a starting point for the explanation of alienation of the characters in the novels of Haruki Murakami, i.e. individuals in the modern society, it is convenient to mention the chapter *The Automat Versus the Glad Hand* in the book *The Lonely Crowd*, written by David Riesman, an American sociologist, in co-authorship with Nathan Glazer and Reuel Denney. Namely, in this chapter there is introduced and explained the meaning of small shops and salesmen devoted to their customers, as opposed to the new ones, modernised, large and depersonalised place full of people, but not interested in and not devoted to shopping, due to the fast way of living and inability to do the shopping calmly, which is followed by the inability of salesmen to devote themselves to the customers (Riesman, Glazer, Denney 1969: 271–272). That kind of disproportion and alienation among people and creation of distances in interpersonal relationships, as a result of a modern way of living, could be completed and explained with an automaton instead of devoted salesmen and their "glad hand". Despite the fact that this book analyses the American society, we notice its wide usage in explanation of a modern society nowadays.

That approach, which is not unfamiliar in Japan, a country which is a synonym for advanced technologies, could be symbolically connected to a motif recognised in Murakami's novels, that is "touching or holding someone's hand" between two people, either two women or a man and a woman. The emphasis is on the importance of that touch at the moment when one of those two people need it – as closeness and touch bring back the safety and self-confidence in the era of alienation. At the same time, we recognise the influence of modern life and, consequently, alienation of an individual in the world we live in.

With regard to the automat, or automatons, the term of equality and elimination of differences, Erich Fromm discusses these issues in his book *The Art of Loving*, which was published in 1956, which shows and at the same time confirms the previously mentioned hypothesis about alienated individuals in society and their longing for love and identity. Furthermore, the following quotation is from the chapter *Is Love an Art* and subchapter *Love, the Answer to the Problem of Human Existence*, which confirms the meaning of the existence of love as a precondition for the existence of a human. Erich Fromm emphasises the interpretation of those terms in the modern society: "By equality, one refers to the equality of automatons; of men who have lost their individuality. Equality today means 'sameness', rather than 'oneness' " (Fromm 1956: 15).

In that kind of world there live Murakami's characters, in the modern, depersonalised society in which they lose themselves. People stand next to each other, in the crowd, but they do not seem to form a whole. They do not manage to make contact. We could say that they are lonely individuals in the crowd.

Erich Fromm also says the following about a modern man: "He is alienated from himself, from his fellow men and from nature" (Fromm 1956: 105), as well as the following about the automatons: "Automatons cannot love; they can exchange their personality packages' and hope for a fair bargain" (Fromm 1956: 87).

The impact of alienation on an individual is thoroughly explained in one key sentence in the book *The Sane Society*, written by Erich Fromm: "Alienated man is unhappy" (Fromm 2001: 199).

The Warmth of a Hand

Continuing the previously explained alienation of an individual and the lack of a "glad hand", while analysing Murakami's novels and the characters we notice that one of the motifs which can be distinguished, as we previously mentioned, is the motif of touching or holding someone's hand. Holding or touching someone's hand happens whenever one person is in the most vulnerable emotional state, feeling either insecure because of some physical characteristics or because of certain emotional emptiness and weakness. The moment of touching or holding someone's hand provides warmth, support, strength, and understanding to another person. That moment follows either spoken words or, by its own strength, it replaces every potentially spoken word, i.e., no words are needed. The importance of the warmth of a hand is something that we all are aware of.

In the novel *Sputnik Sweetheart*, by touching Sumire's hand, Miu, the other female character, persuades Sumire how beautiful she is. "She reached out and, quite unaffectedly, lightly touched Sumire's hand that, lay on the table. 'You don't realize how very attractive you are' " (Murakami 2002: 21). That statement warms Sumire's heart, and she falls in love with Miu. Miu is seventeen years older than Sumire. Sumire's mother died when she was almost three years old. That loss influences her personality. She thinks she is not as beautiful as her father is. Miu brings happiness into her life. Sumire feels safe, self-confident and strong while Miu holds her hand, everything she is not when being overwhelmed by fears and insecurity.

The strength which one touch of a hand has can also be noticed in the novel *South of the Border, West of the Sun*. The male character, Hajime, remembers the touch of Shimamoto's, his friend from the elementary school, hand. Even though it lasts only for ten seconds, it has endless power: "The feel of her hand has never left me. It was different from any other hand I'd ever held, different from any touch I've ever known. It was merely the small, warm hand of a twelve-year-old girl, yet those fingers and that palm were like a display case crammed full of everything I wanted to know – and everything I had to know" (Murakami 2003c: 14).

In the novel *After Dark*, we read about two sisters – Mari Asai and Eri Asai. The story happens during one night in Tokyo. Eri Asai is asleep, as she has been for the past two months. Mari Asai is not that beautiful, at least, according to the information given in the novel and according to the information, based on her parents' attitude towards her, which she shares with a male character, Tetsuya Takahashi. Her sister, Eri Asai, is a real beauty. Their parents make distinctions between the two of them based on the fact how beautiful they are. Furthermore, Mari Asai has short, kinky hair, quite unusual for a Japanese girl, while Eri Asai has beautiful long black hair. The fact that their parents make those differences between two of them consequently influences Mari Asai's life and lack of self-confidence and, therefore, the possibility to make contact with other people. That fact also influences her relationship with her sister and even though she tries to show how the lack of that relationship does not affect her, she suffers. Tetsuya Takahashi comes into her life, seemingly out of nowhere, and becomes her friend, but he actually knows her and knows her sister, and they talk about it, and eventually he helps to her remember a piece of memory, as a very important aspect of everyone's life, along with emotions, experienced when she felt very close to her sister. Mari Asai explains that it happened in the elevator during an earthquake when she was in kindergarten, and Eri Asai was a second-grader. Mari Asai was very afraid, and so was Eri Asai, but Eri Asai decided to be strong for both of them. "The important thing is that during that whole time in the dark, Eri was holding me. And it wasn't just some ordinary hug. She squeezed me so hard our two bodies felt as if they were melting into one" (Murakami 2008: 189). This memory, the warmth of a hug, of a touch of her sister's body when she needed it the most, helps Mari Asai to reconnect with her sister and at the end of the novel she enters her sister's room, lies next to her, hugging her and kissing her, trying to transfer warmth from herself to her sister's body, being assured that Eri's flow is blending with hers while thinking to herself. That scene ends in the following way: "Two young sisters sleep peacefully, their bodies pressed together in one small bed" (Murakami 2008: 196).

At the same time, the touch of a hand is described while Mari Asai describes this memory to Tetsuya Takahashi. "Takahashi reaches out and takes Mari's hand. She is momentarily startled but does not pull her hand from his. Takahashi keeps his gentle grip on her hand–her small, soft hand–for a very long time" (Murakami 2008: 191).

With regards to the fact how important memories are, another conversation between Mari Asai and another female character, Korogi, whom she meets during that one night, is presented in this novel. Namely, Korogi emphasises the importance of memories, comparing them with the fuel which people burn to stay alive. Without that fuel, Korogi explains, she would have snapped a long time ago (Murakami 2008: 168–169).

The importance of memories and their influences on someone's life is explained by Sara Kimoto, Tsukuru Tazaki's girlfriend in the novel *Colorless Tsukuru Tazaki and His Years of Pilgrimage*. "You can hide memories, suppress them, but you can't erase the history that produced them" (Murakami 2014: 32).

As a conclusion to the emotions which connect people, transcending all boundaries, the conclusion which Tsukuru Tazaki comes to may be quoted: "One heart is not connected to another through harmony alone. They are, instead, linked deeply through their wounds" (Murakami 2014: 248). This quotation confirms our statement regarding our skills to hide our fears and inner thoughts while being actually "victims" of our inner anxiety. However, while reading Murakami's novels, we recognise our lives in the lives, fears, and thoughts of his characters and we empathise with them and, at the same time, we manage to find hidden parts of ourselves, in the way they find their parts in other characters, as well as the answers for the anxiety influenced by disharmonised world of wounds.

The Meaning of Beauty

If we want to analyse the physical appearance of Murakami's female characters, we notice that their beauty is peculiar. Even if one of them limps, this physical barrier does not diminish her beauty. This physical trait characterises Shimamoto in the novel *South of the Border, West of the Sun.* Despite her physical problem, whenever Hajime thinks of her, her smile comes first to his mind (Murakami 2003c: 5).

Murakami's female characters are usually not women of classic beauty, but more often with a specific beauty. Despite some physical disability or asymmetry, they are beautiful in a special way. We notice this with nearly all his female characters. That special kind of beauty is sometimes quite objectively noticed, and sometimes it is not widely recognised, but, rather, described from the point of view of a narrator, a man who is in love with her or a person who is her partner. Even when some of them are not real beauties, as Sumire in *Sputnik Sweetheart,* with sunken cheeks and upturned nose, there is still something special about them, which draws people to them. "Defining that special something isn't easy, but when you gazed into her eyes, you could always find it, reflected deep down inside"(Murakami 2002: 6).

A similar approach to describing the specific beauty of Aomame can be noticed in the novel *1Q84.* The size and shape of her ears were significantly different since the left one was quite bigger than the right one. Her lips were in the form of a tight straight line, and her nose was small and narrow, while cheekbones were protruding and forehead was broad. "All of these were arranged to sit in a pleasing oval shape, however, and while tastes differ, few would object to calling her a beautiful woman" (Murakami 2012: 15).

In the world of trends and standards imposed upon an individual in order to be a beauty nowadays, Murakami offers us something that slowly becomes forgotten and that is a beauty of each of us, hidden in the details of our faces, expressions of the face, a finger, or the whole hand, or, what is more important, the touch of that hand and strength and emotion given by a look of the eye, a smile or a touch of the hand. Beauty comes from the touch, either physical or emotional, warming up our frightened heart, finding a way to love, hidden or forgotten in our hearts, making it possible for us to feel alive again.

The Importance of Love

Love, as the most important motif, exists very strongly in Murakami's novels, either explicitly or implicitly expressed. It is described in a genuine way, with carefully chosen words and their synonyms, in order to express it in a proper way, with distinctive shades and layers of its importance and intensity. A description of Watanabe's feelings towards Naoko and Midori, in the novel *Norwegian Wood*, is an example of Murakami's gentle approach:

"What I feel for Naoko is a tremendously quiet and gentle and transparent love, but what I feel for Midori is a wholly different emotion. It stands and walks on its own, living and breathing and throbbing and shaking me to the roots of my being" (Murakami 2003b: 353).

The lack of parents' love during their childhood and, consequently, the lack of understanding among peers during the school period make Murakami's character alienated, nearly safe only in their own companionship. However, they yearn for love, for a feeling of belonging to someone, to be loved or to feel love, even then when they are not aware of that feeling.

In the novel *1Q84*, the main female character, Aomame, does not stop thinking and talking about her only and true love, which she was lucky to experience when she was only ten years old, by holding Tengo's hand for a few seconds. They are the same age. Tengo feels the same. Both of them share the same memory which keeps their love safe until they meet again. Despite many difficulties, they manage to meet again, at the end of the novel.

Twenty years later, they take each other's hands again, wordlessly, being again the ten-year-old boy and girl, a lonely boy and a lonely girl, not loved by anyone or truly loving someone else, but each other. "Totally isolated, yet the one place not tainted with loneliness" (Murakami 2012: 1277–1278).

Aomame explains in detail the greatness of her love and her feelings to Ayumi, a woman she meets in the meantime. She does not want to try to find her love. She waits for the moment of meeting him by chance, all of a sudden, unexpectedly. She is convinced she will recognise him, even though twenty years have passed (Murakami 2012: 274–275). The explanation of her strong belief is hidden in the strength of her love, which cannot vanish or be destroyed by anything or anyone. Her belief, equally with her love, does not fade or weaken at any point. Tengo shares the same feeling. She recognises and recalls his strength, intelligence, and kindness – values of the inner beauty.

She says that a touch of his hand will stay with her. "My shuddering emotion will stay. The desire to be in his arms will stay. Even if I become a completely different person, my love for Tengo can never be taken from me" (Murakami 2012: 530).

Aomame's words about the love she feels towards Tengo describe at the same time the true meaning and strength which love has: "If you can love someone with your whole heart, even one person, then there's salvation in life. Even if you can't get together with that person" (Murakami 2012: 276).

We notice the motif of love as the strongest one to encourage Murakami's characters and give them an identity which has been lost earlier or has never been developed before. They suffer from the lack of love of their parents or friends in school, they are trying to find themselves, i.e., the missing parts of their soul in another person, a person they find close to their soul.

Along with the motif of love, which is quite explicitly expressed, we also notice the motif of holding hands. Those two motifs are strongly connected. Moreover, they are mutually influenced.

In the novel *Sputnik Sweetheart,* Miu explains her longing for love, however, she realises the importance of love too late: "But never once did I truly love someone. I didn't have the time. All I could think about was becoming a world-class pianist, and deviating from that path was not an option. Something was missing in me, but by the time I noticed that gap, it was too late" (Murakami 2002: 174). At the same time, the male character, Sumire's friend from the college describes his feelings towards Sumire, despite the fact that this love had no chance to happen. Nevertheless, the beauty of his description of love and emotions towards Sumire is unique and becomes rare in the world around us: "All over again I understood how important, how irreplaceable, Sumire was to me" (Murakami 2002: 193); "I loved Sumire more than anyone else and wanted her more than anything in the world. And I couldn't just shelve those feelings, for there was nothing to take their place" (Murakami 2002: 194). She loves him too, in a different way, or perhaps it is more appropriate to say in her own way, because when she says: " 'I like you, too,' Sumire said. 'In this whole big world, more than anyone else'" (Murakami 2002: 72). However, she cannot explain it more in more words than she said. The way she loves Miu is different, she wants to have her, to make her hers, because she simply has to (Murakami 2002: 72–73). We notice here a motif of belonging to someone, especially if we bear in mind the fact that Sumire misses her mother, whom she meets in her dreams, but never manages to recall her mother's face and to hear what her mother tells her (Murakami 2002: 153). She does not manage to find the answers in the dreams for the life she lives. She likes living in dreams, furthermore, she could live there forever, because there, boundaries do not exist and no distinction between things needs to be made (Murakami 2002: 148).

In the novel *After Dark,* we also notice the fact that Mari Asai hated school and was not able to find a friend there and it is due to the fact that parents gave the sisters life roles – Eri Asai as a Snow White and Mari Asai as a little genius (Murakami 2008: 57). All she actually wanted was to be loved and to feel like an equal member of her family. She suffered a lot, and so did her sister, Eri Asai, even though the parents loved her more, or perhaps only unintentionally showed less love and care towards Mari Asai.

Conclusion

We, as members of different culture and living in different surroundings, do not feel the barrier and difference while reading Murakami's description of his characters. On the contrary, we identify with them in terms of problems we are faced with, doubts or inner fears, no matter when or where we live. Furthermore, it makes no difference whether we are reading about male or female characters. Even though we are aware of the fact that they exist within the lines of one novel, that does not stop us from identifying with the timeless inner human struggles, thoughts, turmoil and insecurity and, thanks to those facts, from finding strength in ourselves, realising our dilemmas and sometimes being able to overcome them more easily. Whatever side we choose, either being on the side of his (un)real, fictional characters or on the side of real, everyday life circumstances, we are convinced that hope is somewhere there, we should not give up hope, and that is what matters at the end of a day. That is something that Aomame confirms while thinking of her love towards Tengo: "This is what it means to live on. When granted hope, a person uses it as fuel, as a guidepost to life. It is impossible to live without hope" (Murakami 2012: 912).

Murakami's novels sometimes do not offer us the end we might expect, but that is the point. We do not know whether something happened or not, whether it was a matter of inspiration from real life scenes or it was a part of an imaginary world. Such seemingly incomplete, unfinished endings of the novels give us the opportunity to continue to imagine and to revive and preserve our waking memories and feelings.

Bibliography

Fromm, Erich (1956). *The Art Of Loving.* New York: Harper & Row
—— (2001). *The Sane Society.* London: Routledge

Goleman, Daniel (1996). *Emotional Intelligence: Why It Can Matter More Than IQ.* London: Bloomsbury Publishing Plc.

Murakami Haruki (2002). *Sputnik Sweetheart.* Translated From Japanese By Philip Gabriel. London: Vintage

—— (2003a). *Hard-Boiled Wonderland And The End Of The World.* Translated From Japanese By Alfred Birnbaum. London: Vintage

—— (2003b). *Norwegian Wood.* Translated From Japanese By Jay Rubin. London: Vintage

—— (2003c). *South Of The Border, West Of The Sun.* Translated From Japanese By Philip Gabriel. London: Vintage

—— (2008). *After Dark.* Translated From Japanese By Jay Rubin. London: Vintage

—— (2012). *1Q84.* Books One And Two Translated From Japanese By Jay Rubin And Book Three Translated From Japanese By Philip Gabriel. London: Vintage

—— (2014). *Colorless Tsukuru Tazaki And His Years Of Pilgrimage.* Translated From The Japanese By Philip Gabriel. London: Vintage.

Riesman, David, Glazer, Nathan, Denney, Reuel (1969). *The Lonely Crowd: A Study Of The Changing American Character.* New Haven: Yale University Press.

Chapter 16

The Role of Translation in Identity Formation: A Case Study of Turkish Translations of *Martine*

Gözde Begüm Uyanık, *Istanbul University/Turkey*
Harika Karavin, *Istanbul University/Turkey*

Introduction

Throughout the world, children spend their childhood periods by listening to or reading various stories. As it is known, children books have an important place in the personal, emotional and pedagogical development of children. These books help children to discover themselves and perceive the external world. Thanks to children's literature, their language, and emotional development are enriched (Yalçın and Aytaş 2002: 5–6). In addition, children's literature enables the values of a specific culture to be spread to the future generations. In the modern pedagogical approach, which encourages life-long learning, children mimic their immediate surroundings and try to understand the values of society through the models created by children's literature. Through reading children stories, their limited experiences get richer and, hence, it becomes possible for them to make more complicated judgements. In other words, children stories improve children's adaptiveness to the social and cultural environment in which they live. However, it should not be forgotten that the social or cultural values transferred through children's literature do not always affect the child's world in a positive way. The worldview imposed upon the child with literary works can also affect their socialisation in a negative way.

As it is seen, children's literature is accepted as an important part of child development. However, the fact that most of the stories children fondly listen to or read are "translated works" in Turkey literary system should not be ignored. Children who grow up with such stories as *Pinocchio, Snow White and the Seven Dwarfs, Hansel and Gretel* get acquainted with the notion of translation from a very early age and thus enter into different worlds. For this reason, translation of children's literature plays a key role in the socio-cultural and pedagogical development of children. According to Radegundis Stolze, who made important studies in this area, the most important topic to be regarded in the translation of children's literature is the pedagogical view to be transferred to the child in the target culture (Stolze 2013: 219). Emphasising that the primary aim of translated works for children is to develop their pedagogy, Stolze mentions that the worldview of the source text is transferred to the child in the target culture. For this reason, translators can impose a specific worldview on the children in the target culture by selecting certain works to translate (ibid.). As is observed in other translation types, the ideology of the translator or the publishing house determines some translational decisions, including the selection of a text to be translated and the translation strategy to be adopted.

An important linguist, Sandor Hervey claims that the translator starting to translate a children book encounters the following dilemma: (a) whether the target text should reflect the ideology of the target text and target text author; (b) whether the target text should be adapted to the ideological or social needs of the target culture (Hervey 1997: 61). In other words, he questions whether translation serves the source culture or if it tries to develop or change the target culture.

In order to analyse the issues mentioned above in a clearer manner, this study will examine the way translations affect the target system as a "culture planner", considering the socio-cultural and pedagogical reflections of *Ayşegül* stories, which were first translated into Turkish in 1965. As Gideon Toury mentioned, translators resort to translation in order to fulfil a gap in the target culture. It is seen that such translations generally differ from the target text norms in various respects (Toury 2002: 148–155). As a result, translations transfer new thoughts and paradigms from the source to the target culture and affect the target literary norms to some extent. Faruk Yücel explains this issue as follows:

> "As a product of complex relations on social, cultural and political level, translation both affects and becomes affected by the target literature. For instance, the fact that translation affects the target literature to fill a gap in the target culture can create new genres and narrative opportunities in this literature while some of the developments of the target culture that direct the readers' tendencies and cause some sub-

jects to come to the agenda can determine the types of books and the specialty of the authors to be translated" (Yücel 2007: 156–57).

As it is seen, translations can change the social structure of the target culture by affecting the needs, thoughts, and expectations of the target system. These changes can sometimes be carried out as a result of a conscious preference or sometimes unconsciously. The effect of translation is first realised in the target culture. In other words, translation starts to affect the target culture through the target literature. Apparently supporting this opinion, Stolze mentions that the first response is observed in the target readers. According to Stolze, the innovations or the differences affect the target readers in the first instance (Stolze 2013: 165). However, the permanence of these effects depends on the (non)integration of these "transferred" factors into the target system (Even-Zohar 1997).

Based on this theoretical framework and background knowledge, this study will deal with the changes or innovations that the target system aims to create through the *Ayşegül* stories. For this purpose, the characteristics of woman figure "transferred" or "tried to be transferred" with these stories will be foregrounded. However, in order to understand these characteristics, it is necessary to examine the target system in which the translations were carried out with the aim of describing the socio-cultural context in terms of women image. Before starting to discuss the features of an ideal woman figure as described in the *Ayşegül* stories, brief information will be presented regarding the authors and their books.

Information on the Corpus

The original story, entitled *Martine*, was written by Belgian Marcel Marlier and Gilbert Delahaye in French. The series was first published by Casterman as children stories. The first book of the series, *Martine à la Ferme*, dates back to 1954. Following this book, fifty-nine more stories were published. As it was an illustrated storybook, *Martine*'s pictures were drawn by Marcel Marlier. When Gilbert Delahaye died in 1997, the remaining books of the series were continued by his son, Jean-Louis Marlier. The last book of the *Martine* series, which sold more than a hundred million copies throughout the world, was published in 2010 with the title *Martine et le Prince Mystérieux*. Because of the death of Marcel Marlier, it was not possible to publish more books for the series.

Turkish translations of the series were published by Alpagut and Marsık Publishing Houses with the title *Ayşegül* and *Küçük Ayşegül* (*Little Ayşegül*).

The name of the hero was Debbie in the USA, Christina in Italy, Steffi in Germany, Emma in England and Anita in Portugal. The target readership of the series included children who could not read or just started to learn reading (Arı 2015: 65). The stories aim to make the readers experience and join in Ayşegül's adventures. The first Turkish translation was published by Alpagut Publishing House in the 1960s while the second translation was published by Marsık Publishing House in the 1980s. Since its first publication, the series has managed to gain the attention of the readers all around Turkey. The series was even given as a gift for the buyers of the *Sabah* and *Hürriyet* newspapers during the 1990s. The latest translations were made by Füsun Önen and published by Yapı Kredi Publishing House in 2011.

In the translations published by Marsık and Alpagut Publishing Houses, no information was provided regarding the publication date, the original name of the work or the name of the translator. On the other hand, it is possible to find such information in Yapı Kredi's translated versions. In his article published in 2011, Necdet Neydim mentions that "ignoring to note down the publication date and number on children's books during the 1970s is most probably a common trend, for this reason we can predict the publication date of the book approximately" (Neydim, quoted in Arı 2015: 69). For this reason, it would not be wrong to claim that the main reason behind such a tendency may result from the nonexistence of copyright laws for translated books in Turkey.

Analysis of the Socio-cultural Context

When *Ayşegül* started to enter the Turkish literary system, the country was busy with modernisation movements that had started with the foundation of the Turkish Republic. As in many parts of the society, women's position in both social and political areas started to be redefined. Mustafa Kemal Atatürk defined the ideal woman figure "as a woman who has equal opportunities with the men in family, society and the state" (Gelgeç Bakacak 2009: 628). Traditional women, confined to the inside of the home and defined only with their productive skills, were bestowed significant roles "in the cultural and civil formations of nations with their citizen rights and responsibilities" (Yuval–Davis 1997: 17–19). To put it differently, the visibility of women in society increased. Within the framework of this modernisation movement, women were integrated into the working life while attempts were made to strengthen their roles in the family (Gelgeç Bakacak 2009: 628). With this newly created "modern" woman figure, they gained some rights and freedom, but it was also underlined that their primary duty was to be "a mother". The main writings published at that time include such topics as children education, marriage, morality, household management, childcare and fashion (ibid.). To put it in brief terms, the ideal woman image, as attempted to be created after the foundation of the Republic, referred to such kind of a woman who has equal rights with men in social and economic terms, adapts herself to the requirements of the modern age, educates herself, brings up a child in the best way.

The *Ayşegül* stories are significant in terms of representing the characteristics of a "modern" woman in the target system through a character of a little girl. It would not be wrong to mention that these series serve the purpose of creating a modern woman character in the target culture as the girls of the 1960s and the 1980s would become the adults of the 2000s who would have their own jobs as well as trying to fulfil their duty of being a good mother.

This series, introduced into Turkish literary system through translation, gained high success when it was first translated and read by numerous readers. Even though fifty years have passed since its publication, Turkish readers are still interested in reading them. The fact that one of the leading Turkish publishing houses, Yapı Kredi, reprinted the series proves this tendency. However, it is possible to conclude that the aim for its retranslation after fifty years may not be similar. It is a known fact that there are differences both in the periods and the requirements of the periods in which the books were translated. Mentioning that the *Ayşegül* stories aided in creating a modern figure in Turkey and that the current translations contribute to emphasising the characteristics of such a modern woman display a contradictory issue. However, as the translations of the stories have been going on for the last fifty years, it is possible to claim that the latest translations may aim to foreground different aspects of a woman figure. To put it in a clearer way, while the 1960s aimed for women's freedom by providing them with another identity apart from being mothers, the women of the modern world have already gained such kind of freedom and started to move away from their homes. For this reason, it would not be wrong to conclude that these stories were re-translated with the aim of reminding the women of their roles as mothers. In other words, it is possible to mention that different women roles were tried to be foregrounded with the translations produced in two different periods.

Different Reflections of Women Image in the *Ayşegül* Stories

In this chapter of the study, three stories – namely, *Ayşegül Mutfakta, Ayşegül Küçük Anne, Ayşegül Ata Biniyor* – will be handled as the corpus of the study so as to examine both the series in their own periods and their representation of women image. The reason why these three stories have been chosen as the corpus is the eligibility of the translations of these stories' from Alpagut (TT1) and Yapı Kredi (TT2) Publishing Houses as well as their richness to provide examples in describing images of women. Before discussing the corpus in detail, it would be helpful to touch upon the ways Ayşegül has been described in the series in general. For this purpose, other books in the series in addition to the books selected for the corpus have also been analysed, and it was seen that Ayşegül travels, does household duties, does social activities with her friends, goes skiing, rides a horse and dances in ballet. We need to deal with concrete examples so as to better understand the different identities described within the character of Ayşegül. For this reason, first of all, examples from *Ayşegül Küçük Anne* where Ayşegül's role of motherhood stands out will be dwelt upon. In *Ayşegül Küçük Anne,* we see that Ayşegül replaces her mother for a day and takes care of her little brother. Ayşegül gets up early, gives a bath to her brother, feeds him, and finally takes her brother to the park. In this book, we see that during a baby's bath, some points to be paid attention are given as advice.

<u>Example 1:</u>

TT1: "A baby starts a day with a bath. One should pay attention not to heat water too much. Giving a bath to Ali is not such an easy job. It is necessary not to frighten him. He should be helped to splash the water with his hands so that the red fish and duck in the bathtub can dance. Sometimes he wants to stand up in the tub. He splashes water in his face and sticks out his tongue. Ouch! We should be very careful that the soap does not get into his eyes. The bath is over" (Alpagut: 4).

TT2: "The day of the baby started with the bath. But it was necessary to pay attention to the heat of the water. Giving bath to Ali is not such an easy job. He kept on splashing the water with his hands to make the red fish and the plastic duck move. He wanted to stand up in his tub. He was covering his face and eyes with soap and sticking out his tongue. It was necessary to be careful that the soap does not get into his eyes. The bath was over" (YKY: 5).

When we look at the first translation, it can be concluded that the text has the characteristics of a piece of advice. The narrator speaks as if he/she is giving advice. Therefore, the use of modal verbs implying necessity is frequently observed. This kind of use creates an impression on the readers as if they were, in fact, reading a textbook. General information is provided within the context of necessity and what happens during this process is not presented to the readers. However, when we take a look at the picture above the example, we can see that Ayşegül is giving a bath to the baby, the baby is playing with the soap in his hand and, meanwhile, there are a cat and a dog with them. In other words, it is possible to say that the incident is transferred to the readership as general information rather than a narrative. Only in the sentence "He splashes water in his face and sticks out his tongue.", we can observe a description of the moment. The exclamation "Ouch!" used in the last sentence of the example, tries to attract the attention of the readership. The narrator, at this point, also includes himself/herself in these rules. In other words, advice given is first of all for Ayşegül and then for other young women. In Yapı Kredi Publishing House's translation, the narrative is different. Instead of the use of modal verbs, we see the use of past tenses. Such kind of language use makes the book a story in Turkish language and highlights the process of narrating. Moreover, in this translation, it is also possible to see that there are fewer sentences giving advice than in the first translation. In the YKY's translation the translator narrates the situation rather than giving advice, thus highlighting more the actions of the characters. After describing differences at linguistic level, we need to take a look at how much these translations contribute to describing the motherhood role of women.

It will not be wrong to say that the first translation has pedagogical effects since it uses an advice-giving narrative. We can conclude that such kind of a narration method is related to the mothers being uneducated and in need of education at that time. In the first translation, we observe much more expressions on how women should be as a mother. Therefore, we can conclude that the first translation has the aim of changing the image of the mother of the time. However, in the second translation, we cannot see such a strong pedagogical effect. The reason for this could be that women are nowadays more conscious and educated than they used to be. In another example of the book, Ayşegül's preparing dinner for her brother is described. In this part, we see expressions answering the question of "how should baby food be prepared?"

Example 2:

TT1: "The baby cried and got angry. Ayşegül knew the reason of this impatience. It was time for the baby bottle. When a baby gets hungry, you shouldn't make him wait for so long. Thus, Ayşegül heated the water immediately. Where is the dried milk? Or the sugar? Has the baby bottle been washed? Now, everything is ready. The thing left to do was arranging the quantity of milk, water, and sugar. Her mother showed [her] the bottle and said: 'The milk should be right on this level'" (Alpagut: 7).

TT2: "The baby got angry and cried. Ayşegül knew the reason of his impatience very well. It was time for the baby bottle. When the baby gets hungry, you shouldn't make him wait any more. Thus, Ayşegül heated the water. Where was the baby bottle? She needed to find the bottle. Had the baby bottle been washed? Now, everything was ready. The only thing left was to put water and baby food according to the level on the bottle. Her mother showed [her] the bottle and said: 'The milk should be right on this level'" (YKY: 8).

In both translations, advice is given regarding the points to pay attention to in preparing food for a baby. In the translations, attention is paid to milk, sugar and baby bottle, which are needed for babies' nutrition. With question sentences, it is aimed to make mothers question themselves on this matter, and to make them pay attention to issues such as the warmth of the milk and the cleanness of the baby bottle. In other words, some clues for mothers on how to prepare baby food correctly are given in the translations. Another function of these question sentences could be transferring message to mothers to test themselves on these matters. Therefore, it is possible to say that both translations have the aim of directing mothers in childcare. However, when we compare the directions of both translations, we can come to different conclusions. In the first translation, the word "dried milk" is used as a nutrient, while in the second translation we see the use of "baby food". When we consider the period of the first translation, it should be recalled that nourishing children used to be carried out primarily by means of breast milk, and only a minority of people used baby food in Turkey. Although baby food first entered into Turkish market via Nestlé in 1875[1], or, to put it in a different way, before the first translation of the book in Turkish, only a limited number of people could use baby food. Mothers at that period used to stay at home for a year or two, taking care of their children after giving birth. Therefore, the idea of using dried

---

[1] See. http://www.hurriyet.com.tr/nestle-ve-bebek-mamasi-20789322 (Accessed: 05.06.2016).

milk in instances when breast milk is not present is depicted in the book, implying that mothers could have a work life outside home after they give birth to their children. When we think that women's entry into work life was seen intensely in the 1970s, it is possible to conclude that the first translation gives a message that women should enter the work life. As a result, we can suggest that this translation contributes to the idea of modern women working in the market, which is an ideal women image after Proclamation of Turkish Republic. Although same messages are emphasised, it can be said that it aims at reminding women of her responsibilities at home other than work life. When we assume that mothers at our age are more educated, thus, the number of mothers working is higher than that in the 1970s, and they already use ready-made baby food more, it is obvious that it does not have the same function as that of the first translation. Rather, it can contribute to reminding mothers of their responsibilities inside the house. Let us examine an example from *Ayşegül Mutfakta* by Alpagut Publishing House, and *Ayşegül Yemek Yapıyor* by Yapı Kredi Publishing House.

Example 3:

TT1: "Like every girl, Ayşegül likes helping her mother with the household. She does not want to leave her mother, especially while she is cooking. A good cook should know what to do, she should be imaginative and patient like her mother. Patience... Isn't it what is required to shell one and a half kilos of beans" (Alpagut: 3).

TT2: "A master cook has high imagination and knowledge. And also patience! It really required patience to shell one and a half kilos of beans with her mother for five people (her mother, father, herself, Orhan, her cousin Ersin)" (YKY: 7).

The ideal role of women in the kitchen can easily be inferred from this example, although most of the book is composed of recipes. Women are "cooks" in this book besides "mothers", which is also the case in *Küçük Anne*. When we analyse the first translation by Alpagut, it will not be wrong to say that there is a description of what the role of girls as future women should be. In this translation, Ayşegül likes helping her mother on household "like every girl does", which leads the reader think that a mother manages the household in a family and that the daughter should help her mother. We also cannot see any duties on the household for the father and/or the son. Cooking is the duty of the women, and saying a good cook should be creative and patient is also provided in this book with the use of didactic language and modal verbs. Even without using modal verbs, it could be said that the message is given in the same way. This is because when we look at the example "Like every girl, Ayşegül likes helping her mother with the household.", we easily understand that the message "daughters should help their mothers on the household" is given. When we look at the second translation by YKY, again we see the criteria on how a good cook should be being given, we also understand that women should be in the kitchen and cook for the whole family, the rest of which are men. The language use is softer here, for this message could not be given to women of our age.

Examples below can be more representative of the roles of women and men, since these examples illustrate the behaviours of girls and boys, e.g., adults of the future. We have included an example here which can be seen in YKY translation and which is not present in Alpagut translation so as to observe these gender roles.

Example 4:

TT1: "Arda suddenly got in the kitchen and said 'Look what I have found in the attic'" (Alpagut: 10).

TT2: "Egg yolk is cooked well! If our mother is not at home, it is so necessary to know how to make soft-boiled egg when our little brother gets hungry! (YKY: 6)

But suddenly…

Orhan yelled 'Look what I have found in the attic!' getting into the kitchen like a storm" (YKY: 14).

When we analyse the example that is not present in the Alpagut translation "Egg yolk is cooked well! If our mother is not at home, it is so necessary to know how to make soft-boiled egg when our little brother gets hungry!", we observe the motherhood role of a daughter when her mother is not at home. Although feeding a child should be the parents' (irrespective of the gender; both mother's and father's) duty, in this book this responsibility is undertaken by the daughter when her mother is not present. The girl in a family is considered to be a little mother, and an adult woman, although she herself is also a child. Ayşegül is considered to take care of herself, moreover, she undertakes the childcare duty, which is already represented in the series as the duty of a woman(!). However, this is not the case for men in the series. We can take a look at Ayşegül's little brother's actions, which are present in both translations. Ayşegül's little brother represents the future adult man, and we can easily observe that he has no responsibility and he is even naughty. Although there is a woman character (Ayşegül) busy with cooking in the kitchen, the naughty little boy of the family gets there, thus causing the meal to burn. We can observe on this example that boys can be naughty at home and they do not need to take any responsibilities at all. At this point, it will not be wrong to say that even when illustrating the role of men, the message on how girls should behave is also given.

In the last part of the study, *Ayşegül Ata Biniyor* has been chosen to be analysed, since this book provides a different view on woman image within the series. In this book, we see Ayşegül's first acquaintance with a horse and her learning process concerning how to ride. When we think of the riding history in the world and in Turkey, it is possible to say that horse riding as an action dates back to old times, although the purposes differ in that horses were ridden for military purposes, but today horse riding has gained importance as a sport. The fact that the first riding school was founded almost 60 years before the first translation and the first race was organised in the mid-1930s, we can say that horse riding as a developing sports branch was tried to be transferred to the target culture by means of the *Ayşegül* stories. However, the reason why this transfer is realised by means of a female gender could be due to creating a new woman image. When we compare the translations in terms of content, in the first translation Ayşegül decides to ride a horse as a result of the persistence of her uncle, who is a horse breeder, although in the second translation Ayşegül takes horse riding courses from an instructor:

Example 5:

TT1: "Ayşegül's uncle was a horse breeder. He owned a big farm. One day, he said to Ayşegül: 'Now that you have grown up, you can learn how to ride a horse'" (Alpagut: 3).

TT2: "Ayşegül went to Uncle Fırat – a horse riding instructor – to take horse riding lessons" (YKY: 3).

The difference between the translations could be associated with the educational levels in times of the translations. When the first translation was published, horse riding was a developing sport mostly undertaken by men. Therefore, it was thought that women could ride a horse only with the encouragement of another person. We can infer from the text that women were less educated at that time and should be encouraged. In the second translation, however, the fact that women are getting more conscious in horse riding today and get training courses professionally is highlighted. Except for the differences in educational levels of the times, the common thing in both translations is that Ayşegül becomes a better horse rider in time. In addition to the roles attributed in the other examples, Ayşegül is attributed another role outside home. Ayşegül can now ride a horse, which has generally been identified with men, apart from her skills at home. This story has an effective role in creating a new woman image within the target culture, to put it differently. However, at this very point, it will not be wrong to say that the effect of the first translation is more obvious. When we take a look at Turkish horse riding history, horse riding as a sport used to be performed by men in the 1970s except for two women.[2] Therefore, the effect of the first translation that narrates Ayşegül as a little girl taking horse riding courses is more obvious in creating modern woman. It will not be possible to see a similar effect in the second translation because of the fact that borders between men and women have decreased and that women's experience in horse riding has increased. *Ayşegül Ata Biniyor* also draws up a woman figure that has active roles outside home and socially interacts with the opposite sex. After long training, Ayşegül becomes a good horse rider, she participates in a horse riding race where the rest of the participants are male and achieves the first place despite all obstacles she faces. Although we observe that the story is transferred similarly in both translations, the effect of creating a new women image is more obvious in the first translation. The "woman figure" represented by Ayşegül has been presented with characteristics that modern women should have. First and foremost, Ayşegül has the right to make time for herself and develop herself physically apart from her responsibilities at home. Moreover, Ayşegül is described as a successful, brave and strong woman having the ability to compete with males. Therefore, the status of women within society is redefined by the first translation. By presenting a young woman as successful in a sports branch mostly performed by men, translations could have the aim of doing away with the secondary position of women within society. Similarly, it is proven here that women can compete with the opposite sex.

Conclusion

This study has aimed to show the effect of translation on identity formation in the target literary system through an example of translated children's literature. In the analysis of the selected corpus, an attempt was made to explain the effects of the translated stories, taking their socio-cultural and pedagogical reflections into consideration. In line with the findings of the study, it is

---

[2] See: http://www.nkfu.com/unlu-biniciler-binicilik-sporculari-ve-hayatlari/ (Accessed: 05.06.2016).

possible to conclude that translations of *Martine* by two different publishing houses contribute to the formation of a new role for women in Turkish culture. In addition, the study has problematised the possible different functions of the examined translations. Within this framework, it has been assumed that the translations published by Alpagut Publishing House served the purpose of creating a new image of a modern woman who should have freedom and life outside the house. However, it seems that the translations of Yapı Kredi Publishing House have the aim for reminding the "modern" women of their household duties apart from those of their working lives. Although both Turkish versions seem to foreground the idea that women should fulfil their responsibilities both at home and outside it, they emphasise different aspects of these responsibilities. While the earlier translations have an innovatory function by forcing women to overcome borders of their predefined roles, the latest translations aim to remind the women of their roles inside the home that they tended to ignore for a while. The results of the analysis also confirm the hypothesis that translations may be carried out for different purposes in different time periods in accordance with the needs of the target culture and system. In conclusion, this study has shown that the notion of translation as a "cultural planner" has the role of creating and shaping identities by imposing certain perspectives or worldviews within the target system.

Bibliography

Arı, Sevinç (2015). "Çocuk Kitapları Çevirilerinin ÇocuğUn Dünyasına Ve Toplumsal DönüŞüme Etkisi: Martine Mi Ayşegül Mü?" [The Effect Of Translation Of Children's Books On Children's World And Social Transformation: Martine Or AyşEgüL]. *Uluslararası Sosyal Araştırmalar Dergisi* [*The Journal of International Social Research*] 41: 64–73. On-line publication availabe at: http://www.sosyalarastirmalar.com/cilt8/sayi41_pdf/1dil_edebiyat/ari_sevinc.pdf [accessed: May 16, 2016].

Even-Zohar, Itamar (1997). "The Making Of Culture Repertoire And The Role Of Transfer". *Target* 9 (2): 355–363.

Gelgeç Bakacak, Ayça (2009). "Cumhuriyet Dönemi Kadın İmgesi Üzerine Bir Değerlendirme". [An Assessment On Image Of Women In Republican Period]. *Ankara Üniversitesi Türk İnkılâp Tarihi Enstitüsü Atatürk Yolu Dergisi* 44: 627–638.

Hervey, Sandor G.J. (1997). "Ideology And Strategy In Translating Children's Literature". *Oxford Journals.* 33:1. On-Line Publication Available At: http://fmls.oxfordjournals.org/ cgi/reprint/xxxiii/1/60 / [Accessed: February 10, 2017].

Marlier, Marcel, Gilbert Delahaye (unknown). *Ayşegül Küçük Anne* [*Ayşegül Little Mother*]. Trans. Unknown. Alpagut Yayınevi.

—— (2011). *Ayşegül Küçük Anne* [*Ayşegül Little Mother*]. Trans. Füsun Önen. Yapı Kredi Yayınları.

—— (unknown). *Ayşegül Mutfakta* [*Ayşegül in the Kitchen*]. Trans. Unknown. Alpagut Yayınevi.

—— (2011). *Ayşegül Yemek Yapıyor* [*Ayşegül is Cooking*]. Trans. Füsun Önen. Yapı Kredi Yayınları.

—— (unknown). *Ayşegül Ata Biniyor* [*Ayşegül is Riding a Horse*]. Trans. Unknown. Alpagut Yayınevi.

—— (2011). *Ayşegül Ata Biniyor* [*Ayşegül is Riding a Horse*]. Trans. Füsun Önen. Yapı Kredi Yayınları.

Stolze, Radegundis (2013). *Çeviri Kuramları Giriş [Translation Theories]*. Trans. Emra Durukan. İstanbul: Değişim Yayınları.

Toury, Gideon (2002). "Translation As A Means Of Planning And The Planning Of Translation: A Theoretical Framework And An Exemplary Case". *Translations: (Re)Shaping Of Literature And Culture*, Ed. Saliha Paker. İstanbul: Boğaziçi Üniversitesi Yayınları, 148-165.

Yalçın, Alemdar, Gıyasettin Aytaş (2002). *Çocuk Edebiyatı* [*Children's Literature*]. Ankara: Akçağ Yayınları.

Yuval-Davis, Nira (1997). *Cinsiyet Ve Millet* [*Gender And Nation*]. Trans. Ayşin Bektaş. İstanbul: İletişim Yayınları.

Yücel, Faruk (2007). *Tarihsel ve Kuramsal Açıdan Çeviri Edimi [Translation Performance in terms of History and Theory*]. Ankara: Dost Kitabevi.

Chapter 17

The Story of Isamiga: An Analysis of a Miyakoan Epic Song

Aleksandra Jarosz, *Nicolaus Copernicus University/Poland*

1. Foreword

This paper is devoted to an analysis of *The Story of Isamiga*, a folk song in Miyakoan representative of the genre of epic songs known as *aagu* or *ajagu*.

Miyakoan is an endangered minority language of Japan. It is spoken in the Miyako sub-archipelago of the Ryukyu islands, about 300 kilometres south of Okinawa. The language is genetically related to Japanese, although the respective protolanguages are dated to have split by the eighth century (Nara period) at the latest, and likely several centuries earlier[1]. Miyakoan belongs to the Sakishima subgroup of the Ryukyuan group in the Japonic family, while mainland Japanese varieties, including the Hachijō language (cf. Moseley 2010), constitute the other Japonic language group.

Like all Ryukyuan ethnolects, Miyakoan is mutually unintelligible with Japanese. In terms of the phonological system alone, Miyakoan is distinguished by a number of archaic Japonic features on the one hand, such as the retention of word-initial /p/, as well as highly specific innovations on the other, such as several consonant clusters and syllabic consonants. Miyakoan is rather archaic also in terms of its morphology (the lack of ombin in the infinitive/gerundive verb forms) and vocabulary (items related to Old/Early Modern but not modern Japanese lexemes, such as *kuvva* "lungs" cf. *kobura, niv* "to sleep" cf. *nebu* "to get late, to grow old", idiz "to leave" cf. *idu/izu*; a productive system of native numerals up to at least "a thousand").

In spite of a surge in the quantity and quality of the research on Miyakoan in the last fifteen years, Miyakoan remains a severely underdocumented lan-

---

[1] Cf. Jarosz 2015:171–174 for a brief overview of the existing theories on the history of Japonic languages with a particular focus on Miyakoan.

guage (cf. Jarosz 2015:371–385 for an account of this question). One of the areas that have traditionally attracted a lot of research attention is Miyakoan folk songs. They are considered very archaic, some of them are estimated to be older than songs recorded in the eighth-century Japanese chronicles *Kojiki* and *Nihon-Shoki* (Uemura 2003:19). Their genres vary significantly in terms of forms and themes, the epic characteristics of a large part of them considered a uniquely Miyakoan feature in the scale of Japan. Miyakoan *aagu* in the narrow sense that is the long pieces devoted to the stories of heroes or the plight of the common people are considered to have originated in the late 15th century; they are unlikely to have any parallel elsewhere in the Ryukyus (Hokama and Shinzato 1972: 341–342), and they contrast with the history of oral literature in mainland Japan, where the last traces of epic poetry could be observed in the late eight-century anthology *Man'yōshū*.

The earliest research on Miyakoan folk songs, collectively also named *aagu* in the broader sense, was conducted by an Okinawan teacher Risaburō Tajima in the late 19th century. A Russian linguist and ethnographer Nikolay Nevskiy undertook his study of Miyakoan songs in the 1920s; the research of the field then apparently went dormant until about the 1960s, when it was revived by native Ryukyuan academics such as Shuzen Hokama. Owing to such efforts, Miyakoan oral literature has been recorded in relatively large amounts. Nevertheless, these records usually lack a linguistic analysis of the material and commentaries on the content, meaning that even if a given song has been translated (which is not always the case), it cannot be readily used for the purpose of studying the language, nor can its meaning be immediately grasped. This state of affairs is also reflected in the following comment on the overall state of documentation of Ryukyuan oral literature.

> Of the numerous songs and folktales found throughout the archipelago, from Amami to Yaeyama, many have been recorded in recent years in Japanese syllabic script, which only incompletely captures the pronunciation, and only a very few have been phonologically transcribed by language researchers (Uemura 2003:18).

This paper is a sketchy attempt to fill such a gap concerning *The Story of Isamiga* by translating directly from Miyakoan and comparing three versions of the lyrics recorded in different sources: by Tajima (Moromi et al. 2008: 208–210), by Nevskiy (1978: 144–147), and by Hokama and Shinzato (1972:184–187). When necessary, a phonological transliteration of the original notation has also been supplemented. Translations and language analyses have been based chiefly on Nevskiy's lexicographic Miyakoan notes (Nevskiy 2013) and this author's language description pertaining to those notes (Jarosz 2015).

2. About the Song

The Story of Isamiga (henceforth *Isamiga*) is a piece which apparently used to be sung all over Miyako islands, and as such, it has multiple versions, three of which, mentioned above, are currently available to this author. It is very likely that its area of origin is Karimata, a village by the northern coast of the Miyako main island, which is also where the story takes place. Hokama/Shinzato's version explicitly marks the song as representing the Karimata ethnolect of Miyakoan; in Nevskiy's and Tajima's case the Karimata origins are implicit but highly plausible.

The lyrics tell the story of a young woman, named Isamiga or Kiçamiga, who is mistreated by her mother-in-law. The events of one day are depicted when the heroine goes down to the sea with her friends to do some seafood hunting on the occasion of an ebbing tide. What follows are descriptions of her conversation with friends, nit- and lice-picking enjoyed as a pastime, the search for sea creatures thrown ashore, and the confrontation with the in-laws back home. The song thus offers several noteworthy glimpses into the traditional daily and family life of Miyakoans, especially women.

The song in question can be considered a long epic song, or *aagu* in the narrow meaning (Hokama 1968: 90). In fact, however, Hokama and Shinzato identified Isamiga as *kuitɕa* (*kuicha* in Hepburn romanisation). Unlike the two other main genres, the ritual god-praising *niiri,* and the purely epic *aagu, kuitɕa* involve both epic and lyrical elements. As songs involving group singing and dancing, they probably originated in ceremonial settings and gradually gained an increasingly "civil" character. Many of the early *kuitɕa* "optimistically told of the joys of life or of careless people, but gradually the lyrics would shift to hardships tied to the tax system or to emotional anguish" (Hokama 1968: 96). *Isamiga* clearly represents the latter trend.

Like other Miyakoan genres and unlike Japanese *waka* or Okinawan *ryūka, kuitɕa* do not have a fixed moraic rhythm of phrases. Lyrics are based on many repetitions, an important unit being the so-called *parallel phrases* (*tsuiku* 対句 in Japanese) which involve anaphoric or epiphoric repetitions of portions of text. A phrase is rarely repeated in its entirety; instead, a replacement of a word or expression with a synonym is usually observed.

As a traditional community song, *Isamiga* cannot be linked to a specific author. There are also no firm grounds to help establish the time of the creation of the song. Nevertheless, based on Iha's observation that the song cannot be "that old" due to its very limited usage of archaic forms (Iha 2000:315; cf. remarks on *hayashi* in 7 below) and the fact that a change in the general mood of *kuitɕa* followed the enforcement of a crippling tax system (the poll-tax) upon the Sakishima islands in the 17th century, the origins of the song can be approximated at the 17th or the 18th century.

The lyrics of Isamiga involve phrases sung from different points of view. It remains unclear, however, if they used to be sung by an ensemble with role-switching or if the whole song could be performed by a single person. Role-switching apparently did take place in different *kuitɕa*, such as *Pstu-jumja-nu aagu* (Nevskiy 1978:44).

3. Tajima's Version

The following transcript has been based on Tajima's record combined with its 1927 critical rendition by Iha (2000:312–314). Both records have been written in the *ryūkyūgana*[2] with a slight addition of Chinese characters, making the sound form of the lyrics difficult to decode; hence the decision to transliterate, or retranscribe, the text into a simplified IPA notation. Tajima's text contains multiple lexical annotations, but no actual translation. On the other hand, Iha included a complete Japanese translation of the lyrics. The texts are further differentiated by a more extensive usage of Chinese characters on Iha's part, while Tajima for these particular lyrics used almost none, except for the place names. In other words, Iha took the liberty to interpret several Miyakoan lexical morphemes as cognates of certain Japanese words and used the same characters as in their Japanese counterparts to represent them.

A number of discrepancies can also be observed in the syllabic notation of both researchers: while Iha consistently applied the *hiragana*, employing a notation system closely reminiscent of the one observed in *Omorosōshi* (cf. footnote 2), Tajima experimented with a mixed *hiragana* and (lower index only) *katakana* usage, possibly in an attempt to indicate specifically Miyako-

---

[2] The term *ryūkyūgana* refers here to a particular usage of the Japanese *hiragana* script as applied for transcribing Ryukyuan ethnolects, the most notable example being perhaps *Omorosōshi*, a twenty-two volume collection of mostly ritual songs compiled in the 16th and 17th century by command of the royal dynasty Shō. The correspondence between the *kana* graphemes and Ryukyuan syllables is not straightforward; for instance, syllables with close-vowel nuclei are often written as if they had a mid-close-vowel nucleus, thus <け> for /ki/, も for /mu/, etc. For specific examples cf. Jarosz 2015:108–119, 130–133, 136–138.

an sounds and sound distribution patterns. Iha took on several other minor alternations, such as transcribing *zima* "where" with a voiced hiragana <tsu> character, づま, as opposed to Tajima's voiced <su>, ずま. Iha also consistently omitted the *hayashi*, or refrain; on the other hand, the lack of the word *siɕɕa* in the *Mjutu-daku-juba ban turadi siɕɕa* line is most likely an accidental omission on Iha's part.

This author's transcript combines both versions with a complete song text intended as the outcome. Whenever notation discrepancies arose, the version closest to the Miyakoan data recorded by Nevskiy (1998, 2013) has been preferred.

Kazmata-nu Isamiga

Kazmata-nu Isamiga
Mnaguzi-nu mjarabi
Andaki-nu suuʋtsi-n
Kandaki-nu suupjari-n
Im urida, jaa ummu?
Pama fumada, bʑi-ummu?
Zuju zuu, kjuu-ja im urjuu.
Zuju zuu, kjuu-ja pama fumadi.

Iza im-ga uridi-ka?
Zima pama-ga fumadi-ka?
Uri-naraz im dara
Fum-naraz pama dara

Baga nuzuki miriba-du
Jaara nuzuki miriba-du
Suu-ja psada uriba
Asaparada uriba
Pstu-nu jumi-durja-ja si
Nasan ffa-durja-ja si
Adangi-ga sitara-n
Pstumutu-ga ukagi-n
Ssamzim ɕi-uz-kja-du
Gissa-guru ɕi-uz-kja-du
Suu-ja pɕi-du uriba
Asapara-du uriba
Ba-ga tirjaa turimutɕi,

Isu-dirjaa turimutɕi
Nau-nu zzu-ga turi-ngidi-ga,
Ikja zzu-ga turi-piradi-ga
Nisi-nu anoo[3] *miagiriba-du,*
Mjutu-daku-nu bʑi-uriba
Pai-nu anoo miagiriba-du,
Mjutu-zzu-nu bʑi-uriba
Mjutu-zzu-juba vva turi, tungara
Mjutu-daku-juba ban turadi siɕɕa
Ba-ga tirjaa-n mtiz-kja
Isu-tirjaa-n mtiz-kja
Mutsi-na mutɕi-ikiba-du
Kami-na kami-muduriba-du

Situmma-nu janamunu,
Sitasazza-nu janamunu,
"Midum turidakoo-aran
Bunaz turizzoo-aran.
Zuributu-nu turidaku.
Sitaurja-nu turizzu."
Ba-ga piraba situmma,
Ukamafutsi-n bizari-uri
Ba-ga piraba sitasazza,
saɕi-nu mizzu, kui-numi

Isamiga from Kazmata

Isamiga from Kazmata
A young girl of the Mnaguzi[4]
When there is a tide that large,
When there is an ebb this great,
Are you going to stay home and not descend to the sea?
Are you going to sit still and not step onto the beach?
Hey hey, today let's descend to the sea
Hey hey, today let's step onto the beach

Which is the sea we should descend to?

---

[3] The text says <wo> (hiragana を).

[4] *Mnaguzi,* literally "the land of sand", can be interpreted as a family name (Hokama and Shinzato 1972:184).

Which is the beach we should step onto?
It is the sea we always descend to, certainly
It is the beach we always step onto, certainly

When I glanced
When myself glanced
The tide had not yet fallen
The field had not yet become shallow
Let's gather other wives
Let's gather other daughters-in-law

Under a pandanus tree
Under a single tree
While we are picking one another's lice
While we are smashing nits with our nails
The tide has fallen
The field has become shallow

So I take a basket
So I take a seashore basket
Which fish do I catch and take back home?
Which fish do I catch and go away?

When I look up to a northern hole
There is a married couple of octopuses sitting there
When I look up to a southern hole
There is a married couple of fish sitting there
You catch the couple of fish, friend
Because I will catch the couple of octopuses
Until my basket is full of them
Until the seashore basket is full of them

When I have brought as many as I could bring
When I have carried on my head as many as I could carry
My awful mother-in-law
My awful father-in-law [they said]:
"These are not octopuses caught by a woman.
These are not fish caught by a female.
These are the octopuses of your lover
These are the fish of your lover"

If I leave, mother-in-law,

may you be sitting by the stove
If I leave, father-in-law
may you beg for your water from the ladle

4. Hokama/Shinzato's Version

The song recorded in Hokama and Shinzato's volume, entitled simply *Isamiga*, clearly tells the same story as the lyrics collected by Tajima and edited by Iha, structural and storytelling differences notwithstanding. Hokama and Shinzato provided two transcripts, one in a phonetic IPA notation and one in *katakana*; unlike the *ryūkyūgana* widely used by the local students of Ryukyuan at the turn of the centuries, both notations are clearly intended to approximate the sound of the lyrics as straightforwardly as possible.

There are multiple differences in the interpretation of the Karimata ethnolect phonetics to be observed between Nevskiy's and Hokama/Shinzato versions. These will not be subject to a discussion in this paper. On the other hand, in order to account for the content discrepancies among the three records analyzed in this paper, a translation of the Hokama/Shinzato lyrics has been included below.

Isamiga

"Isamiga of the Nnaguzi
A young girl from Kazmata
As you are rich
As you are a wealthy fishing girl
Get up early in the morning
Get up at dawn
Go and draw some water, child
Bring a ladle with you, the young one

What will you do with the water?
What will you do with the ladle?

We will wash our hands, child
We will get our hands clean, the young one

So you are going to wash your hands?
So you are going to get your hands clean?
You will eat your rice
You will drink the sacred wine
When you have finished eating

When you have finished drinking
I will walk around the neighborhood
I will walk around the village

Are there my friends?
Are my companions sitting there?
What should I be doing at home?
Why should Miga[5] be sitting home?
Hey, hey, today let's descend to the sea
Hey, today let's step onto the beach

Which is the sea we will descend to?
Which is the beach we will step onto?
Certainly the sea we always descend to
Certainly the beach we always step onto

I have rushed to the northern sea
I have rushed to Panabutsi
When I glanced
When myself glanced
The tide had not yet fallen
The field had not yet become shallow
While the tide is falling
While the field is becoming shallow
Today is the day to pick the lice, certainly
Now is the time to pick the nits, certainly

While we are picking the lice
While we are picking the nits
Today is the day to bash our mothers-in-law, certainly
Now is the time to condemn our husbands' mothers, certainly
You speak first, our friend
You talk first, Miga, our companion

The mother-in-law of my house
The mother-in-law of this child's house
She scorches me like wax tree firewood

---

[5] This self-referent usage of the diminutive of *Isamiga* is, in fact, a reportedly frequent technique encountered in Miyakoan songs. Miga was a popular feminine name and so it was used in songs to refer to any woman as well as a female first-person "pronoun" (Nevskiy 2013:383).

She scorches me like pandanus firewood

You speak too, our friend,
You talk too, Miga, our companion

The mother-in-law of my house
The mother-in-law of this child's house
She is as violent as the summer southern wind
She is as violent as the wind straight in the face

As we were doing that, really
The tide had fallen
As we were doing that, definitely
The field had become shallow

And in the northern hole
A married couple of fish
And in the eastern hole
A married couple of octopuses

My basket became full
The seashore basket became full
I was overjoyed
I was really glad

When I showed it to my mother-in-law
When I presented it to my mother-in-law
This is what she said
This is what she told me

"These are not fish caught by a female
These are not octopuses caught by a woman
These are fish caught by your man[6]
These are octopuses caught by your lover"

So I was told by my mother-in-law

[6] The lyrics say *budu* "husband", which imposes a significant difference in the interpretation of the reproach by the in-laws; while here the heroine is ridiculed as having brought her husband's sea catch as if it were her own, in both other versions the in-laws throw an accusation that the heroine has an extramarital affair (i.e. is cheating on her husband and their son). The parallel phrase word *jubai-simja*, however, implies that *budu* may have the meaning of "a lover" here too, after all.

So I was spoken to by my mother-in-law
I am so heartbroken
I really am heartbroken

The mother-in-law, more and more,
And the brother-in-law too
Keep scolding me

The mother-in-law, extremely,
And the sister-in-law[7] too
Are so horrible to me[8]"

5. Nevskiy's Version

The exact dates of when Nevskiy recorded his versions of the song discussed in this paper are unknown. In all likelihood, however, he did it during his first trip to the Miyako islands in 1922, and more specifically, in the interval of August 11–14, which was when he recorded other traditional songs from Karimata and the adjacent villages of Shimajiri, Ōura and Nishihara (cf. Jarosz 2015:43).

Nevskiy's records of the song were only released posthumously, in the 1978 Russian compilation of Nevskiy's handwritten materials on Miyakoan oral literature. The volume contains two distinct Russian translations of a song identifiable as *The Story of Isamiga*, but there is only one original text provided (Nevskiy 1978: 69–73, 144–147). Several final lines are missing from the translation number one. As no actual differences content-wise can be detected between the two translations, it seems that translation number two is simply a verified and corrected version of the first version.

In the 1998 Japanese edition of Nevskiy 1978, both Russian translations have been translated into standard Japanese (Nevskiy 1998: 240–256), and the original Miyakoan text has been retranslated into Japanese directly from the source material, as well as supplemented with a transliteration of the phonetic lyrics into *hiragana*. Like in the Hokama/Shinzato *katakana* transliteration, the *hiragana* notation has been adjusted to meet the needs of the syllabic representation of Miyakoan.

---

[7] The lyrics say *ani-gama*, which is an affectionate form of "older sister" (*ani*), but the context implies that a "sister-in-law" (either a husband's own sister or the wife of a husband's brother) rather than "one's biological sister" is the intended meaning here.

[8] The interpretation of the last six verses is uncertain.

In Nevskiy's transcript, an unusual notation has been used: instead of the regular IPA-based system observed, among others, in Nevskiy 2013, a peculiar mixture of Cyrillic and phonetic symbols was applied. The result can be regarded as highly idiosyncratic and counterintuitive. Due to the space concerns, an IPA retranscription of Nevskiy's transcript will not be provided here. It bears mentioning, however, that Nevskiy's version contains numerous traces in support of the theory that Nevskiy recorded the song at an early stage of his Miyakoan studies. His notation is highly phonetical and unstable, producing different written forms of specific morphemes (such as *fudu*/*hudu* "about, as much as", *naripada*/*narihada* "companion", *tul*/*tui* "to take"). A number of morphemes found in the lyrics appear in a different form in the later Nevskiy 2013.

Kiɕamiga from Kalmata

Kiɕamiga from Kalmata
A young girl of the Mnaguzi
Kiɕamiga, are you home?
Our childhood friend, are you sitting at home?

And what if I am home?
What if I am sitting home?

On a moonlit night like this
When there is such an ebb like that
How could we not descend to the sea?
How could we not step onto the beach?
Hey hey, today let's descend to the sea
Hey hey, today let's step onto the beach

Which is the sea we should descend to?
Which is the beach we should step onto?
It is the sea we always descend to, certainly
It is the beach we always step onto, certainly

When we descended to the northern sea
When we descended to the surging shore
I glanced and saw that
Myself glanced and saw that
The tide had not fallen yet
It had not become shallow yet

As the tide was falling
As it was getting shallow
Under a pandanus tree
By the evening shadow of a single tree
Wives, they gathered
Daughters-in-law, they gathered
This is the day for picking lice
Now is the time for removing nits

As we are picking lice
As we are removing nits
This is, indeed, the day for our mothers-in-law
Now is, indeed, the time for our husbands' mothers

You speak first, our friend
You talk first, our companion

The mother-in-law of my house
The mother of the house of Miga's husband
She is just like the crescent moon
She is a mother-in-law I want to respect
She is a husband's mother I want to look up to

Now you speak, our friend
Now you talk, our companion

The mother-in-law of my house
The mother of the house of Miga's husband
She is just like scorching firewood
She is a quarrelsome mother-in-law

While we were doing this
While we were spending our time like that
The tide had completely fallen
It had got completely shallow

So I took my basket
I took a seashore basket
When I groped through all the holes
When I looked through all the pits
In a northern hole
There was indeed a married couple of octopuses

In a southern hole
There were indeed wobbly-armed octopuses

Until my basket became full
Until the seashore basket was filled to the edge
I took as much as I could and brought it home
I carried on my head as much as I could and brought it home

And I found my mother-in-law saying
And I found my husband's mother saying
"These are not octopuses caught by a female
These are not octopuses caught by a woman
It was your lover who caught these octopuses
It was your secret man who caught these octopuses
Carry them on your head and run, my daughter-in-law
Take them and run, you child I did not give birth to"

If I do take them and run, my mother-in-law
If I do carry them on my head and run, my husband's mother
You go sitting in the kitchen
You go sitting by the fireplace
You go begging for some water from a jug
You go begging for some water from a mug

6. Elements Shared by All Versions

The three records presented above essentially revolve around the same story, an account of how a young wife went with her girlfriends down to the beach to collect some seafood, and upon her return home ended up bashed by her in-laws with the allegations of being untrue to her husband and their son. The following are the details of the content as encountered chronologically in all three lyrics.

1. The story focuses on a single heroine named Isamiga or Kiçamiga, born or married into (the lyrics do not specify the interpretation) the family Mnaguzi/Nnaguzi and living in the village of Kazmata (Japanese Karimata). The heroine is a young girl living, as the custom had it, together with her husband's family.
2. The story sets off when the heroine is invited by her friends to gather some seafood, taking the opportunity given by the ebbing tide. The lyrics imply that these women would meet up every so often to conduct the seafood hunting at their favorite spot. It was a woman's job to walk down

the shore during the ebb, looking for the edible sea creatures left ashore. As Iha (2000: 316) explains, the task was usually conducted by mothers and their children, but since Isamiga responds to the invitation by leaving the house on her own (i.e., there is no mentioning of her taking a child with her), it can be inferred that at the time she is still childless. This fact has certainly significant implications for Isamiga's position in the patriarchal structure of her family. Since she has not yet given birth to a future successor, and since she is not a mother, her status must be extremely low.
3. The women reach the shore to find out that the tide has not yet fallen and the beach is not yet exposed. They decide to wait for the fishing conditions to improve; in the meantime, they choose to rest under a *pandanus* tree and enjoy some mutual lice-picking. Again, Iha (ibid.) clarifies that lice picking used to be considered a pleasurable pastime in a Ryukyuan province.
4. Once the tide has fallen, Isamiga descends to the shore with her friends. She finds a couple of octopuses in one sand hole and a couple of fish in another. She is lucky to fill up her basket with all the food she has found on the shore.
5. Happy and proud about her catch, Isamiga returns home only to be scolded by her in-laws who find it impossible that a woman should have caught such a basketful of seafood by herself, so they conclude she must have had her lover do this in her stead.

The three versions also share the following structural characteristics.

1. There are at least three speakers (or groups of speakers) that appear in the lyrics, meaning that the point of view presented in the story shifts freely among the subsequent "voices". The "voices" belong to Isamiga herself, Isamiga's girlfriends, and the in-laws. There are no specific cues to indicate that the speaker has just changed, at least not in the lyrical sphere; to grasp the changes of the speakers, a comprehension of the lyrics is necessary.
   Due to the punctuation possibilities offered by Russian, Nevskiy's translations are the only available versions of Isamiga in which the role-switching among the "voices" is indicated, namely the parts sung by different characters are marked with inverted commas.
2. The refrain, Japanese *hayashi*, appears following every two verses. *Hayashi* imbues the lyrics with rhythm and emotion, and it is not directly related to the story told in the song. For that reason, it is often removed

from the record of the lyrics. The exact form of the refrain in Isamiga is *aga sumjaa joo* in Tajima and in Nevskiy (2013), *aga sumjoo joo* in Hokama/Shinzato, and *aga sumjee joo* in Nevskiy (1978). The phrase means "oh, my beloved", "oh, my dearest one", and it involves the usage of an archaic first-person genitive form *aga* (*baga* in contemporary Miyakoan, as well as elsewhere in the song).

3. There are multiple parallel phrases recurring in all three lyrics. They include pairs of expressions such as:
   - *Isamiga* and *mjarabi/ mijarabi*, the first being a proper name and the second meaning "young woman", both referring to the heroine;
   - *iza/ida im-ga uridi-ga/ka* "which is the sea we should descend to?" and *zima pama-ga fumadi-ga/ka* "which is the beach we should step onto?"; in Hokama/Shinzato these phrases have a slightly different grammar, namely *iza im-du uridi-ga* and *zima pama-du uridi-ga*, with declarative sentence focus marker *-du* replacing the wh-question focus marker *-ga*;
   - *uri-naraz im* "the sea that we always descend to" and *fum-naraz pama* "the beach that we always step onto";
   - *baga nuzuki/nuziki miriba* "when I glanced" and *ja(a)ra nuzuki/nuziki miriba* "when myself glanced";
   - *midum turidakoo-aran* "these are not octopuses caught by a female" and *bunaz turizzoo-aran* "these are not fish caught by a woman" in Tajima's version; in Nevskiy's version these phrases have a slightly different grammar and vocabulary: *midum-nu tul-daku jaran* and *bunagu-nu tul-daku jaran*, with the nominative-genitive marker *-nu* inserted after the subject, a more analytic copula negation (*taku jaran* instead of *takoo aran*), the word *taku* "octopus" repeated twice instead of *taku* and *zzu* "fish", and the word *bunaz* replaced by a synonymic *bunagu*; in Hokama/Shinzato the order of *tako* and *zzu* is reversed, but otherwise the phrases resemble closely those by Tajima: *midum tuz zzoo-aran* and *bunarja tuz takoo*[9]*-aran*, *bunarja* being a yet another Miyakoan word for "woman".

[9] The transcript (Hokama and Shinzato 1972:187) says *kaku* instead of *taku*, but it is considered a spelling error here.

7. Essential Discrepancies Among the Versions

The three stories presented in the lyrics above differ in terms of plot details. Some of these differences introduce new angles to the otherwise identical plotline, while others indicate mutually exclusive contrasts in the story.

Tajima's version is the shortest, which explains why it lacks several of the particulars present in the other lyrics. It can be therefore called the basic version of the *Isamiga* story, the remaining two constituting the more elaborate variations. Furthermore, while the other versions focus on the conflict between the heroine and the mother-in-law alone, Tajima's record tells of both parents-in-law, putting an emphasis on the dire circumstances of a woman married into a family governed by her husband's parents rather than just on the mother/daughter-in-law relationship dynamics.

Hokama/Shinzato's variant introduces, among others, several pieces of background information on the heroine. One learns that she comes from a wealthy fisherman family. This is the only lyrics which include a dialogue with the mother-in-law prior to Isamiga's meeting with her friends. Through that conversation one catches a glimpse of the servant-like manner in which Isamiga is treated at home ("get up early in the morning", "go get a ladle and draw water for us"[10]). When Isamiga is done with her labor, she goes for a stroll around the village, and there she encounters her friends going to the sea for the seafood catch. That is when she spontaneously decides to join them, the course of events clearly distinct from Tajima's and Nevskiy's versions, in which the friends apparently come by Isamiga's house to invite her for the hunting. The Hokama/Shinzato variant is the only to reveal Panabutsi, a proper name for the beach where the women customarily conducted their hunting.

Once the women realise the water upon the shore is not yet shallow enough to allow for collecting the sea creatures thrown ashore, they sit beneath a *pandanus* tree, picking each other's lice as they are waiting for the water to recede. That much is a part shared by all versions of the lyrics; what is absent from Tajima's record and present in two others is the women's simultaneous gossip on their mothers-in-law. In Hokama/Shinzato it is specified that the gossip be limited to the foul-mouthing of their in-laws, and the women, two of which are explicitly quoted, exchange their experiences of the in-law abuse. In both Nevskiy and Hokama/Shinzato's variants two distinct words

---

[10] Until water mains were installed, which apparently did not happen in all of the Miyakos until the post-war period (cf. Saigazoku 2002:104), water had to be drawn physically from the underground cave wells. It was a strenuous labor to draw water from there and carry it back home.

referring to "mother-in-law", *situmma* and *maiɕeeza*/ *maiɕaiza*, are introduced as parallel phrases; the absence of the latter in Tajima's record can be explained by the fact that Tajima's plotline revolves around the relationship with both in-laws, so *sitasazza* "father-in-law" replaces *maiɕaiza* in the function of parallel phrase.

The act of seafood hunting as depicted afterward in Hokama/Shinzato does not differ significantly from Tajima's or Nevskiy's variants, the exceptions being indeed slight, such as the "married couple of fish" (*mjuutu-zzu*) being found in the *northern* (instead of *southern*) sand hole, and the "married couple of octopuses" (*mjuutu-daku*) discovered in the *eastern* (instead of *northern*) hole. At home, Isamiga gets scoffed by her mother-in-law. While the two other versions emphasise that the confrontation led to a heated argument, here the heroine dwells on her feelings of sadness and despondency for being thus ridiculed and taken for granted. The lyrics end rather abruptly with unspecific complaints on Isamiga's part about her brother- and sister-in-law, too, leaving doubts as to whether originally this version of the song had been longer, but there were no more people who remembered it completely by the time Hokama and Shinzato recorded it at the turn of 1960s/1970s.

Nevskiy's version could probably be best described as an expanded edition of Tajima's variant. It fills in several gaps of the shorter Tajima's record, mostly without introducing any contradicting material. It does differ from the Hokama/Shinzato version by indicating specifically that the women conducted their seafood hunting in the evening[11]. The scene of the "in-law gossip" is also different in that here the first speaker actually praises her mother-in-law for being benevolent and respectable, and it is only second speaker – one can guess it is Isamiga (Kiçamiga) herself – that complains about the abusive treatment she receives from her husband's mother. The description of gathering the seafood involves the same holes as in Tajima's, "northern" and "southern" respectively, in which Isamiga finds her catch; unlike both other versions, however, the heroine finds only octopuses, with no mentioning of fish (hence the consequent usage of parallel phrases *mjuutu-daku* and *tjura-daku* instead of *mjuutu-daku* and *mjuutu-zzu*). The very scene of the seafood search is also depicted with slightly greater precision, stating that Isamiga had to "grope" (*ɕaduz*) and "look through" (*fuzi*) the sand pits in the darkness to find her catch.

The final confrontation between the heroine and her mother-in-law is essentially an expanded version of what can be found in Tajima's record, with

---

[11] Which, on the other hand, perhaps was self-explanatory for the community members – maybe ebbing tide hunting was something to undertake during the night alone.

only the mother-in-law, however, participating: the older woman mockingly tells Isamiga to take her "lover's" catch back to the sea, to which Isamiga responds essentially with the same curses as in Tajima's variant. The curses that Isamiga throws towards her in-laws way can be essentially summarised as "if you want me gone so bad, then try and manage your daily life without me", including the kitchen chores and asking somebody to give her some drinking water from the well, the latter linking the content of these lyrics with the Hokama/Shinzato version.

8. Endnote

The present description has been a prelude to an intended in-depth research of the Miyakoan songs which had been collected but not analysed or analysed only superficially. It has hopefully confirmed the ethnolinguistic value of traditional *aagu* as a record of not only the language but also traditional lifestyle and worldviews of the island communities.

At present, the youngest native speakers of Miyakoan have reached a very advanced age, and they have hardly anyone in younger generations to communicate within the vernacular. In the face of such devastating decline in language use, the study of Miyakoan oral traditions gains paramount importance.

It does not concern only understanding and preserving the language in its linguistic essence. It also concerns using the language as a key to the past, to a world which does not exist anymore, in this case, a pre-Japanese, pre-modern Miyako. In order for a language to disappear, first, the world in which it was used and which it described must disappear, too. Conversely, by reclaiming the reflections of that world as fossilised in oral texts such as songs, tales, proverbs or riddles, one can certainly reclaim the language itself, too – if not as a primary communication tool, then at least as an understandable and relatable part of the community heritage.

Bibliography

Hokama Shuzen, ed. (1968). "Miyako-no bungaku [Miyakoan literature]". In: Ryūkyū Daigaku Okinawa Bunka Kenkyūjo. *Miyako shotō gakujutsu chōsa kenkyū hōkokusho. Gengo/bungaku-hen* [a report of academic study of Miyako islands, the volume on language and literature]. Naha: Ryūkyū Daigaku Okinawa Bunka Kenkyūjo. 63–166.///外間守善編「宮古の文学」琉球大学沖縄文化研究所『宮古諸島学術調査研究報告書』那覇市・琉球大学沖縄文化研究所 。

Hokama Shuzen, Kōshō Shinzato (1972). *Miyakojima-no kamiuta* [holy songs from the Miyako island]. Tokyo: San'ichi Shobō.///外間守善、新里幸昭『宮古島の神歌』東京都・三一書房。

Iha Fuyū (2000). *Ko-Ryūkyū* [old Rykyus]. Revised by Shuzen Hokama. Tokyo: Iwanami Shoten.///伊波普猷『古琉球』外間守善校訂　東京都・岩波書店。

Jarosz, Aleksandra (2015). *Nikolay Nevskiy's Miyakoan Dictionary: reconstruction from the manuscript and its ethnolinguistic analysis. Studies on the manuscript.* Unpublished doctoral dissertation. Poznan: Adam Mickiewicz University, Faculty of Modern Languages and Literature, Chair of Oriental Studies.

Moromi Nana, Junko Maeshiro, Masami Tamaki et al. (2008). "Honkoku. Tajima Risaburō *Miyakojima-no uta* (Ryūkyū Daigaku Fuzoku-Toshokan Iha Fuyū Bunko shozō) [*Songs from Miyako islands* by Risaburō Tajima (preserved in the Fuyū Iha Archive of the Ryukyu University Library), transcript]". In: Tamaki Masami (research team representative). *Okinawa-ken Miyakoshotō-ni okeru girei kayō-no shūshū/kenkyū-to dētabēsuka* [collection, research and creating a database of ritual songs of the Miyako islands in Okinawa Prefecture]. Nishihara: Ryūkyū Daigaku Hōbungakubu [Faculty of Law and Letters, University of the Ryukyus]. 171–280.///諸見菜々、前城淳子、玉城政美、高橋俊三　「翻刻　田島利三郎『宮古島の歌』（琉球大学付属図書館伊波普猷文庫所蔵）」玉城政美研究代表者『沖縄県宮古諸島における儀礼歌謡の収集・研究とデータベース化』　西原町・琉球大学法文学部。

Moseley, Christopher, ed. (2010). *Atlas of the World's Languages in Danger, 3rd ed.* Paris: UNESCO Publishing. Online version: http://www.unesco.org/culture/en/endangeredlanguages/atlas

Nevskiy, N[ikolay]. A[leksandrovich] (1978). *Folklor ostrovov Miyako* [folklore of the Miyako islands]. Edited by Lidia Gromkovskaya. Moscow: Nauka.///Н. А. Невский 1978. Фольклор островов Мияко. Москва: Издательство Наука.

Nevskiy, Nikolay (1998). *Miyako-no fōkuroa* [Miyakoan folklore]. Edited by Lidia Gromkovskaya. Translated by Shigehisa Karimata, Yukiko Tokuyama, Yoriko Takaesu, Masami Tamaki, Masago Hamakawa and Takako Hasekura. Tokyo: Sunagoya Shobō.///ニコライ•A•　ネフスキー著　『宮古のフォークロア』リヂア・グロムコフスカヤ編　狩俣繁久　渡久山由紀子　高江洲頼子　玉城政美　濱川真砂　支倉隆子共訳　東京都・砂子屋書房。

—— (2013). *Nikolay Nevskiy's Miyakoan Dictionary. Recovered from the manuscript by Aleksandra Jarosz.* Stęszew: International Institue of Ethnolinguistic and Oriental Studies. Preprint 50.

Saigazoku (2002). *Yomeba Miyako! Araragama paradaizu dokuhon* [you read it, you have Miyako! A reading about a damn paradise[12]]. Naha: Bōdā Inku.///さいが族『読めば宮古！あららがまパラダイズ読本』那覇市・ボーダーインク。

Uemura, Yukio (2003). *The Ryukyuan language.* Suita, Osaka: Endangered Languages of the Pacific Rim.

[12] *Araragama* is an expressive word in Miyakoan (or in a miyakoanised variety of Japanese) which may serve as a mild swearword.

Chapter 18

Crossing Boundaries: From Private to Public Space. Memoirs of Antarjanam

Olga Nowicka, *Jagiellonian University/Poland*

> "Most antharjanams observe ghosha [seclusion]. They have eyes but are prohibited from seeing anything pleasant. They have legs but their movement is circumscribed. Their state is quite like that of household utensils. In short, the antharjanam is a jailed creature. Antharjanams are constantly watched; they are not permitted to breathe fresh air, to see the world. An antharjanam is born crying, lives her life in tears and dies weeping." (Devika 2015: xxv)

In these very words registered during the speech in the Assembly in 1937, K. Devaki Antharjanam, who became a member of the Sree Mulam Legislative Assembly in the princely State of Travancore[1], described the state of being one of Nambudiri[2] women, who are traditionally called *antarjanams* (literally: *the indoor people*)[3]. Through these words, K. Devaki Antharjanam, who herself was a representant of the culture in question, was stressing the lack of agency among antarjanams, which was implied through a reduction of women to the instruments of their domestic, everyday labour. After attaining puberty, the antarjanam women were living their lives in the elaborate seclusion

---

[1] The Kingdom of Travancore was a kingdom in South India from 1729 until 1949. It covered the territory of contemporary central and southern Kerala state together with the Kanyakumari district (today in the Tamil Nadu state). In the beginning of the 19th century it became a princely state of the British Empire.

[2] Nambudiris – one of the brahmin communities of Kerala, constituting an upper class in the social hierarchy.

[3] *Antarjanam* – "antar" (inside) and "janam" (person, people). It is a name for Nambudiri women which means "those who stay indoors".

(mal. *ghōṣā*)[4] of their houses (mal. *illam*)[5]. They could leave homes only while wearing a cloak (mal. *putappu*) and large cadjan umbrella (mal. *kuṭa*), escorted by maids or male family members – being by that means shielded from public view (Nilayamgode 2015: 43). Separated from the outside world, likewise, they were denied access to the education. Their domesticity was highly ritualised. However, this situation started to slowly change with the nascence of reformist movement within the Nambudiri community (that is Nambudiri Yoga Kshema Sabha) at the beginning of the twentieth century. The movement led to radical reformulations in the structure of the Nambudiri family and the power equations within it, thus breaking the silence and allowing the antarjanams' voice to be heard. (Devika 2015: xviii) These circumstances turned out to be favorable to the Malayalam works of literature authored by brahmin women from Kerala.

The above-mentioned Yoga Kshema Sabha – a reformist movement within the Nambudiri community – was formed with broad objectives, with a major aim to uproot the illiteracy and lack of modern education among Nambudiri brahmins. It was one of the resolutions of the second annual meeting in 1910. Thus, at the beginning of the 20th century, the Yoga Kshema Sabha took in action progressive plans for the purpose of social change. One of the steps was to comprehend the problems which the antarjanams were facing. It was one of the Sabha's objectives to find a proper solution to the problem of the silent oppresion among the Nambudiri women. Due to the revolutionary activities of the Yogakshema Sabha, the antarjanams abandoned their traditional confinement (*ghōṣā*) and began to be equal to the needs of a social change. The leadership in this movement was taken by such personalities as Parvathy Nenminimangalam, Parvathy Nilayangod, Parvathy Manazhi, Arya Pallam, Neeli Mangalass and Lalithambika Antarjanam. Thus the sub-branch of Yogakshema Sabha was born – which was called Antarjana Samājam[6]. A few sub-groups of Antarjana Samājam were then organised under the leadership of Arya Pallam and other women, but what started the proper Samājam was the one that trooped in Namboothiri Vidyālayam at Thrissur in 1939. The

---

[4] *Ghōṣā* – the custom prevalent among Nambudiri brahmins which forbade woman to step outside of her house without carrying palm leaf umbrella, shawl covering her face and body, and without a woman servant.

[5] Illam – a Nambudiri homestead.

[6] Matamp Narayanan Namboodiri (9.11.2000). *Namboothiri Yogakshema Mahaasabha. A Historical Perspective.* On-line publication available at: http://www.namboothiri.com/ [accessed: April 15, 2017].

organisation was revived during 1945, at the time when the Yogakshema Sabha congregated under the leadership of E. M. S. Namboodiripad[7]. The fraction of women which has been working since the revival of the Yogakshema Sabha in 1961, continues to function as the Antarjana Samājam even to this day. What turned out to be significant for the instigation of the social change appeared to be the foundation of the training centres which conducted classes in sewing and tailoring, spinning, weaving cloth, making paper envelopes and other minor activities, with support from the Social Welfare Board of the Government of India. That enabled women to become more independent and self-sufficient and led, as a result, to the gradual appearance of the Nambudiri women in the public space of Kerala[8].

In 1968 the Antarjana Samājam also established a women's library. It is considered to be an A-grade library with ca. 7,000 books. An important celebration was organised at Katambazhipuram (Palakkad district) to honour the famous Malayalam writer – Lalithambka Antharjanam – when she received a Central Government award for her work entitled *Sītā mutal Satyavatī vare* (*From Sītā to Satyavatī*). The Antarjana Samājam was registered under the Societies Registration Act in Palakkad in 1977[9].

It was due to the social revolution in Kerala that the Malayalam autobiographic literature authored by the Nambudiri women started to sprout. One of the first such female writers, nowadays well known throughout Kerala was – the abovementioned Lalitambika Antharjanam[10]. She was a prominent writer and a social reformist. Lalitambika published nine volumes of short stories, six collections of poems, two books for children, and a famous novel, *Agnisakshi* (1976), which won the Kendra Sahitya Akademi Award in 1977 and was translated into English in 1980. She also wrote an autobiography *Ātmakathakkoru āmukhaṃ* (*An Introduction to Autobiography*) a very significant work which was an inspiration for her future followers[11].

---

[7] E.M.S. Namboodiripad (1909–1998) – an Indian communist politician who was the first Chief Minister of the Kerala state in 1957–59 and in 1967–69. As a social reformist he introduced radical land and educational reforms in Kerala.

[8] C.K. Parvathy (16.02.2001). *Antharjana Samaajam.* On-line publication available at: http://www.namboothiri.com/ [accessed: April 15, 2017].

[9] Ibid.

[10] Born in 1909 in Punalur, Kollam. Deceased in 1987.

[11] Lalithambika Antharjanam's biography. On-line publication available at: http://www.keralasahityaakademi.org/sp/Writers/PROFILES/Lalithambika/Html/Lalit

Another prominent author, also an antarjanam, was Devaki Nilayamgode. What seems to be worthy of attention is the fact that Nilayamgode, unlike Lalitambika Antharjanam, who composed mainly literary fiction, was more inclined towards autobiographic writing. All literary pieces she published are her own personal histories based on the social context of the particular region, which in this case was Kerala. What is interesting is that she started to write only after her 75th birthday, encouraged to do so by her grandson. In 2003 she published her first piece – a slim book of memoirs – *Naṣṭabōdhaṅa-lillate* (which means: *with no sense of loss or regret*), where she described growing up in the loveless, shadowed environment of a Nambudiri household in central Kerala. The response of the Malayalam-reading public to the book appeared to be very enthusiastic, which influenced Nilayamgode to publish another book three years later – *Yātra: kāṭṭilum, nāṭṭilum* (which means: *a journey through lands and forests*). Nilayamgode also wrote some articles which were published in various Malayalam periodicals. (Nilayamgode 2015: vii–viii)

In 2011 she published another autobiographic piece of writing, this time in English, entitled *Antharjanam: Memoir of a Nambudiri Woman*, which appears to be an important book contributing to broadening the perception of the Kerala social landscape. As Devaki Nilayamgode stresses, it was meant to be an autobiography authored indeed by an antarjanam and exclusively about Nambudiri women. (Nilayamgode 2015: 156) Being the first antarjanam's memoir published in English, her book certainly played a significant part in correcting myths and legends that have surrounded women of the Nambudiri community for a century. "Antharjanams have always been a source of a great fascination in the popular imagination in Kerala" – as notices Radhika Menon, the translator of Nilayamgode's autobiography to English – "to an outsider's eyes, they were living exotica. Cocooned in luxury, shielded from public view, always escorted by an entourage of obsequious attendants and endlessly enjoying a hedonistic life full of festivals and elaborate feasts, these upper-caste women appeared to led a charmed existence." (Menon 2015: xii). However, nobody suspected that, in fact, under the veil of mystery there was hidden one of the most merciless forms of patriarchal oppression, which for many centuries deprived antarjanams of all basic human rights, such as independence, education or even the most innocent joys of everyday life. Thus, Nilayamgode's book causes the crossing of boundaries – that which was hidden for a long time in the intensely shielded Nambudiri illam (house of a Nambudiri) crossed into the public sphere. Her autobiography broke

hambikagraphy.htm [accessed: April 15, 2017].

centuries of silence – being the first full-length account of a Nambudiri woman's life featuring the world already belonging to the past. Without a doubt, Nilayamgode's work can be considered a significant step forward in the domain of personal and social history. Her memoirs were translated into English by Malayalee scholars, Indira Menon and Radhika Menon, in 2011. The peculiar feature of Devaki's writing style, as emphasised both translators, is language that is very simple, unadorned, almost bare and stark to the point. Thus, because of the use of the minimal language, her story seems to be told without a trace of self-pity, with no sense of loss or regret, as the author herself stresses. However, behind the apparent softness there hides, in fact, the strength that any woman or girl in her position needs to possess in order not to lose her sanity. Certainly, acceptance was less difficult for Devaki because of her upbringing, but beyond such silent consent there hides afterthought, challenging and questioning coming from an intelligent woman who rejects the doubtful values of Nambudiri community. Seemingly, Nilayamgode's prose appears smooth and tranquil, but, in fact, this stylistic manner brings the emotional upheaval to the surface and, at the same time, avoids making them obtrusive. While reading the book, one can feel Devaki's silent, hopeless suffering. Her suffering transgresses cultural spaces to speak to a wide audience. The author's work is an attempt to feature a realistic image of antarjanas' existence, which so far was usually painted by the outsiders in flattering and flamboyant colours. In her autobiographic writing, Devaki describes, in an honest way, some of the Nambudiri's beliefs, practises, rituals and customs which made life within this hermetic community unbearable for women[12].

Devaki Nilayamgode was born in 1928 in Pakaravoor mana at Mookkuthala in Malappuram district[13] to Pakaravoor Krishnan Somayajippad[14] and Parvathy Antharjanam. She was brought up in an orthodox Nambudiri family. She has never been formally educated other than acquiring the basic knowledge of English received traditionally at home. She was given in marriage at the age of fifteen and thus sent to the Nilayamgode illam of a great feudal family; the place turned to be a home of progressive minds, such as her husband – Ravi Nambudiri. (Nilayamgode 2015: 3–4)

---

[12] Translators' Notes: ix-xv. In: Devaki Nilayamgode (2015). *Antharjanam. Memoirs of a Nambudiri Woman.* Trans. Indira Menon, Radhika P. Menon. New Delhi: Oxford University Press.

[13] A district in central Kerala.

[14] *Somayajippad* – a brahmin who has performed a Vedic ritual of soma, fire sacrifice.

The crucial moment in Devaki's life, as in all other antarjanams' lives, was the peculiar rite of passage called *uṭuttu tuṭaṅṅal* (mal.): a ritual which constructed her social identity as a Nambudiri woman. It was a formal ceremony marking a girl's entry into womanhood, usually at the age of 9, during which she is made to wear a cotton loincloth instead of the previous one which was made of leaves. For Devaki that was the end of childhood, the end of relative freedom. The ceremony socially constructed her as a proper antarjanam – the person kept indoors. Nilayamgode describes this transformation in her autobiography in these words:

> "Uduthu thudangal was the first step towards womanhood and it brought tremendous changes in my daily routine. Wearing a cloth meant that it could get [ritually] defiled; so a girl had to take a bath every time she touched an outsider or a person from another caste. Thus gradually, my life was confined to the inner rooms and to the company of my elder sisters. I could go to pray at the temple but not stay back to play. I could look at the boys and walk in the portico or the courtyard only until puberty." (Nilayamgode 2015: 31)

From that point, there started Devaki's confinement in her family *nālukeṭṭu* (mal.)[15]. As Nilayamgode writes in her autobiography, with attaining the puberty she was forbidden to set out on any journey, even to go to the temple. She could not attend any social function which took place at another Nambudiri household. The only place where she was allowed to go out was the kitchen-tank in the complex of her illam. She "retreated then into her illam like a bird with clipped wings" as she describes. Until the time she left home after her wedding, Devaki could see the sky only during her walk to the kitchen-tank (Nilayamgode 2015: 46, 111).

To mark their high social status, as they belonged to the brahmnin aristocracy, antarjanams had also to follow the peculiar dressing code. Thus, "the Nambudiri women had to dress very simply and without any redeeming colour. They must have longed to ensure that their clothes remained constnatly white. [...] What is more, Antharajanams never wore any flowers – colourful and sweet-smelling flowers were used only in the pujas for the deities [...]" (Nilayamgode 2015: 24, 16). The Nambudiri women, although belonging to prosperous families, wore only bronze bangles because they were not allowed

[15] Mal. *nālukeṭṭu* – the word means literally "quadrangle". This term customarily refers to an illam (Nambudiri house). The reason for this is the square plan of this typical Keralan architectural structure.

to wear the gold ones. Their designs varied according to the financial status of the particular family – richer women enjoyed rounded bangles while the others had to be satisfied with flat ones (Nilayamgode 2015: 37). Thus, one can notice that the status differences within the Nambudiri brahmins' community itself were also emphasised. For Devaki the first moment in her life when she realised her own miserable appearance took place only after the confrontation with Nayar women[16] who once visited her in the *illam*. Nayar women were wearing colourful blouses, brocade-bordered *muṇṭu*[17] with an upper cloth, plenty of gold ornaments and perfume as well. In her memoirs Nilayamgode features the striking contrast by giving a detailed description of her sister appearance:

> "My elder sister was almost as old as Bharati (Nayar women), but how different she looked! Her hair was not properly brushed. She didn't wear a blouse, had neither brocared-bordered mundu nor any jewellery. So she refused to enter the room and stood behind the door, trying to conceal herself as much as she could. Even I, though only six or seven years then, felt inferior, being conscious of my loincloth and lice-infested hair" (Nilayamgode 2015: 36)

Antarjanams, according to tradition, were not allowed to look at men not belonging to the family; they also should not be seen by the strangers. As Nilamgayode recalls: "Whenever Namboodriris entered the nalukettu, they usually announced their presence by clanging the chain that hung from the door. It was a warning to some antharjanams to keep out of sight" (Nilayamgode 2015: 17). Even in the case of a severe illness antarjanams were refused a proper medical examination because of the strict observance of *ghōṣā* (seclusion):

> "The doctor visited only when the men fell ill. He was not sent for when the women were indisposed. Nobody payed much attention when women were unwell. [...] Women were confined to the vadakke ara – a room in the north of the house – and treated only by vaidyans[18] – indigenous physicians – brought up in the tradition of their forefathers" (Nilayamgode 2015: 107)

---

[16] Nāyar (also known as Nairs)– a community in Kerala, an upper caste among Hindus, although lower in social hierarchy compared with the Nambudiris.

[17] Muṇṭu – cloth worn around the waist by men and women of Kerala.

[18] Vaidyan – an ayurvedic doctor.

Then Nilayamgode continues with more striking details:

> "Since women were not allowed to see men other than family members, the vaidyan would stand leaning against the door and would not venture close enough to either touch the patient or even to observe her symptoms, confining himself to asking her in loud tones what the problem was. The treatment depended on her answer or on the reply of those who stood near her." (Nilayamgode 2015: 107)

Atarjanams were strictly prohibited from leaving illam alone – in the case of necessary travel they were always accompanied by female servants. Nambudiri women were then obliged to also wear a cloak (mal. *putappu*) and a large cadjan umbrella (mal. *kuṭa*) – thus being carefully shielded from the public view. What is more, according to another custom which made antarjanams subordinate and inferior, they could not possess even small amounts of money on their own. Thus, in order to make a rare trip to their mother's houses, they were forced to acquire an income by selling, in secret, small quantities of illam rice, as by tradition women were not given any money by the family (Nilayamgode 2015: 43). To quote Nilayamgode: "Antharjanams had nothing on their own [...], their marriages were merely concessions made to their existence" (Nilayamgode 2015: 83).

However, the winds of change began to sweep over the Nambudiri community in the 1930s and 1940s with such organisations as Yogaksema Sabha and Antarjana Samājam. In 1945, the noted Ongallur meeting took place. It was when the famous declaration was made by E.M.S. Namboodiripad: "Let's make the Nambudiri a human being."[19]. Many women took part in the Ongallur Convention[20]. The social activists of that time were spreading awareness about the importance of education and employment among antarjanams. The Antarjana Samājam's meetings started to be held regularly. Devaki Nilayamgode also became a member of this reformist movement. In her memoirs, she extensively describes the process of social changes in Kerala. In one chapter of her autobiography, she writes about the Antarjana Samājam assemblies in which she had participated:

---

[19] A speech delivered in 1930 by E.M.S. Namboodiripad.

[20] The 34th annual conference of the Nambudiri Yogakshema Sabha which took place at Ongallur in 1944.

> "Every meeting began with the question: 'Should we let our children suffer our fate?'. Then we elaborated our point: 'We have neither education nor knowledge; no idea about the outside world either. We are born and we die in the dark interiors of our nalukettu. Having no jobs, we have to beg for money. To get jobs, we should be educated. So let us educate our children and equip them for employment.' – this was what we said" (Nilayamgode 2015: 149–150).

As Devaki Nilayamgode stresses, it was the last stage of a reform movement within the Nambudiri community, which caused a crucial change among antarjanams. The founding of the training centres for Nambudiri women across the Kerala state succeeded in bringing the thus far enprisoned beings – including Devaki – to the forefront of public life; thus causing them to cross the boundary between the private and public space (Nilayamgode 2015: 148–154). As Nilayamgode concludes her memoirs:

> "On looking back, I find little similarity between my present-day life and the childhood I spent in my old illam. How much and how fast things have changed in fifty-sixty years! I can emphatically state that life today is better than ever before. [...] Today there is no sorrow specific to a Nambudiri family. It has the same joys and sorrow as any other family. Time, the great leveller, has ironed out most differences" (Nilayamgode 2015: 155).

By 1969, when the first pieces of Malayalam autobiographic literature authored by antarjanams started to appear, the traditional world of Nambudiri brahmins had retreated considerably. (Devika 2015: xvii) Thus, due to the reformist movements resulting in the social change which had taken place in Kerala, in the 20th century, the voice of Devaki Nilayamgode – as well as other antarjanams – could be heard, hereby breaking the centuries of suffering in silence.

Bibliography

Aiyappan, Ayinipalli (1965). *Social Revolution In Kerala Village: A Study In Cultural Change.* Bombay: Asia Publishing House.

Antharjanam, Lalithambika (2015). *Agnisakshi. Fire, My Witness.* Trans. Vasanthi Sankaranarayanan. New Delhi: Oxford University Press.

Devika, Jayakumari (2013). *Woman Writing = Man Reading?.* New Delhi: Zubaan.

—— (2015). *Introduction. The Namboodiris Of Kerala.* In: Devaki Nilayamgode. *Antharjanam. Memoirs Of A Namboodiri Woman.* Trans. Indira Menon, Radhika P. Menon. New Delhi: Oxford University Press.

Galewicz, Cezary (2015). *Żyjące Biblioteki Indii: Rygweda Braminów Nambudiri.* Kraków: Wydawnictwo Uniwersytetu Jagiellońskiego.

Kpm (2005). "Are Women Weak? ". In: *Her-Self: Early Writings On Gender By Malayalee Women.* Ed. Jayakumari Devika. Kolkata: Stree.

Menon, A. Sreedhara (1970). *A Survey Of Kerala History.* Kottayam: National Book Stall.

—— (1978). *Cultural Heritage Of Kerala. An Introduction.* Cochin: East-West Publications Private Ltd.

—— (1979). *Social And Cultural History Of Kerala.* New Delhi: Sterling Publishers Pvt Ltd.

Namboothiri Website Trusts (2017). On-line publication available at: http://www.namboothiri.com/ [accessed: April 15, 2017].

Nilayamgode, Devaki (2015). *Antharjanam. Memoirs of a Namboodiri Woman.* Trans. Indira Menon, Radhika P. Menon. New Delhi: Oxford University Press.

Panikkar, T.K. Gopal (1983). *Malabar And Its Folk.* New Delhi: Asian Educational Services.

Parpola, Marjatta (2000). *Kerala Brahmins In Transition. A Study Of A Nampūtiri Family.* Helsinki: Gummerus Printing.

Pillai, T. Meena (2013). "The Celluloid Women Of Kerala ". *Economic And Political Weekly,* November 30.

Report Of The Nambuthiri Female Educational Commission (1927). Thrissur: Mangalodayam Press.

Unni, N.P. Trans. (2003). *Śāṅkarasmṛti.* Torino.

Veluthat, Kesavan (2013). *Brahman Settlements In Kerala. Historical Studies.* Thrissur: Cosmo Books.

Wood, E. Amanda (1985). *Knowledge Before Printing And After. The Indian Tradition In Changing Kerala.* Delhi: Oxford University Press.

Index of Names

A

B

C

D

E

F

G

H

I

J

K

L

M

N

O

P

Q

R

S

T

U

V

W

Y

Z

CPSIA information can be obtained
at www.ICGtesting.com
Printed in the USA
BVHW051248060623
665472BV00013B/1027

9 781622 735006